PIRATES, TRAITORS, AND APOSTATES

Renegade Identities in Early Modern English Writing

Pirates, Traitors, and Apostates

Renegade Identities in Early Modern English Writing

LAURIE ELLINGHAUSEN

UNIVERSITY OF TORONTO PRESS
Toronto Buffalo London

ISBN 978-1-4875-0268-3

Printed on acid-free, 100% post-consumer recycled paper with vegetable-based inks.

Library and Archives Canada Cataloguing in Publication

Ellinghausen, Laurie, 1972–, author
Pirates, traitors, and apostates : renegade identities in early
modern English writing / Laurie Ellinghausen.

Includes bibliographical references and index.
ISBN 978-1-4875-0268-3 (hardcover)

1. English literature – Early modern, 1500–1700 – History and criticism.
2. Rogues and vagabonds in literature.   3. Outlaws in literature.
4. Outsiders in literature.   5. Outcasts in literature. 6. Social classes in
literature. I. Title.

PR428.R63E455 2017   820.9'35269409031   C2017-905211-X

University of Toronto Press acknowledges the financial assistance to its
publishing program of the Canada Council for the Arts and the Ontario Arts
Council, an agency of the Government of Ontario.

Canada Council **Conseil des Arts**
for the Arts **du Canada**

ONTARIO ARTS COUNCIL
CONSEIL DES ARTS DE L'ONTARIO
an Ontario government agency
un organisme du gouvernement de l'Ontario

Funded by the   Financé par le
Government   gouvernement
of Canada   du Canada

Contents

Illustrations

Acknowledgments

Thanks first to my friends, students, and colleagues at the University of Missouri – Kansas City for their support of this work. A research grant from the University of Missouri Research Board funded a leave to support the book's completion; the Office of Research Support, the College of Arts and Sciences, and the Department of English at UMKC supported the final stages of production. Portions of chapter 3 were presented at the department's colloquium series, where I received valuable feedback.

Thanks also to my colleagues in the field for their constructive criticism and support. Portions of each chapter were presented at meetings of the Shakespeare Association of America and the Renaissance Society of America; this book has benefitted greatly from the camaraderie, community, and rich intellectual exchange I regularly enjoy at these meetings. I also wish to thank the Empire Studies group at the University of Houston for the stimulating conversation that shaped the final version of chapter 2; thanks especially to Ann Christensen for facilitating that opportunity. Additionally, I wish to thank the two anonymous readers at University of Toronto Press, as well as acquisitions editor Suzanne Rancourt, for their valuable guidance on the final stages of the manuscript.

Portions of chapter 1 were originally published under the title "Melancholy and Spleen: Models of Masculinity in *The Famous History of Captain Thomas Stukeley*," in *Violent Masculinities*, ed. Catherine E. Thomas and Jennifer Feather (Palgrave Macmillan, 2013), 213–30. Portions of chapter 2 were originally published under the title "'We Are of the Sea!': Masterless Identity and Transnational Context in *A

Christian Turned Turk," *Explorations in Renaissance Culture* 41.2 (Fall 2015): 178–201.

Above all I am grateful for the unwavering support of my husband, Jeff Callan, whose love gives me the strength and confidence to persevere in all my scholarly endeavors. Finally, I dedicate this book to the memory of Gobi, my little runagate.

PIRATES, TRAITORS, AND APOSTATES

Renegade Identities in Early Modern English Writing

Running Down the "Runagate"

John Ward grew up in Plymouth, England, as the son of a poor fisherman and became a fisherman himself, an occupation that Elizabethans scorned as "masterless" – paltry, contingent, and outside protective guild structures. Fishermen were highly susceptible to impressment into the navy – an institution hated for its meagre pay and slave-like conditions. The navy conscripted Ward in 1603, but he would not serve for long. One night after a drinking bout, he and several comrades seized a merchant ship in Portsmouth Harbour and sailed away. Elected captain, Ward thus began his career as one of the age's most dreaded pirates. He terrorized Mediterranean merchants, sold his own countrymen in slave markets, and, most notoriously in the eyes of his Christian contemporaries, converted to Islam.

In a 1609 play treating Ward's life, Robert Daborne imagined the corsair dying in ignominy on African shores, betrayed by his alliances and bemoaning the day he ever aspired above his lowly station. But according to the shipmaster Andrew Barker, the real Captain Ward had retired in a Tunisian palace, living "in a most princely and magnificent state," wearing "curious and costly" clothing, and eating "sumptuous" food. "I do not know any Peere in England," Barker wrote, "that beares up his post in more dignitie, nor hath his Attendants more obsequious unto him" (C2ᵛ). John Ward died not in the humiliating state that Daborne assigned him, but rather as a wealthy apostate, as far from the Plymouth fishing waters as the English could imagine.

Of Ward's many crimes, the worst of all in Daborne's view was his conversion to Islam, as the play's title – *A Christian Turned Turk* – suggests. This act made Ward a "renegado" – a person who, in renouncing the Christian faith, also renounces his country and thus becomes a traitor.

But the several contemporaneous texts that detailed Ward's story suggest something else – that his aspirations above his social station in fact constituted his worst sin. They portray him as the vilest of overreachers, a vulgar man never content with the lot decreed by his birth. The alleged defiance that led Ward to desert the queen's service links him to another version of the word "renegado" – that is, the "runagate" – defined in the *Oxford English Dictionary* as "a vagabond, a wanderer; a restless roving person" who defies the stabilizing norms of his society. This older cognate of "renegade" roots Ward's colourful legend in a more homely phenomenon – that of the runaway apprentice or disobedient labourer, the fearsome and unruly "masterless man" that statutes such as the 1563 Statute of Artificers, the 1572 Vagrancy and Poor Relief Act, and the 1601 Poor Relief Act all sought to manage. Effectively, the term "runagate" situates the transnational figure of the "renegado" in a history of resistance to domestic oppression.

This book explores how literary representations of renegades in late Tudor and early Jacobean England – an era of both "masterlessness" at home and increasing commercial activity abroad – marshalled history to make the renegade speak provocatively to diverse audiences. In tracing the projection of domestic discourses outside English borders, I make several claims. First, by expanding the repertoire of vagrancy to include mercenaries, pirates, and adventurers, *Pirates, Traitors, and Apostates* argues that these figures do not merely threaten English identity through their "outsider" status, as some critics claim. Rather, I find a pattern that at first may seem counterintuitive – that renegades invite critical reflection on English identity by demonstrating their enduring *connection* to the land and its people, a bond expressed through languages of social class. From this stems my second claim: that the commonalities, not the differences, between renegades and their public made these tales successful, leading writers to produce multiple versions of renegades' individual stories across decades or even centuries. Third, I find that versions of renegade tales change in significant ways not only across time but across different types of writing – ballads, plays, travel accounts, romances, and polemical prose. This mutability argues for the centrality of genre in renegade representations. Finally, I note that the narrative capaciousness enabled by generic diversity accompanies a rhetorical construction of audiences that are themselves socially diverse, sharing with the renegade a range of experiences, including poverty, itineracy, and social and economic aspiration. The blurring of distinctions between the settled English subject and the putative English "other" expands the political conversation about renegades beyond standard moral condemnations into new and subversive directions. In fact I have discovered that these tales, by drawing connections between the renegade and the obedient English subject, foreshadow emancipatory potential in England's transition to a capitalist economy – a revelation that stokes, rather than contains, the cultivation of renegade desire.

Barker's sneering description of Ward's ersatz "dignitie" lends a distinct class-based dimension to Ward's religious and political transgression. As such, Barker extends the domestic languages of hierarchy to rhetorically rein in a figure who is, strictly speaking, no longer domestic. This transposition anticipates habits of thought that David Cannadine finds in later centuries. Specifically, Cannadine argues that the British Empire's very organization reflected a preoccupation with status that made the entire empire into a projection of the British class system. This extension of hierarchical thinking across borders, he elaborates, characterizes a people "at least as likely to envisage the social structure of their empire – as their predecessors had done before them – by analogy to what they knew of 'home,' or in replication of it, or in parallel to it, or in extension of it, or (sometimes) in idealization of it, or (even, and increasingly) in nostalgia for it." Cannadine characterizes this thinking as "hallowed by time and precedent." Thus his argument invites a look backwards into the early modern roots of a deeply embedded mindset (4–5, 4).

I propose that the conceptual link between the domestic vagrant and the world traveller resides in the concept of *mobility* as a pressure point on the coherence of "Englishness." The specter of "masterlessness" – that is, the omnipresence of the itinerant poor in the towns, in the countryside, and on the roads – presented a major crisis to Tudor society. The late medieval enclosure laws led to a sharp increase in destitute men, women, and children migrating from town to town, begging for relief, and attempting to eke out meagre wages for daily subsistence.[1] The poor flocked especially to London in search of such relief, resulting in a population boom that the city's institutions and infrastructure strained to accommodate.[2] Statutes imposing harsh labour discipline on the poor and punishing those who shirked service, ran away from a master, or bilked parishes out of poor relief reflected these pressures.

Writers such as Thomas Awdeley, Thomas Harman, Robert Greene, and Thomas Dekker appropriated the moral category of the undeserving poor for popular entertainment, as their "coney-catching" tales of criminal trickery detailed the alleged cleverness of shifty migrants.[3] The possibility that such men and women would transform their itineracy into opportunity, as Ward had, helped construct poverty as inchoate criminality awaiting discipline.

At the heart of it all lurked a deep layer of cultural anxiety about social mobility. As Linda Woodbridge argues, "[F]ulminations against vagrants' geographical mobility project or displace other kinds of change and mobility: religious and intellectual change, social mobility" (26). That writers such as Daborne would cast Ward's religious apostasy as an internationalized form of domestic masterlessness then comes as no surprise. Vagrancy was a fruitful topic for writers because it made England's political and economic difficulties manifest and visible. Contemporaries saw vagrancies as a blot on the health of the nation and an embarrassment. Woodbridge describes "upbeat Renaissance publicists" who struggled to incorporate this aspect of social reality into their vision; these nationalists considered vagrancy a threat to national pride (13).

Cultural suspicion towards the itinerant poor raises the question of the degree to which normative English identity was a matter of being (in Patricia Fumerton's term) *settled*, and how exactly that settledness was meant to register in the context of an individual life. English attitudes towards travellers hint at expectations similar to those governing perceptions of the masterless. Despite the country's rapidly increasing commercial and diplomatic openness to the rest of the world, English culture and attitudes remained notably insular throughout the period. There was a general resistance towards travel.[4] Newly returned English merchants and sailors attracted suspicion owing to their recent exposure to strange customs, fashions, and religious practices; travellers thus faced intense pressure to demonstrate a core of orthodox "Englishness" uncorrupted by foreign contact.[5] To English people, Andrew Hadfield argues, travellers resembled "nomads who have no rooted sense of place and no means of establishing proper, settled communities" (106).[6]

Different types of travellers were regarded with suspicion. "Factors," for example, who negotiated on behalf of English merchants with foreign agents, required a great deal of trust from their employers, owing to the factor's potential to deceive, flatter, and assimilate.[7] English prejudices against foreign contact extended such suspicions of cultural malleability to merchants themselves and even passengers on trading ships, particularly those outside the nobility.[8] Even peers of the realm who undertook diplomatic missions had to do so with clear royal dispensation and had to demonstrate their resistance to the influences of foreign culture and religion. Travel advice aimed at such emissaries instructed readers to remain stolidly "English" when conducting business abroad, even while, paradoxically, attributing a veneer of learned sophistication to exposure to the best of foreign cultures.[9]

Thus, on the one hand, English travellers risked corruption merely by the act of transporting themselves physically abroad; yet, as books and pamphlets offering advice to travellers commonly suggested, remaining "English" was largely a matter of stolid inward character. This nexus of ideals converges on – and is disrupted by – the renegade as a creature both English *and* foreign. Renegade texts, as they struggle to describe a transnational social identity, respond by deploying class descriptions that bind the renegade to the home country. The 1682 poem "Apostasy Punish'd," which treats the "deserved death" of the renegade Jonas Rowland, illustrates the pattern. Rowland's story mingles the temptations of foreign religion with suggestions of underclass insubordination. The poem's anonymous author asserts that Rowland's alleged murder of the Morrocan ambassador was a natural consequence of his apostasy, "A thing that's against the Rules of Nature," and thus affirms Rowland's "unnatural" disposition (n.p.). Invoking the spectre of the runaway apprentice to characterize Rowland's crimes, the poem describes him as a "Renegado" who "from his Master run [*sic*]" – in other words, as a "runagate" who fled his country, his god, and perhaps his literal master in order "to be free." Ultimately, the poem explains this will to freedom as resulting from "travells of the brain" – that is, a disposition towards roaming. "Apostasy Punish'd" assigns a series of causes and effects to the moral fable of Jonas Rowland – *first*, he possesses "travels of the brain," and *then* he breaks away from his "Master," making himself "free" to betray his god and *then* commit murder.

"Apostasy Punish'd" provides one example of how doctrines of religious and social obedience mutually reinforced one another, casting social rebellion as violation of divine order. The Judeo-Christian scriptures rely heavily on vocabularies of debt, bondage, and redemption to articulate religious authority; these references are not mere metaphors but reflective of actual master-servant and master-slave relationships

at the time of the scriptures' writing.[10] Early modern sermons addressing renegades similarly conflate the religious and the economic. William Gouge's *Recovery from Apostasy* (1639), for example, invokes the
putative sinfulness of "abandoning" or "running" from one's economic
obligations and, by extension, one's obligations to society. Drawing on
the parable of the prodigal son, Gouge uses the term "Father" to conflate God, father, and master into something from which the renegade
runs: "when [the renegade] went out of his Fathers house he proved
an Apostate. His Fathers house was the church, wherein alone were
the means of salvation" (C). This church, Gouge later comments, was
"a prison" to the apostate, who rails against it in quest of some illusory notion of liberty until he returns to obedience and thus, paradoxically, becomes "the Lords freeman," subject to a master who "dearely
bought" him (I4^v, C2^v, D4^v). In a rhetorical move that denies the specific-
ity of captive experience – a situation in which a captured Englishman,
especially a common one unlikely to be ransomed, might accept his
captor's religion to free himself – Gouge renders the actual experience
of chains, torments, and confinement illusory when compared to "slavery under sinne and Satan" (C4). For Gouge, who compares the peni-
tent apostate to a wife returning to her husband after having "formerly
lived loosely" (M3^v), apostasy represents rebellion against patriarchal
control, an act of defiance that belies the physical and psychological
hardships that might lead one to "turn" in the first place.[11]

Renegade tales similarly appropriate, extend, and refigure literary
tropes of masterlessness within the rapidly expanding sphere of international commerce, but the range of texts addressed in this book reveals
a more complex conversation about mobility than "Apostasy Punish'd"
or Gouge's sermon indicate on their own. *Pirates, Traitors, and Apostates*
adds an overlooked but crucial dimension to previous scholarly discussions that draw on interlocking discourses of race, religion, gender,
and nationality to account for renegade behaviour. According to Ania
Loomba, converting to Islam violated the trifecta of "common heri-
tage, bloodline, and religion" that defined the English as a "race," thus
awakening a nexus of religious, racial, and national anxieties about
invasion, miscegenation, and foreignness in general (*Shakespeare* 24).
Apostasy also raised the threat of English emasculation, as Jonathan
Burton shows in his discussion of dramatic episodes that portrayed
"compromised Christian male bodies," especially the circumcision
rituals (widely misunderstood as castration) prevalent in the period's
"Turk" plays (*Traffic* 111). Daniel Vitkus, who also notes themes of

anxious masculinity and sexual transgression, expands the context for apostasy to include Anglo-Ottoman commercial and cultural exchange. The renegade, in Vitkus's account, embodies the cultural and economic vulnerabilities that belied mutually beneficial commercial and diplomatic relations between England and the Mediterranean world.[12] In other words, the renegade testified to the cost of participating in the Mediterranean marketplace, which was both violent and multicultural and therefore placed intense pressure on concepts of national identity as fixed and innate (*Turning* 113, 162).

To be sure, contemporary writers drew on a multiplicity of overlapping discourses to understand and explain the confounding spectacle of the Englishman who "turned" to Islam. As Patricia Parker points out, they often applied the word "preposterous" to such conversions. Further, she writes, that word associates the phenomenon of Christians "turning Turk" with spiritual and sexual degeneracy as well as with aspiring above one's social class. As chapter 2 will describe, the case of *A Christian Turned Turk*'s renegade character, Gismund, who invokes what Parker terms "the original luciferic upstart," exemplifies this point.[13] The implied connection between religious apostasy and lowly ambition, as displayed by such figures, invites a more thorough investigation of how class discourses measured the renegade's divergence from social norms.[14]

Recent work on early capitalist expansion argues further for class as a category for analysis, because in the early modern period, states, merchants, diplomats, military personnel, and even criminal outliers such as pirates facilitated developments that persist today, such as capital's reliance on cheap labour across the world. Linda Colley demonstrates how enterprises in North Africa, the Americas, and India depended on the forced expulsion of the English poor to these sites, many of whom were eventually left to languish in captivity, unransomed, never seeing England again. David Armitage points to such practices to suggest that early English colonial enterprise had as much to do with managing the domestic population as it did the acquisition of wealth and power abroad.[15] Mark Netzloff also has examined underclass experience from the vantage point of global capitalism, noting in particular how texts "racialized" the poor as ethnically inferior and thus rationalized deportation and forced labour. Crucially, Netzloff's study demonstrates the evolving dialectical relationship between domestic social crises and international expansion – a just emphasis, given that the industries employing labourers at home had come to depend on expansion into foreign markets. Patricia Fumerton's work on the English seaman as well as Amanda Bailey's and Crystal Bartolovich's work on indentured labour in the Americas further illustrate the evolving nature of socio-economic experience as both domestic *and* international.[16] These studies lend a material dimension to literary analyses that treat class on a more purely discursive level, such as Barbara Fuchs's study of pirates whose activities troubled class-based distinctions between the lowly pirate and the gentleman privateer.[17]

All of these analyses, while local and specific, also gesture towards enduring forms of labour and entrepreneurship in which global contexts both confirm and disrupt status hierarchies forged within national borders. Renegade tales make those disruptions not only visible, but entertaining, provocative, and even inspiring. Their capacity to evoke such responses resides not only in their fantastical subject matter, but in the particular ways they construct and engage diverse audiences.

Some renegade texts address audiences with a clear didactic purpose, which is to portray the inhumanity of the renegade and dissuade audiences from following his path. But other texts borrow from these conventional approaches only to complicate the very moral message they impart. Such contradictions often follow the lines of admiring the renegade's defiance while at the same time critiquing the individualism thought to underpin that defiance. This complicated dynamic suggests that early modern English audiences may have been drawn to renegades for reasons that differ significantly from how audiences respond to renegades today.

The embeddedness of the apparently singular figure of the renegade in common experience – that is, in the *un*singular – largely has been lost to modern audiences. Today the word "renegade" carries a romantic connotation, suggesting independence, free thinking, and self-determination in the face of conformist pressures. Individualistic cultures frequently valorize renegade behaviour as an effort to preserve personal autonomy against totalizing ideologies and regimes. Looking forward to the cultural potency of today's renegades in Western popular culture, some scholars have viewed early modern renegades as harbingers of Western culture's love affair with individualism – that is, as figures who manage to individuate themselves in the face of politically absolutist, religiously universalist, and socially oppressive ideologies, face consequences for that action, and, for a time at least, get away with it. Jacob Burckhardt, in his classic attempt to tease out the special characteristics of the Renaissance, correlates Italian adventurers' "discovery of the outward universe" with the "high degree of individual development" that characterizes the beginnings of modern identity (171). Historian Lucia Scaraffia distinguishes the "renegade" from the "traitor" on the basis of the former's multiple allegiances, a situation that forced him to build his own identity independent of his "first allegiances" or "roots."[18] Scaraffia reaches this conclusion by studying the early modern religious wars, the widespread persecution that resulted from them, and the consequences of such persecution for the many subjects who, as Mercedes Garcia-Arenal and Gerald Wiegers put it, were forced to "dissimulate their beliefs and find ways to legitimize the dissimulation, often with a skepticism that may have led to the first stirrings of atheism" (131).[19] The experience of the early modern renegade subject, the story goes, heralds the eventual emergence of the secular, the personal, the individual, and the private – that is, the transcendent Person – over the claims of politico-religious regimes that purported to suppress such individuality.

In light of this history, contemporaneous outrage at early modern renegade behaviour at first might seem a relic of a less tolerant, more authoritarian, and less individualistic age – although the heroic status of contemporary renegades in popular culture suggests audiences still experience a vicarious thrill watching struggling, ordinary individuals reinvent themselves as disruptive figures of subversive power, figures inspiring fear rather than ridicule from those accustomed to dominating them. That being said, while the cult status of such figures speaks to at least latent defiance of the oppressive structures of late capitalism, the popularity of the early modern renegade stems just as much from issues of community as it does from the territory of individual self-interest, which was at the time largely forbidden. In his work on credit networks in early modern England, Craig Muldrew describes a socio-economic landscape heavily rooted in community and neighbourhood, where "individual" economic actions linked inextricably to a web of human relationships. This localized system, which Muldrew describes as forged by emotive bonds as well as bonds of material necessity, would have informed audience responses to the renegade's allegedly selfish calculation. Yet this conditioning does not automatically mean that audiences viewed the renegade as radically separate from themselves. Alexandra Shepard has argued recently that – the period's growth of seemingly inward-looking spiritual autobiography notwithstanding – ordinary English subjects largely understood themselves and others in terms of connection at least as much as distinction. Shepard explains: "social identities were forged within the parameters necessitated by the need for broader consensus on the shape of the social order. While often founded on the intricacies of individual differentiation, the articulation of identity also depended on collective sanction and thereby worked indirectly to connect individuals to groups" (26). Discursive attempts to isolate the renegade from his fellow English men and women would have had to confront, and be complicated by, this bias in favour of "connect[ing] individuals to groups." This bias also would have accompanied audiences to the playhouse, the bookstalls, and the myriad settings in which ballads were sung. While both contemporary discourse and modern scholarship variously describe the figures examined in *Pirates, Traitors, and Apostates* as masterless, deviant, foolish, and even comically deluded, this book suggests that some early modern readers and playgoers empathized with and even cheered on the renegade. His exploits entertained in part because he on some level remained an *English* creature tied to the homeland and thus relevant to their own lives. This dynamic suggests that even a figure who broke away as spectacularly as the renegade was not always understood as abandoning his country, nor did all audiences see him as an anti-English monster.

To be sure, it would be methodologically difficult to ascertain in what direction a given audience's response to a particular text ultimately tended. But this very indeterminacy argues that renegade texts, in spite of their moralistic veneer, in fact required a complex engagement of emotion and thought. To encounter a renegade – a figure at once repulsive *and* attractive, frightening *and* entertaining, treacherous *and* loyal – was to encounter a unique opportunity to look at the contradictions within one's country and oneself. The case of John Ward, which I explore in chapter 2, well illustrates how even the most villainous men could acquire long-term status as touchstones for reflection, discussion, and even vicarious adventure. His durability as a figure of interest over the centuries testifies to the flexible interpretations his story invited. According to polemical prose works such as Barker's account, the anonymous *Newes from Sea*, and the account of the Scottish traveller William Lithgow,[20] Ward was a bad man who, despite the luxury he enjoyed, surely would receive his comeuppance on earth and in heaven. Daborne as well as Thomas Dekker, whose play *If It Be Not*

Good, the Divel Is in It features the lord of the underworld, Pluto, inquiring after Ward's whereabouts, describe this comeuppance. Yet the very proliferation of these printed accounts suggests that Ward's story held continual interest for audiences beyond any pat moralistic conclusions. Ballads relating Ward's seaborne exploits entertained audiences well into the early modern period; by the nineteenth century, proponents of worldwide free trade were citing Ward as a harbinger of international entrepreneurship.[21]

It is entirely possible that the widespread knowledge of Ward's actual fate – that is, his putatively undeserved luxury and prosperity – played a role in stoking popular fascination and thus disrupting the impact of Daborne's moralistic conclusion. Yet other pirates of similar fame did not share his fate. Chapter 3 will address a pair who received their comeuppance yet also gained popular attention. The pirates known as "Purser and Clinton" operated successfully off the English coast, provided stolen goods to sustain local communities, and received protection from local authorities until their luck ran out in 1583 and the state hanged them both. Their story appears in several late Tudor ballads, an early Jacobean chronicle history, a Jacobean play, and a Caroline prose pamphlet – a textual history spanning three English monarchs. Each text offers a different perspective on the significance of the men's crimes and, most particularly, the justice of their punishment. If Ward's prominent role in popular culture owed something to his luxurious retirement, it was in part in comparison to such figures, whose own, lesser fate was no barrier to fame.

Indeed, tales of transgressive figures – sustained over a proliferation of genres and thematic emphases – held audience attention long after the renegade in question died or disappeared. Men such as Ward, Purser, and Clinton lived on in the realms of narrative, fantasy, and imagination, and the early modern markets for popular print and drama facilitated this endurance. The potency of these markets suggests a crucial role for early modern audiences in the construction of renegade tales. Through their entertainment choices, audiences acquired a level of independent agency that remains unaccounted for in existing readings of these renegade tales, which tend to focus on ways in which the plots both affirm and critique state policies towards continental Catholicism, seaborne crime, and military engagement abroad.[22] While such readings usefully illuminate the political contexts of these tales, their specific focus does not account for how the diversity of audiences in the early modern markets for print and drama – markets that highlight a variety of individual experiences and biases reflecting both domestic and international influences – influenced how these tales would be read, seen, and understood.[23] In the early modern literary canon, examples abound of texts that appeared to affirm orthodoxy and yet lent themselves to subversive readings, such as Shakespeare's *Richard II* and *Henry V* and Marlowe's *Doctor Faustus*. The potential for divergent readings played out among diverse audiences and continues to generate debate about these texts. This ongoing vitality well exemplifies Stuart Hall's "encoding/decoding" theory of reception, which accounts for what he calls the "hegemonic," "oppositional," and "ambivalent" reception of texts among audiences.[24] Hall's theory of multivalent response well describes the complex ways in which renegade tales construct and engage their public.

I should mention here that, by connecting the renegade to the broad socio-economic experiences of popular audiences, *Pirates, Traitors, and Apostates* distinguishes the renegade from the traitor, figures such as Anthony Babington and the second Earl of Essex. Traitors' plans and actions were consciously political, idealistic, and ideological, while renegades sought their own gain. Certainly renegades and traitors share similar characteristics and actions, such as Ward's apostasy, which earned him the "traitor" label. Both are, as Karen Cunningham describes traitors, "fearsome border-dwellers" who trouble distinctions between self and other, domestic and foreign (20). And, indeed, there is evidence that the renegades Thomas Stukeley and the Sherley brothers, whom I discuss in chapters 1 and 4, respectively, considered Essex a source of inspiration. However, their evident self-interest and malleable loyalties indicate motivations different from those of Essex and other traitors who sought to reshape the English realm along specific political and religious lines. Traitors such as Essex, Babington, Mary Queen of Scots, and Guy Fawkes, who directly threatened monarchs and their governments, might inspire political defiance by renegades, but the socio-economic discourses embedded in renegade representations merit a level of attention in their own right. These discourses necessarily lie outside the scope of previously published studies addressing traitors.[25]

Although he may possess religious or social principles of his own, the renegade's crimes stem primarily from the will to transgress his "place" – that is, his social status and the forms of economic agency assumed by that status. As England became more of a player on the international scene – striving to compete with Spain, Portugal, and the Netherlands – new markets opened up for the traffic of cash, goods, and human commodities. These markets brought new opportunities for wealth, status, and political influence at home and abroad, which led to the rise of the mercantile "middle sort." Travel stories proliferated in the print market and on the stage, allowing even English subjects remaining at home the opportunity to satisfy their curiosity and expand their knowledge about exotic "new" places far from home. As the ensuing chapters will show, renegade tales drew heavily on these contexts in their consideration of renegades' "bad" deeds. The danger and the thrill of such badness, when played out over a range of potentially emancipatory settings, both terrify and tease audiences with stories that originate in everyday, *un*exotic lives.

The case of Thomas Stukeley, which chapter 1 will explore in detail, illustrates how a seeming turncoat – one who wilfully renders himself foreign – can still remain "English" and, in so doing, inspire his country's audiences to entertain their own innate susceptibility to wandering and rebellion. Popularly known as "lusty Stukeley," this son of minor Devonshire gentry briefly served the first Duke of Somerset until the duke's arrest in 1551, when Stukeley fled to France and served in that nation's army. After unsuccessfully attempting to play the French and the English against one another, he found himself in heavy debt and attempted to remedy the situation by marrying a wealthy heiress, whom he abandoned to pursue a career in piracy. All along he proved a thorn in the side of Elizabeth I, whom he tended to address presumptuously, exploiting the rumour that he was Henry VIII's illegitimate son. Sometime after a military stint in Ireland, he came into the employ of King Philip II of Spain, at whose court he plotted an invasion of Ireland. He also found favour with the pope, who had excommunicated his queen, in Rome. His final adventure happened in the service of King Sebastian of Portugal, who employed him in an invasion of Morocco. The campaign culminated in Stukeley's allegedly heroic death at the Battle of Alcácer Quibir in 1578.

Stukeley's story – full of danger, violence, and international intrigue – demonstrates the renegade's potential to resonate differently with different audiences, thus stimulating a larger conversation about the relationship between national identity and obedience to sociocultural norms. While Elizabeth I undoubtedly considered the recusant Stukeley's vainglorious actions treason, writers and readers seem to have recognized the draw of his adventures: ballads, prose romances, and two plays detailed his life in heroic, tragic, and even comic veins. Seeking to complicate Stukeley's traitor status, Brian C. Lockey reads those two plays – George Peele's *The Battle of Alcazar* and the anonymous *The Famous History of the Life and Death of Captain Thomas Stukeley* – to suggest that, for all Stukeley's self-serving ambition, his courage and his quasi-knightly manners retain him as an English figure, just one devoted to a more "cosmopolitan" ideal than Protestant England tolerated at the time. While Lockey offers an important corrective to prevailing opinion surrounding Stukeley, the argument nonetheless reinforces a conceptual "English-other" binary that cannot account for the ways in which each version of Stukeley's tale negotiates such categories anew. As an alternative, I propose that, on the question of whether Stukeley ultimately is "English" or a self-made "other," he is neither and both. Similar to Georg Simmel's "stranger," Stukeley is both distant (geographically) and near (culturally); he is a part of the national body and yet outside of it; and, most importantly, his status as English other makes him into a testing ground for a subversive cultural imaginary.[26]

The potential for subversion exists in the particular way each renegade tale connects its hero to native English contexts. In Stukeley's case, this connection occurs largely within an intersection of class and gender – he is an English *gentleman* and, as such, follows an old script of knightly crusading that remained popular in the period's literature and drama. But the play *Famous History* investigates the gendered nature of the renegade even further by rooting it in humoral discourse. In the play's language, Stukeley is a creature of excessive "heat"; the abundance of this masculine quality accounts for both his resistance to domestic English life (i.e., a burning desire to leave England, culminating in the abandonment of his wife) and the bravery that even readers most aware of his reputation nonetheless found themselves admiring. Some contemporaneous medical texts, particularly Robert Burton's *Anatomy of Melancholy*, describe excessive "heat" as lending itself to political rebellion; however, other texts describe this same "heat" as indigenous to the English, a people widely considered to be humorally predisposed to wandering. In fact, in a departure from its sources, the play adds two fictional English male characters – Stukeley's friend Vernon and his rival Captain Harbert – as proximate figures who inspire further reflection on Stukeley as an essentially English creature, one bred from the very air and soil that his more settled counterparts occupied.

At first glance, as a mercenary English gentleman, Stukeley may appear to have little in common with the fisherman-cum-pirate John Ward. Yet I find that early modern texts applied the lowly and criminal associations of the "runagate" to rebels across a range of classes as a way to explain defiant behaviour. In fact, of the figures examined in *Pirates, Traitors, and Apostates*, only Ward is recognizably "low"; Stukeley, the Sherley brothers, and Clinton all come from the minor gentry. But the ever-wandering Sherley brothers nonetheless earned the epithet "masterless," a term originally associated with the swelling class of itinerant poor thought to be evading service. Likewise, Elizabeth's chief minister, William Cecil, imagined Stukeley wandering the country, hiding in dark corners, picking up masterless riff-raff and rallying them to his treasonous causes. He therefore assigned Stukeley to the lowest social strata. Clinton and Purser endured a typical commoner's hanging at Wapping Dock for their piracy, which suggests that their transgression ultimately determined their social status. In each case, signifiers of lowly criminality abound to manage the transgressive appeal of renegades across the social spectrum. These rhetorical moves suggest that class in the early modern period was not merely an ontological identity, but rather an identity constructed in discourse and in response to acts that challenged pseudo-religious representations of the "natural" social order.

The literary record of Captain Ward, which I examine more closely in chapter 2, demonstrates vividly how writers could deploy the renegade's social origins strategically not only to rationalize his behaviour, but to contain his potential to inspire others to live similarly. The prose sources for Daborne's play repeatedly underscore Ward's birth, his original occupation, and the vulgarity implied to go hand-in-hand with these attributes. Given how little most readers could have known about the "real" life of a common fisherman, these representations assume the status of explanatory fact – Ward was poor, itinerant, and therefore masterless; his grumbling and ambitious character merely confirms this status; deserting the navy to go corsair is the natural result. Daborne represents Ward in similar terms; yet at the same time, the play strains against this conventional profile in ways that invite the possibility of sympathetic, even empathetic, responses to Ward and his men. Instead of simply presenting audiences with the one-sided tale of a morally bankrupt bad guy, Daborne sprinkles the play with references to poverty and injustice at home, conditions that pose a very different explanation for piracy than the moral sociology undertaken in the pamphlets. While the play's attention to the socio-economic causes and conditions of renegade behaviour does not serve to excuse the men's deeds, it does draw on a set of experiences recognizable to commoners who also struggled with daily existence. Thus, the play's attention to domestic hardship plants the seed for divergent responses, including some along the lines of social resistance that the orthodoxies typically describing the renegade would not allow.

As with Stukeley, the construction of Ward's social identity relies on a particular intersection between class and gender. While both men foolishly pursue personal honour, Ward recalls the spectre of the rebellious apprentice – or even the unruly and dangerous workingman. Representations of male labourers in early modern literature frequently present them as threatening, owing to a lethal combination of physical strength and a propensity for unruly behaviour; Jack Cade and his gang of artisanal rebels in Shakespeare's *Henry VI, Part 2* provide a case in point.[27] While the sources treating Ward do not describe him as particularly strong – in fact one anonymous Italian describes him as "very short"[28] – his unruly temperament, thought to derive from his social origins, makes him physically dangerous nonetheless. Ward possesses another form of strength indigenous to the working man: skill – in his case, navigational know-how acquired as a fisherman that serves his own ends just as well as it could serve the navy. These skills combine with his bold, reckless, and profane nature to create a villain not only prone to acts of violence, but *good* at them as well. This fact raises the question of who, among Daborne's audiences, also possessed skills their social betters took for granted, skills that potentially could be put to a more lucrative or emancipatory purpose.

Further, both Ward's and Stukeley's cases raise an issue of paramount concern in this book: the role of genre in constructing renegade tales. While Peele and the anonymous author of *Famous History* cast Stukeley in a tragic vein – his death signifying a loss of one foolhardy English gentleman's heroic potential – ballads and popular prose repurposed him for the sake of merriment, including material such as bawdy tales about his wedding night and the ironies of a planned pirate expedition gone awry. Such multiple versions, I argue, make renegade tales available not only for multiple audiences but also for multiple interpretations of the character's story. Accounts of Ward also vary from ballad to prose narrative to play, but that play presents the fascinating example of generic confusion within a single text. *A Christian Turned Turk* has proven notoriously difficult to classify in terms of the period's popular drama. Because it focuses on a villain and does not counterpose him with a hero of consequence, it cannot be called a tragicomedy; because the villain is of meagre origin and seems to have no redeeming qualities, the play cannot be a tragedy, although Gerald MacLean reads in it a "tragic design" borrowed from Shakespeare's *Othello* (243). Most unusually, though, the play pays serious attention to social reality, injecting the voices of England's itinerant poor into an adventure story / morality tale. These multiple and seemingly irreconcilable agendas, I argue, signify the dynamism of the renegade tale itself as an opportunity for collective introspection, conversation, and debate about economic migration, social mobility, religious identity, and domestic social practices.

A conversation among genres also occurs in the case of Purser and Clinton, the subjects of chapter 3. This time, however, the texts draw more specifically on audiences' agency as co-creators of the story. The spectators who would have crowded the scaffold at the pirates' execution thematize that agency. Historians inspired by the work of Michel Foucault have variously described public executions as sites of contest between state justice and popular response, assigning different levels of agency to the crowd. In the context of this body of work, I find that the crowd, as represented in texts depicting Purser and Clinton, prefigures a larger field of emotive response beyond the site of execution. Audiences for the hanging ballads, the chronicle history, the play, and the prose pamphlet would return Purser and Clinton to public attention over the reign of the next three monarchs. The hanging ballads in particular, circulated close to (indeed, even before) the pirates' deaths, give voice to the condemned and invoke the spectators as a court of public opinion that, much more than the state, might empathize with the pirates. Thus, these ballads complicate the state's justice by appealing to the kinds of common English subjects to whom Purser and Clinton gave stolen goods, subjects who might have known them personally, and who might have stood at Wapping Dock themselves on that day in 1583.

When the Purser and Clinton of the hanging ballads beg the spectators for "pity," they seek understanding and connection from subjects who might otherwise condemn them. This emotive engagement dramatizes the fact that, as pirates serving communities in the south of England, Purser and Clinton regularly infused those communities with money and goods; while the mayor of Exeter and the local admiralty official may have been bribed to keep Purser and Clinton out of the hands of the law, these officials might also have recognized the importance of the pirates' activities in sustaining the local people. This system of mutual care illustrates the enduring nature of pre-capitalist socioeconomic relationships – relationships based on charity, hospitality, and kinship networks – and suggests that those relationships held meaning even for pirates, those creatures of supposedly cold, self-interested calculation seeking to exploit markets for their own benefit. The emotive quality of these economic bonds between friends, families, and neighbours also sows a field of dissenting response to state justice. Like the other renegades I examine, Purser and Clinton possess underlying connections to their public, ties that challenge the moral thrust of writers who wholeheartedly condemn their activities.

The case of Purser and Clinton illustrates a major contention of this book: that renegade tales speak in multivalent ways, in many voices and to multiple audiences, and this multiplicity itself means that state interests and the interests of diverse audiences are not always coterminous. The Sherley brothers exploit these differences perhaps most explicitly of all. Chapter 4 unfolds their textual history, much of which they penned themselves or commissioned from writers such as Anthony Nixon, who wrote the pamphlet *The Three English Brothers*, and John Day, William Rowley, and George Wilkins, authors of the play *The Travels of the Three English Brothers*. All of these texts display a distinct awareness of the family's unsavoury reputation – despite their status as minor gentry, their travels and business exploits earned them the image as masterless, faithless men whose services were available to the highest bidder, regardless of that bidder's relationship to the English monarch. But the brothers' travel narratives, Nixon's pamphlet, and the play variously seek to engage the collective imagination of an insular and settled English audience, speaking in particular to "gentlemen" who shared their interest in undertaking feats of "honour" on behalf of their sovereign and themselves. Not only do such gestures rewrite the "runagate" trope as a mode of adventurous risk-taking, but they also erect bold action – even when unsanctioned and punished – as a virtue laying the groundwork for a future English empire.

The texts that defend the Sherleys do so largely by blurring the demarcations of hero versus traitor, and bold visionary versus faithless runagate. But they also attempt to restore the brothers to the good opinion of the English public by appealing directly to the bold imagination and latent ambition of the settled English subject who might share what Nixon terms – in a rewrite of the brothers' minor gentry status – "modest beginnings." After all, like the renegades in chapters 1 through 3, the Sherleys appeared regularly in books and plays throughout the sixteenth and seventeenth centuries, reflecting their enduring fascination. But while scholarship has described the brothers as singular and eccentric figures of curiosity, the Sherley texts suggest that only the brothers' actions – not their origins or their desires – distinguish them from their settled English counterparts. By addressing this public in a patriotic vein, these texts construct a *shared* desire – as opposed to a singular self-serving desire – for commercial greatness on the international stage.

Chapter 4 highlights the inherent theatricality of the renegade tale and how this theatricality facilitates its appeal, a theme that appears in other chapters in the form of analyses of at least one work of drama per chapter. The language of *The Travels of the English Brothers* strategically crafts the public playhouse as, on the one hand, a bounded space in which a fictional world can unfold but, on the other hand, as a venue open to the air and thus spatially engaged with the larger city and with the nearby Thames, which feeds the English Channel and the vast ocean beyond. The play both confirms the boundedness of the settled subject and seeks to awaken that subject's excursive, largely forbidden, desires – desires that, as will see in chapter 1, contemporaneous writers considered indigenous to the English physical body and its native climate. While the colourful drama of the Sherley adventures played out widely in print, the connection between renegade ambition and the public's own potential for such desire plays out most vividly in front of a live audience, a collective body whose physical immediacy enhances the Sherley story as shared experience.

The topics that emerge in the chapters of this book, then, span a wide range of early modern experience: social mobility, economic migrancy, the deleterious effects of poverty, and the freedoms and consequences of disobedience to earthly "masters." These subjects are reflected variously in recent scholarship on early capitalist development in Europe. Among this vast body of work, literary studies have brought the complex nexus of developments wrought by historical change to bear on the study of prose, poetry, and plays that reflect, respond to, and imagine cultural change. Similarly, *Pirates, Traitors, and Apostates* treats such texts as part of a collective conversation – a mingling of orthodox, subversive, and ambivalent voices – about social identity, economic participation, and national belonging as England opened up to new opportunities abroad. Through the figure of the renegade, the texts explored in this book all take up challenges to common ways of thinking about social and economic mobility, and the most imaginative of these works suggest daring new perspectives on notorious figures who appeared to flout that thinking.

The chapters proceed in rough chronological order, according to the probable birth date of each central figure. However, each case incorporates a range of texts written over several reigns, decades, or even centuries, which makes further chronological ordering of chapters futile. Thus, *Pirates, Traitors, and Apostates* opens up the context of these reigns to include textual history and audience reception, considerations that do not always align neatly with historical chronology. The chapters as a whole, then, constitute clusters of tales that raise new questions and revisit old ones across the late sixteenth and early seventeenth centuries – and indeed, these clusters overlap, speak to, and complicate one another as well. The coda extends this historical focus towards later articulations of the renegade in post-Restoration English criminal biography.

Although *Pirates, Traitors, and Apostates* culminates in a glance at the eighteenth century, the chapters preceding it do not chart a teleology so much as explore a range of avenues for engagement – humoral, social, economic, and political – between renegades and their audiences. This diversity of approaches suggests the multidimensional cultivation of critical and self-reflective publics whose awareness may tend in any number of directions: anti-hierarchy, pro–local community, pro-corporate, and even patriotic in ways that paradoxically flout state authority.[29] Such capaciousness, in and of itself, foregrounds the complex narrative constructions of the novel – a genre that will bring the early modern renegade tale's themes of economic migration, social mobility, religious identity, and domestic hardship to bear on the burgeoning empire, Britain's most morally fraught endeavour of all.

Chapter One

"Unquiet Hotspurs": Stukeley, Vernon, and the Renegade Humour

And out of Ireland ranne away one Thomas Stukeley, a defamed person almost through all Christendome, and a faithlesse beast rather than a man, fleeing first out of England for notable piracies, and out of Ireland for treacheries not pardonable, which two were the first ringleaders of the rest of the rebelles ... not only all the rabble of the foresaid traitors that were before fled, but also all other persons that had forsaken their native countries, being of divers conditions and qualities, some not able to live at home but in beggerie, some discontented for lacke of preferments, which they gaped for unworthily in Universities and other places, some bankerupt Marchants, some in a sort learned to contentions, being not contented to learne to obey the Lawes of the lande, have many yeeres running up and downe, from countrey to countrey, practiced some in one corner, some in another ...

> William Cecil, Lord Burghley, *The Execution of Justice* (1583 A2ᵛ–A3)

"Almost" all of Christendom realized the "faithlesse" nature of Captain Thomas Stukeley – pirate, mercenary, and rumoured illegitimate son of Henry VIII. Yet, to the dismay of William Cecil, Elizabeth I's chief administrator, "almost" was not enough to prevent the fascination that Stukeley held for his contemporaries. According to Cecil, Stukeley's greatest danger resided in his talent as a "ringleader" – that is, his ability to yoke malcontents across social classes into "rabble," "running up and downe" like vagrants, hiding "some in one corner, some in another," undetectable to the authorities. Stukeley may or may not have induced such legions to go "runagate," but he certainly held strong appeal for early modern England's readers and playgoers, who enjoyed ballads, romances, and two plays treating Stukeley's life. This array of texts can be described as a collective meditation on the ambiguous line between swashbuckling heroism and "faithlesse" treason – an ambiguity perhaps most famously displayed in the case of the second Earl of Essex, condemned for treason and executed in 1601.

The later of the two plays, the anonymous *Famous History of the Life and Death of Captain Thomas Stukeley* (c. 1596, pub. 1605), in particular addresses this doubleness differently than Cecil's pamphlet does. For Cecil, Stukeley succeeds as a rebel because he is constantly on the move – first in England, then nearby in Ireland, then further abroad, continually evading capture as he sweeps "other persons" into his wake. Cecil's Stukeley strategically resists grounding himself anywhere on English soil, a strategy that both symptomatizes and feeds his rebellion. But according to *Famous History*, Stukeley's rebelliousness does not, ultimately, represent detachment from England but in fact a prior *attachment* to its very air and soil. Specifically, the play reduces Stukeley's rebellion to his blood, an essence nurtured by the English climate and, according to rumour, stemming from the queen's own family line. By attending to Stukeley's humoral profile, *Famous History* introduces the somatic makeup of the renegade body into the political conversation he inspires, shifting the cause of renegadism away from wilful, aberrant behaviour to something more endemic – the English body itself. Not only does the play's Stukeley spread the disease of sedition among what Cecil calls the "simple people" (A2), but he carries disease within him, and this condition, thematized as "heat," marks him as irreducibly English and thus not so deviant after all.

While critics typically discuss Stukeley in terms of his discursive status as a folk hero/traitor, a closer look at his humoral body unlocks a deeper dimension to his political significance for the audiences of early modern England. *Famous History*'s humoral language, this chapter will argue, necessitates an investigation into the causes and conditions of treason by highlighting the porousness of the English male body and, by extension, the porousness of the national body. The play supports that investigation by comparing and contrasting Stukeley not to foreign characters, but to an *English* character – the fictional Vernon – who appears alongside him on his journey from England, to Ireland, to Iberia, and finally to both their deaths in North Africa. Vernon, an introverted man who suffers from bad "air" in Stukeley's presence yet cannot escape him, serves as a device for exploring questions about the origins of treasonous male behaviour. The melancholic Vernon, in continual interaction with the overheated Stukeley, redirects the terms of contemporary conversation about the causes of treason away from exterior causes – such as "heretic" religion and the allure of foreign gold – towards a look at England itself. This redirection provides audiences with the opportunity to contemplate how native English conditions – conditions that audiences themselves experience – create English renegades. This move neutralizes the putative threat of foreign enemies that officials like Cecil invoked to rhetorically manipulate audiences and opens those audiences up to a more introspective mood that, while open-ended, nonetheless fosters a counterdiscourse to the state's representation of renegades as radically "other."

By focusing on the somatic body as it appears in medical texts and in the play itself, this chapter will explore one vehicle by which the renegade brings to the forefront what Daniel Carey calls the "fiction of incommensurability" between English self and foreign other. The most widely discussed humoral treatise of the period, Robert Burton's *Anatomy of Melancholy* (1621), will be analysed to expose blurred demarcations between putatively un-English renegade traits and the traits of obedient English subjects. The interrogation of such "fictions" through humoral language may well have been more apparent to audiences than any representation of Stukeley as a "traitor" or even as a "cosmopolitan" figure. In his critique of scholarship that relies on "the nation" as a category, Brian C. Lockey describes Stukeley, a Catholic recusant, as more cosmopolitan than traitor; Stukeley, Lockey argues, is "the product of a dialectical relationship existing between his English identity and the transnational or 'cosmopolitan' identity that his Englishness enables." Lockey thus concludes that "the Stukeley plays ultimately present Stukeley's Englishness as a window onto an imagined network of Christian sovereigns that should ideally act as caretakers for one another" (187). This perspective, while offering an important corrective to recent criticism that privileges English nationalism as the dominant model for identity, nonetheless overlooks Stukeley's deep and organic connection to the heart of the English state – a connection that the play expresses in its focus on Stukeley's somatic imbalance and its correspondence to other English men. It is the play's apprehension of renegadism as beginning *in* the body, rather than beginning in any overt action *against* the state, that endows this particular renegade with the potential to inspire critical dialogue about renegadism as an affliction stemming from within the nation, rather than from outside it.

As with all of the historical figures in this book, the "truth" about Thomas Stukeley varied over a range of imaginative retellings. The record of ballads, romances, and chronicles reveals what biographer Richard Simpson calls the "complete cloud of traditions" surrounding Stukeley (4); each text highlights aspects of the legend and downplays or omits others. Among such treatments, the earlier play, George Peele's *Battle of Alcazar* (c. 1590), centres mainly on the conflicts between the Iberian and North African kings, conflicts that lead up to the eponymous battle, where Stukeley meets his death. Peele's Stukeley appears mostly in brief moments to declare his bravery as well as his single ambition – to attain royal status:

> There shall no action pass my hand or sword
> That cannot make a step to gain a crown,
> No word shall pass the office of my tongue
> That sounds not of affectation to a crown,
> No thought have being in my lordly breast
> That works not every way to win a crown. (2.2.69–73)

In contrast to Peele's exclusive focus on the drama of political ambition on foreign soil, *Famous History* includes scenes in England, in Ireland, and between three English men – Stukeley, Captain Harbert, and Vernon.

The additions in *Famous History* bring the Stukeley story closer to home. While Peele's play opens in Morocco, *Famous History* begins in London with Stukeley's wooing of Nell Curtis, the daughter of a wealthy alderman; although Vernon wooed the lady first, Stukeley wins her hand. These early scenes allow glimpses of the flaws that belie Stukeley's gallant image. Nell's father considers, and then dismisses, his son-in-law's wild reputation. Stukeley's own father visits his son at the Inns of Court to find that the younger man has no regard for "scratching things out of a standish" (2.177–8) – that is, poring over law books and copying out statutes – and that his son intends to make his fortune instead by marrying Nell. At the wedding, one Captain Jack Harbert earns Stukeley's ire by openly objecting to the marriage. Soon enough, Stukeley exhausts Nell's fortune by settling his debts to London merchants and then abandons her. Claiming gentlemanly liberality, devotion to honour, and a fervent desire to serve his queen, Stukeley abruptly departs from London to fight in the Irish wars, leaving Nell behind.

Stukeley proceeds to Ireland, then to Europe, then further abroad. Vernon, who also turns up as a soldier in Ireland, rues Stukeley's presence, although he never states the reason. As the English forces battle the rebel Shane O'Neill, Stukeley shows himself to be vainglorious and concerned primarily with his own honour. There he meets Captain Harbert again, who confronts him. The standoff concludes with Stukeley abruptly leaving the campaign in the middle of a siege.

Stukeley sails to the Iberian Peninsula. The Governor of Cales (Cadiz) takes him prisoner, but he gains his freedom by appealing to King Philip II of Spain. Philip confirms a common English stereotype of the Spanish by behaving in a wily and deceitful manner, promising aid which he has no intention of actually delivering. Philip convinces Don Sebastian of Portugal to take Stukeley to Tangier to intervene on behalf of the displaced sovereign Muly Muhamet. Meanwhile, Vernon turns up in Spain as the passenger of a captured ship. He is unhappy to meet Stukeley again, saying "Either was he created for my scourge / Or I was born the foil to his fair haps, / Or in our birth our stars were retrograde" (17.56–9). He leaves, saying he will "range this universe about" (70) but meets Stukeley again at the battle of Alcazar, fighting on the side of the Portuguese in support of Muly Mahamet. The Portuguese lose and rogue Italian soldiers kill both Stukeley and Vernon. In dying they proclaim friendship at last – "in our birth we two / Were so ordained to be of one self heart / To love one woman, breathe one country air" (28.23–5). They comfort each other in the knowledge that their spilt blood will mingle with that of kings.

Recent critical commentary on *Famous History* and *The Battle of Alcazar* has focused on two interrelated topics: the plays' wide international scope and the significance of Stukeley's treason within that context. While scholars such as Lockey and Eric Griffin read the plays in terms of cosmopolitan identity and transnational networks, others read them in terms of the class and gender discourses that they invoke. Jean Howard situates Stukeley's "renegade masculinity" within the generic context of the early modern adventure play, a kind of drama that treats "the aspirations of social and economic interlopers who rise above their stations and in so doing signify both national self-assertion and vulnerability" (*Gender* 247).[1] While some of adventure drama's heroes – such as the merchant Vitelli from Philip Massinger's *The Renegado* (pub. 1630) and the tavern wench Bess Bridges from Thomas Heywood's *Fair Maid of the West, Parts I and II* (1630) – succeed in these aspirations, others go too far and thus fall to their destruction, as in the case of

Stukeley. Also considering Stukeley's status as transgressor, Claire Jowitt extends the spectacle of "unruly masculinity" into the realm of political critique. She argues that Stukeley stimulates debate about "the limits of appropriate male behavior" in a way that explores English masculinity in general and in the context of Elizabeth I's rule (*Voyage Drama* 82, 94). In comparison to the supposed liabilities of female rule, Stukeley's warlike courage presents a strength. Yet paradoxically, this same strength, put into action, makes Stukeley into a traitor, one whose "rampant individualism" threatens national stability (65). "Individualism," in Jowitt's analysis, captures the paradox of the hero/traitor whose manly self-definition at once stimulates both fear and admiration. This description of Stukeley as "rampant" individual resembles Barbara Fuchs's view of pirates as exhibiting so much "self-will" that their talents for warfare become liabilities ("Faithless" 46). In this sense, Stukeley fits the discursive pattern of the renegade as a man apart, one radically and wilfully disconnected from his origins, his religion, and from all of society's stabilizing structures – in Cecil's word, "faithlesse."

While I do not deny that Stukeley's story, in its various articulations, seems to fit the pattern Fuchs identifies, I propose that the humoral language employed in *Famous History* undercuts Stukeley's "individualism" and ultimately renders it superficial. In doing so, the play suggests that the English renegade is not an extraordinary deviant, but a man who remains connected to the English land and people in spite of himself. Stukeley's relationship with Vernon thematizes this connection. I cite again Stukeley's lines from the last scene to demonstrate how the play renders their bond: "in our birth we two / Were so ordained to be of *one self heart* / To love one woman, *breathe one country air*" (emphasis added). Stukeley's claim that he and his friend breathe the same "air" strikes a note of irony, given that the air between them was once the very basis for Vernon's antipathy. When Stukeley turns up in Ireland, Vernon complains, "Is Stukeley come, whom I desire to shun? / And must he needs to Ireland follow me? / I will not draw that air wherein he breathes, / One kingdom shall not hold us if I can" (9.9–12). Yet at the play's conclusion, it turns out that Stukeley's "air" is Vernon's own after all, no matter how hard Vernon has tried to escape it. Moreover, they find in this moment that they share "one self heart" as well. Early modern medical theory held the heart to be not only the seat of the passions, but the internal organ most endowed with "heat."[2] Stukeley and Vernon share the same "heat" source as well as the same air. Thus, this heat is not unique to the renegade Stukeley after all. It is as though, despite his best efforts at escape, Vernon has carried Stukeley's essence within him all along.

I suggest that "one self heart" and "one country air" function as rhetorical signposts alerting us to the particular way in which the play represents renegade behaviour – as rooted not solely in a character's actions, but in his very complexion. The English term "complexion" originated in the Greek word *crasis*, or "temperament," which represented the balance of humours – hot, dry, cold, moist – in the human body. Scientific writers in the sixteenth and seventeenth centuries believed that humans, plants, and animals alike had their own individual complexion, a unique mixture with explanatory power for that individual's behaviour.[3] Complexion theory informs Old Stukeley's understanding of his son's temperament:

[h]e shows himself a gentleman,
And though perhaps he shall not know so much,
I do not much mislike that humour in him.
A gentleman of blood and quality,
To sort himself amongst the noblest spirits,
Shows the true sparks of honourable worth
And rightly shows he is mine own. (2.55–61)

In Old Stukeley's view, his son "shows himself a gentleman" due to a "humour" within; the son therefore is a gentleman "of blood," blood being both the source and the carrier of his "gentlemanly" essence. The blood they share, Old Stukeley reasons, "rightly shows he is mine own." The invocation of blood becomes the basis for a claim of social distinction as well, underwriting the son's (and by implication the father's) right to "sort himself amongst the noblest spirits."

The younger Stukeley too understands himself to be a product of his "humour." However, he reads that "humour" in ways that sever, rather than affirm, his bond with his father. Later in the scene, we learn that the son in fact seeks to *differentiate* himself; the first sign of this differentiation occurs when he rebels against his father's wish that he attend the Inns of Court. Howard regards Stukeley's rejection of the Inns as a "transformative moment" in his progress towards full disengagement from England: "Implicitly renouncing the citizen values of thrift, civic duty, domesticity, and fidelity to the monarch, he increasingly embodies a hyperbolic attachment to chivalric honor and self-assertion" ("Gender" 352).[4] Indeed, we learn in Cecil's treatise that rebels hold the "[l]awes of the land" in contempt; Stukeley's disdain for the Inns literalizes this rebellious attitude as a rejection of the nation's legal training grounds. His unwillingness to obey his father also invokes treason. For example, in *Rules to Know a Royall King* (1642), Thomas Jordan equates honouring the king with "honoring thy father and thy mother," because the divine appoints them both (A2); in these terms, Stukeley's actions prefigure his willingness to defy the state.

Stukeley's failure to honour his father extends to rejecting the very "air" surrounding Old Stukeley and the places his father represents. The younger Stukeley seems to regard his own complexional "heat" as something to protect, as we learn when Old Stukeley rebukes him for his desire to participate in the Irish wars:

> Father, unless you mean I shall be thought
> A traitor to her majesty, a coward,
> A sleepy dormouse and a carpet-squire,
> *Mix not my forward summer with sharp breath,*
> Nor intercept my purpose, being good. (6.93–7, emphasis added)

Stukeley's "forward summer" represents his ability to take action rather than remain at home. The winds of his father's "sharp breath" threaten to compromise the heat he expresses here. Notably, Stukeley equates lack of such "summer" with duplicity, cowardice, laziness, and the base servile role of a "carpet-squire," all descriptions that deny him his due social privilege.

Stukeley's use of humoral language, like his father's, references his social position, but it otherwise reflects a viewpoint that diverges from that of his father. The two men's perspectives reflect broader cultural and scientific conversations about the origins of the human character. While Old Stukeley sees his son's "gentlemanly" disposition as an expression of inherited blood, the son sees his own spirit as something to be carefully cultivated and protected from outside elements, including the breath of his father and other men less "forward." His words invoke the relationship between the environment and individual psychology, two spheres that early modern medical thought – shaped by classical humoralism – regarded as mutually influential. Early modern psychology, which studied the soul, fell under the larger disciplinary umbrella of natural philosophy; learned writers saw the soul as rooted in nature. Biology and psychology were thus not separate fields, but fields of inquiry in reciprocal relationship.[5] Therefore, as Gail Kern

Paster explains, the relationship between the body and external circumstances also is reciprocal: "In the dynamic reciprocities between self and environment imagined by the psychophysiology of bodily fluids, circumstance engenders humors in the body and humors in the body help to determine circumstance by predisposing the individual subject to a characteristic kind of evaluation and response" (14).[6] While Old Stukeley sees "blood" as preceding external circumstance – that is, as indicating some natural disposition that flows throughout a closed body – his son is much more attuned to the porousness of that body and the "spirit's" dependence on air and other "outside" elements. Given the body's capacity to absorb outside elements, Stukeley sees both the Inns and his father as detrimental to his "purpose," a plan that requires the preservation of what he sees as his special humoral characteristics.

Therefore Stukeley does not fear only the confinements of "thrift, civic duty, domesticity, and fidelity to the monarch." He fears that the very air he breathes will stifle the gallantry that, until this point, has stirred both admiration and condemnation among his fellow Londoners. Before Stukeley even appears on stage, we witness a conversation between Nell's parents that clues us in to the range of perceptions surrounding their future son-in-law:

> CURTIS
> Stukeley is a gallant man,
> And one here in our city much beloved.
> LADY CURTIS
> Nay, husband, both in court and country too,
> A gentleman well born, and as I hear,
> His father's heir ...
> CURTIS
> Passion of me, wife, but I heard last day,
> He's very wild, a quarreler, a fighter,
> Ay, and I doubt a spend-good too.
> LADY CURTIS
> That is but youthfulness – marriage will tame him. (1.100–10)

"Gallant," "well born," "wild," "a quarreler," "a fighter," "a spend-good": these descriptions together capture the paradox of the hero/traitor, with a dash of boyish "wildness" that Lady Curtis surmises, mistakenly, "marriage will tame." Like Old Stukeley, she misunderstands the source of Stukeley's behaviour. While a person's complexion might alter according to age and life circumstances[7] – a point that I will discuss more fully below – Lady Curtis does not realize Stukeley's overriding "purpose," which is to apply his heat to the wider world of international warfare and politics. To do that, he believes that he must escape the *English* influences that stifle the heat he so carefully cultivates. While his "wildness" may indeed reflect his youth, he intends to prolong that wildness well beyond the conventional life stage assumed by Lady Curtis. Once he arrives in Spain, the governor and his wife also refer to his blood:

> GOVERNOR'S LADY
> Surely the confidence of this man's spirit
> Shows that his blood is either great or noble,
> Or that his fortune's at his own command.
> GOVERNOR
> I hold him rather to be some desp'rate pirate,
> That thinks to domineer upon the land
> As he is used amongst his mates at sea. (13.52–7)

This exchange takes place in Cadiz, a setting with special significance for English audiences: at this port, in 1587, Francis Drake achieved a decisive victory for England by raiding several forts and destroying a Spanish fleet. But for every hero like Francis Drake, Walter Raleigh, and Martin Frobisher, there existed a multitude of pirates seeking riches and adventure on their own terms. Further, as Fuchs shows, the line between privateer and pirate was not always distinct (*Mimesis* 119–22). Concerning Stukeley, the debate between the governor and his wife invites audiences to consider these competing representations: they may admire "the confidence of this man's spirit" or condemn him as "some desp'rate pirate." It also demonstrates that Stukeley has managed to keep his "humor" intact and has put it into valiant (according to the lady) and threatening (according to the governor) action.

The ambiguities surrounding Stukeley – hero or traitor, gentleman or rogue – reside in how others identify and interpret his somatic makeup. Although Stukeley views his "forward summer" as an enabling condition, the conversations between these two couples – one in England, one in Spain – indicate the destructiveness of that same nature. By the time he arrives in Spain, he already has proven himself to be a spendthrift, a deserter, and, yes, a pirate. The fact that England's Spanish enemy finds Stukeley's "heat" useful suggests why his "gallant" temperament is a problem for England as well as for the man himself. King

Philip's marshal, Valdes, marvels at Stukeley's bravado: "What a high spirit hath this Englishman. / He tunes his speeches to a kingly key, / Conquers the world, and casts it at his heels" (18.26–8); yet, this same "high spirit" will drive Stukeley to plot an invasion of Ireland, ally himself with the Iberian monarchs, and eventually walk into his own destruction on the battlefield at Alcazar.

Stukeley's "heat," then, both confirms his heroic nature and marks that same nature as foolish at best, dangerous at worst. To call Stukeley a "cosmopolitan" in the sense that he idealistically chooses a world view that only happens to compete with that of his queen is to ignore the extreme deviations in his nature and the fact that those extremes manifest in distinctly destructive, as well as admirably heroic, ways. The Spanish notice the impulsiveness of Stukeley's "heat" and, indeed, take advantage of it, noting that Stukeley is "[h]ardy but rash, witty but overweening, / Else would this English hot-brain weigh the intent / Your highness hath in thus employing him" (16.166–8). His heroism and his impulsiveness make him gullible and useful to foreign agendas. Thus, his blood poses a threat to his country.

Furthermore, the discussions among the Londoners and the Spanish remind us that, while Stukeley may be "gallant" and "beloved," he nonetheless operates in an imbalanced state – that is, in what early moderns would have understood to be a state of disease. Stukeley's heat testifies, on the one hand, to his manliness and nobility; yet, on the other, its excess means he does not live up to the classical ideal of noble masculinity prevalent in early modern England. Mary Floyd-Wilson usefully explains the implications of humoral imbalance for class and gender distinction: "To embody and express masculinity successfully, the classical ideal male must sustain *crasis* or temperance, a harmonious mixture of all four qualities, warm, cold, dry, and moist. Masculinity and social superiority, maintained by temperance, could be undone by the predominance of any one humor" (12–13).[8] Stukeley lacks the control over his own passions that, according to Michael Schoenfeldt, made a man truly the master of himself (11, 79);[9] as Paster elaborates, "once [aristocratic high-spiritedness] escapes such management and escalates into political rebellion, impulsivity is recoded as rusticity, social backwardness, or archaism" (196). Humoral imbalance, then, was a condition imbued with "moral density and spiritual import" (6). A biological undercurrent underwrites Stukeley's doomed rebellion.

However, because humoral and complexional theories held bodily health and the environment to be reciprocal, it would be a mistake to identify Stukeley's excessive heat as an aberration from some standard of normative Englishness. Although Stukeley claims that his spirit makes him unsuitable for England, as if he were an Italian or a Spaniard accidentally born in an Englishman's body, the evidence in the play does not support this understanding. As Andrew Wear reminds us, the humoral understanding credited the influence of the supposed "constitution" of a person's country of birth (126). Although the real-life Stukeley had travelled outside of England before his marriage, the play does not mention this. Instead, it portrays a young man straining against the norms of English manhood, craving adventure outside of those conventional restrictions – his "heat" and "wildness" have been present all along.

Yet the play's portrayal of Stukeley's "heat" as unique to his body reflects a fundamental contradiction in humoral discourse. The ideal of *crasis*, even if theoretically achievable, ultimately could not be achieved because, as scholars of humoralism have shown, humoral theory regarded all bodies as malleable and thus subject to change according to age, diet, climate, and other circumstances.[10] In other words, humoral imbalance over the course of a person's life was expected – vacillation represented the norm, not the exception. My reading of Burton's *Anatomy* will exemplify this idea by showing that discussions of humoral types reflect not a genealogy of discrete personalities, but an exploration of ways in which individuals deviate from an elusive ideal. These deviations may differ in kind, but imbalance itself exists in everyone, a fact that undermines Stukeley's sense that his own "heat" makes him singularly heroic.

This mistake in Stukeley's self-understanding thus raises the question of whether male Englishness itself creates renegadism and, if so, whether Stukeley's behaviour epitomizes a larger phenomenon, one that casts doubt on Stukeley's putative singularity. *Famous History* suggests that the English renegade begins not at sea, not in foreign courts, and not in contact with foreign religion. It begins within the body, living and breathing on English land. My reading of Vernon – a superficially opposite personality type who, in spite of himself, nonetheless shares Stukeley's "heat" – will support this perspective. First, however, I will turn to one of the period's best-known humoral treatises – Burton's *Anatomy of Melacholy*. It sheds light on not only the link between masculine heat and rebellion, but also the particular ripeness of that connection for literary and dramatic explorations of male behaviour.

Even a brief survey of early modern medical texts will reveal a cultural preoccupation with humoral and complexional theories – that is, theories that study the relationship between the health of a living thing and its environment. These writings extended scientific observation into commentary about the habits and practices of everyday life, including religion, superstition, the formation and expression of national character, travel, food, drink, and even clothing. Texts that illuminate the renegade Englishman's humoral profile might include Thomas Wright's *Passions of the Mind in General* (1604), which ties emotional temperance to regional identity, or Thomas Cogan's *The Haven of Health* (1584), which expands on the humoral consequences of England's cold and moist climate.

Robert Burton's voluminous *Anatomy of Melancholy*, first published in 1621 and then published in five revised editions before his death in 1640, was perhaps the most famous reflection on humoral imbalance written in the period. Burton's special relevance for renegade representations lies not only in the sheer volume of attention he devotes to troublesome personalities, but in his distinctly literary, even dramatic and satirical, approach to anatomizing these personalities. In a fashion similar to the "humoral comedy" popularized by playwrights such as Ben Jonson and George Chapman, Burton relies on characters to exemplify the staggering array of causes and symptoms he groups under the broad diagnostic umbrella of "melancholy." As Bridget Gellert Lyons has shown, literary treatments of melancholy help build an imaginary world and thus differ from scientific texts; in similar fashion, Burton infuses scientific discourse with his own descriptive strategies, strategies that draw a vivid and engaging picture of melancholic personalities.

Burton's approach creates at least as many ambiguities as it attempts to resolve. Although one might expect his use of character to concretize, through vivid description, the ways in which melancholy manifests, it does not. The characters we find in the *Anatomy* end up mixing together, borrowing elements from one another, and even contradicting one another, giving the impression that *any* discernible personality trait can lead to a melancholic diagnosis. This lack of distinction among types also raises a question: If nearly anyone can be melancholic, is the theoretical ideal of *crasis* even possible? This question matters for *Famous History*, because of Vernon. He appears to be Stukeley's complete opposite and yet ultimately shares the renegade's traits, as the play's conclusion confirms. Just as the sickness Burton explored seems to echo everywhere – even in his own alter ego, "Democritus Junior" – so do traces of Stukeley's sickness appear in a less obviously threatening character, suggesting that the renegade humour may not be so specific to the designated renegade after all. In fact, the ideal of *crasis* begins to look like merely that – an ideal – with actual personalities representing degrees of deviation from that ideal rather than distinct types in their own right.

The phrase "unquiet hotspurs" signals Burton's distinctly literary approach to exploring the relationship between the humours and political defiance. Readers of Shakespeare's histories will recognize the reference to Henry Percy, the rash face of chivalric rebellion in Shakespeare's *Henry IV, Part 1*. In the preface to *Anatomy*, "Democritus to the Reader," Burton draws on Hotspur to describe the kinds of men who vainly lead soldiers into the miseries of war: "wars are begun, by the persuasion of a few debauched, hairbrain [*sic*], poor, dissolute, hungry captains, parasitical fawners, unquiet hotspurs, restless innovators, green heads, to satisfy one man's private spleen, lust, ambition, avarice" (D3ᵛ). Whether or not Burton had Stukeley in mind, he captures common perceptions surrounding the renegade type and his rabble of followers. As Hotspur, the Earl of Essex, and Stukeley himself illustrate to different degrees, the English rebel frequently assumed the shape of a "hungry captain" and sometimes "parasitical fawner" manipulating monarchs for his own ends, "poor" in cash yet full of "spleen, lust, ambition, avarice." Cecil similarly links Stukeley to treason through the figure of the "restless innovator" or roaming heretic in his pamphlet two decades earlier. Burton's medical diagnosis echoes the language that Cecil uses when describing Stukeley and other rebels who "ranne away." His repurposing of the proper name "Hotspur" captures the stereotypical humoral composition of this type, a man who suffers from excess heat and whose intemperance leads him to dangerous and unruly action.

Effectively, Burton's inclusion of the "unquiet hotspur" in his gallery of melancholics shifts the conversation about renegade warmongering away from the influence of *outside* forces – that is, the foreign religion and politics that putatively influence Stukeley and other renegades – to the inner condition of the body. While Burton does not deny the body's vulnerability to external pathology, his focus on the humours raises the question of where rebellion actually originates: from within or without. This question matters because it apprehends the ultimate permeability of the absolute distinctions – inner/outer, self/other, domestic/

foreign – that designated the renegade as a declared outsider, one wilfully divorced from his country and its people.

Previous critics have noted anxieties about the permeability between countrymen and foreigners emerging in different discourses in the period. For example, David Hillman notes that the word "crisis" – commonly used in reference to political disturbance – also referred to the turning point in an illness; this semantic ambiguity, which blends the discursive realms of the political and the medical, invokes early modern anxieties surrounding the porousness of the human body and, by extension, the porousness of the national body (5). Similarly, Jonathan Gil Harris reads the ambiguities that undermine such absolute distinctions into the writings of seventeenth-century mercantilists, for whom the economic health of the nation increasingly relied on "an ambivalent conception of *transnationality* that works to naturalize the global even as it stigmatizes the foreign" (1). English political and economic power relied on international participation; yet at the same time, such participation served to reify the "foreign" as a source of infection and corruption. The renegade, whose humours reflect and exert influence on both "English" and "foreign" elements, literally embodies these increasingly ambiguous boundaries between "self" and "other." Likewise, Burton's conception of the "unquiet hotspur" as suffering from humoral disruption displays uncertainty about the origins of anti-establishment conduct – whether they come from the interior landscape of the body, the pernicious influence of foreign ideas, or some confluence of both.

Characters, for Burton, offer a way to explore this uncertainty. He considers the possible relationships between interior disorder and exterior influence through a colourful description of personalities recognizable to his seventeenth-century audience. Burton begins by satirizing his own alter ego, "Democritus Junior," who writes from the enclosed space of his "garden" as a withdrawn observer – a position that has only exacerbated his own melancholy. Democritus diagnoses himself by elaborating on conventional binaries of the solitary life of contemplation versus the active life of worldly engagement, polarities that, as I will show, superficially characterize Vernon and Stukeley as well. In self-imposed isolation, Democritus Junior lives apart from the constant influx of "new news every day":

> those ordinary rumours of war, plagues, fire, inundations, thefts, murders, massacres, meteors, comets, spectrums, prodigies, apparitions, of towns taken, cities besieged in France, Germany, Turky, Persia, Poland, &c. daily

musters and preparations, and such like, which these tempestuous times afford, battles fought, so many men slain, monomachies, shipwracks, piracies, and sea-fights ... Amidst the gallantry and misery of the world, jollitie, pride, perplexities and cares, simplicity and vilany, subtletie, knaverie, candour and integrity, mutually mixt and offering themselves, I rub on, *privus privatus*: as I have still lived, so I now continue statu quo prius, left to a solitary life, and mine own domestick discontents. (A2–A2ᵛ)

Democritus, who eschews travel and adventure in favour of scholarly tranquility, at first seems to stand in direct contrast to a man of action such as Stukeley. Unlike the solitary writer, Stukeley avoids the "domestick" and creates "discontents" wherever he goes, openly rejecting his home in favour of glory abroad. For Democritus, simply reading about travel preserves his tranquility enough to keep his melancholy manageable: "I have never travelled but in map or card, in which my unconfined thoughts have freely expatiated, as having ever been especially delighted with the study of cosmography. Saturn was lord of my geniture ... I have little, I want nothing: all my treasure is in Minerva's tower" (A2). Notably, Burton connects Democritus's resistance to travel to "want[ing] nothing." By implication, travel only serves the spiritual ills of ambition and desire, conditions that Democritus studiously avoids by staying at home. Yet this very avoidance suggests that he recognizes within himself a latent form of the desires he ascribes to the "hungry captain." His solitary state is deliberate, cultivated, and sensitive to outside influence; he nurtures it in the same way that Stukeley nurtures his own seemingly opposite temperament. Both bodies – that of the solitary scholar and that of the unquiet hotspur – hold within them same potential for humoral, and thus political, disruption.

Thus Burton's reliance on character sketches as a strategy for differentiating melancholic types ultimately fails to identify the specific causes, conditions, and manifestations of melancholy. The *Anatomy* identifies a spectrum of behaviours, some of which appear – like the withdrawn scholar and the unquiet hotspur, melancholics both – to contradict one another. The frontispiece of Burton's book visually depicts a range of traits associated with melancholia: "jealousy," "solitariness," "enamoredness," "hypochondria," "superstition," and "madness" stemming from anger (Sig. 1.). This illustration indicates that the book will explore much more, reflecting the proliferation of scientific and literary treatments that appeared in the decades before the *Anatomy*'s publication. An orientation towards action and violence distinguishes the "jealous" melancholic. In contrast, Burton describes the "solitary" melancholic as sleeping. Another melancholy figure lives sequestered from the rest of the world, locked in study and contemplation, eschewing human company. Yet the unquiet hotspurs, those aspiring men who make war for their own aggrandizement, suffer from melancholy as well. One character from the frontispiece, the "Superstitious Man," is plainly Catholic – he kneels in a friar's robe, praying the rosary as he looks to the heavens: "He fasts, he prays, on his Idol fixt, / Tormented hope and fear betwixt." While Stukeley's self-appointed role as Catholic crusader never seems to manifest as actual religious devotion, his Catholicism marks him as a "restless innovator" nonetheless. Another character from the frontispiece, the "Madman," suffers primarily from the heat of anger: "see the madman rage down right / With furious looks, a ghastly sight." This fury, while not aligned in this case with the restless captain "hungry" for war, nonetheless exhibits a key aspect of the melancholic's personality that leads to the destruction of himself and others. Once we learn of these varying extremes, the "non-melancholic" alternative appears rather narrow, inhabiting an imprecisely defined mean between passivity and aggression, lethargy and passion. Even so, Burton only describes perfect humoral balance negatively, merely as the absence of extremes. This broad range of behaviours in turn suggests a broad range of possibilities for unruly and threatening behaviour, all of which originate from a discursively pre-political place – that is, from within the body itself.

Two key points about humoral discourse in Burton's text illuminate *Famous History*'s version of the Stukeley legend. First, the proliferation of melancholic personalities that we find in the pages of the *Anatomy* testifies to the wide range of symptoms thought to exhibit the melancholic humour – from withdrawal (and possibly the practice of heresy in contemplation) to overt rebellion, from excessive sleeping to a restless inability to settle. This sheer range of symptoms works against the "unquiet hotspur" as a singular figure of rebellion and connects him to a much wider range of behaviours, some less obviously pathological than others, but all holding the potential for disruption. Second, Burton's brand of "humoral comedy" links scientific writing to dramatic characterization, invoking the stage as a place where an audience might consider characters in humoral imbalance individually and in comparison to other characters. In pairing the legend of Stukeley with an ordinary Englishman, a character who shares his fate but appears in no previous version of the legend, *Famous History* suggests that even the most withdrawn Englishman holds the potential to go rogue. Vernon's connection to Stukeley deepens the play's treatment of masculinity by suggesting that every Englishman, even the most seemingly withdrawn, possesses within himself the potential for disruptive "heat."

꩜

Although critics widely consider *Famous History* a meditation on English masculinity, they have paid surprisingly little attention to the play's other Englishmen. Among those who do mention Vernon, Jowitt implies that that "honest" character exists only as a contrast to enhance the audience's sense of Stukeley's faithlessness and to highlight the "poison" in England and in Stukeley; Lockey succinctly describes Vernon as Stukeley's "cosmopolitan double: a representative of positive English traits who for his own reason has exiled himself from his native land."[11] Both critics take Vernon to be a foil, of sorts, for Stukeley's behaviour – a reasonable assumption, given how different the characters initially appear.

However, their companionate journey reveals that the two men have more in common than critics, and the characters themselves, realize. Vernon and Stukeley share a "heat" that gives them a passionate desire to travel and a sense of revulsion towards remaining in England. This common ground repeatedly pulls them together as they travel throughout the world, and it brings them together at the end, as if dying in the same "air" were inevitable. The men's companionate death indicates an enduring commonality underneath the superficial characteristics of their respective personalities. In fact, while Stukeley is rash and Vernon is introspective, neither man displays a "pure" humoral profile, but rather a mixture of qualities. Moreover, the two men who embody these blended traits share the same fate at the end, roping the introspective, Democritus-like man into the same fate as the unquiet hotspur.

Although the ending scene perhaps expresses the men's essential sameness most dramatically, earlier moments in the play indicate the essence the two men share. One such moment occurs in an observation Stukeley makes, which represents his only explicit criticism of Vernon's character, despite Vernon's own regular expressions of revulsion towards Stukeley. In Spain, where Stukeley saves Vernon from being taken prisoner after the latter's ship is seized, Vernon expresses doubt about the success of the mission to Tunis: he doubts King Philip's intentions and Stukeley's capacity to fulfil them. Stukeley replies, "Friend

Vernon, leave such discontenting speech. / Your melancholy overflows your spleen / Even as the billows over-rack your ship, / Whose loss for my sake will restore" (17.11–15). Stukeley's diagnosis of Vernon as "overflowing" with melancholy partakes of the popular early modern vocabulary of manly self-definition that I discuss above. There are many possible terms Stukeley might use to criticize Vernon's inaction, but here he draws on a common humanist trope of selfhood, one based in classical medical theory, to distinguish Vernon's temperament from his own.

Yet although Stukeley speaks in a way that attempts to distinguish Vernon's temper from his own, the diagnosis of excess "melancholy" itself does not much clarify the difference between the two men. Given the vast amounts of contemporaneous writing on melancholy – not to mention the ambiguity present in texts such as Burton's *Anatomy* – it is difficult to distil Stukeley's diagnosis into a stable set of traits we might attribute to Vernon. We might, then, reframe the issue with more attention to the context for the men's dialogue, as Angus Gowland offers: "Instead of asking why people are afflicted with melancholy, we must ask why people described themselves or others as melancholic, and consider what they meant by this" (83). Specifically, we might ask what Stukeley himself means by calling Vernon "melancholic" and how this attribution defines the two men as *dramatic* figures for the play's audience.

While we have seen that symptoms of melancholy were diverse and often contradictory, the characterization of the melancholic as fearful, passive, and given over to solitary contemplation at the expense of action persisted across scientific writings. These symptoms have received ample scholarly discussion elsewhere; here, however, I would like to note that different genres of writing have distinct uses for the melancholic personality. Melancholics in literature do not merely reflect scientific discourse. Rather, they introduce that discourse into specific generic and historical contexts, inviting audiences to consider melancholy through a particular lens – in the case of *Famous History*, through the lens of unruly English masculinity in foreign contexts. Accordingly, the play invokes "the melancholic" as a dramatic type in order to scrutinize masculine heroic traits. While melancholy held a positive status for many writers, designating (usually the male) melancholic as a humanist individual of extraordinary intellectual and artistic achievement, it seems unlikely that Stukeley intends the term in this way, particularly given the disdain for learning that he displays during his final days at the Inns. If anything, Stukeley prefers action over reflection of any kind; by contrast, Vernon spends a great deal of time reflecting. His speech and behaviour fit common descriptions of the melancholic as "accompanied by groundless fear and sorrow," exhibiting an affinity for "solitariness" and passive spectatorship.[12] Stukeley seems to be using "melancholy" as shorthand for a lack of masculine bravado, particularly since melancholy also was commonly associated with kinds of emotionalism widely attributed to women. Stukeley clearly views Vernon's scepticism towards a military campaign – and perhaps his contemplative questioning of a monarch's integrity – as betraying melancholy in excess of the organ ("spleen") that secretes it. We might say that, in Stukeley's view, Vernon's habit of thinking renders him cowardly and perhaps a shade too circumspect towards the idea of majesty itself.

Based on Stukeley's impression, Vernon is a fearful melancholic, a popular dramatic type. Like Hamlet, Vernon eschews violent action and avoids his duty to fight; like *As You Like It*'s Jaques, he meditates from a position of discontent exacerbated by the compulsion to travel.[13] Yet Vernon ultimately complicates this artificial distinction between himself as "melancholic" and Stukeley as "heroic." Not only does Vernon feel propelled to travel, like Stukeley he claims inner heat – supposedly Stukeley's attribute – as his cause for doing so. He tells his English companions: "I am *fired* with a desire to travel / And see the fashions, state and qualities / Of other countries" (4.53–5; emphasis added). The *Oxford English Dictionary* cites "fire" as a verb as meaning "to inspire with passion or strong feeling or desire" as well as "to kindle or inflame" (v. 1, 3a). The word, when applied to the awakening of Vernon's inner heat, recalls a passage from Wright's *Passions of the Mind* that describes the passions as latent things awaiting "kindling":

> divers sorts of persons be subject to divers sorts of passions, and the same passion affecteth divers persons in divers manners: for, as we see fire applied to drie wood, to yron, to flaxe and gunpowder, worketh divers ways; for in wood it kindleth with some difficultie, and with some difficultie is quenched; but in flaxe soone it kindleth, and quencheth; in yron with great difficultie it is kindled, & with as great exteinguished, but in gunpowder it is kindled in a moment, and never can be quenched till the powder be consumed.[14]

"Gunpowder," the metaphor for the man who most easily "ignites," directly links heat to warfare and violent rebellion. We might say, then, that Stukeley is the "gunpowder" and Vernon the less flammable "iron." Yet the iron, albeit with "great difficultie," kindles nonetheless, and so does Vernon's wandering spirit. Stukeley reminds Vernon of the heat within him when he criticizes Vernon's "overflow" of melancholy as a temporary state, not a permanent condition. He counsels Vernon to "leave such discontenting speech," as though the speech itself exacerbates the melancholy, and promises that action will "restore" the overflowing "ship" of Vernon's body. Only action itself, Stukeley argues, will correct Vernon's melancholy – but it is correctible.

Vernon's claim, that inner fire propels him to wander away from England, reaches considerably beyond what readers frequently understand as his reason for travel: heartbreak over the loss of Nell to a friend. Of course, we also know that Vernon's desire to escape Stukeley plays a major role in his roaming. But the fact that his plan fails to work and ultimately results in the deaths of both men encourages us to see Vernon's aimless desire for travel in the same terms as Stukeley's own – that is, as the effect of too much "heat" and a resistance to England, a land that early modern geohumoral theory commonly held to be "cold."[15] Thus, the play does not allow its audience to dismiss these men as polar and static complexional "types" – one the fiery hero and one the cold melancholic. Rather, Vernon and Stukeley represent the same "heat" in two apparently different personalities who nonetheless follow the same path.

The men's physical and humoral proximity, then, argues against viewing Vernon simply as a foil, a character playing only a bit part in Stukeley's all-consuming drama of "individual" self-will or "cosmopolitan" idealism. If we see the two Englishmen as sharing the same qualities and thus suggesting that those qualities exist in all personality types, then Vernon occupies as important a role as the title character. The two exist in a binary relationship of superficial antagonism, having once pursued the same woman, and yet they cannot seem to escape one another no matter how far they travel from England. Despite this antagonism, the men's similarities mark them less as foils and more as, to borrow a term from Bruce R. Smith, "proximate selves." Smith describes "proximate selves" as different figures who both resemble and contrast with one another, mirroring different variations on certain traits, much as Burton's melancholic types comment on one another through their own play of resemblances and differences. Moreover, Smith argues that "masculine self-definition depends as much on proximate selves as on opposite selves" (104). This recognition is particularly important in an English play depicting exoticized foreign cultures – the presence of the

Spanish Catholic Philip and the Muslim Muly Muhamet as "others" in opposition to Stukeley further complicates Stukeley's relationship to the other Englishmen in the play. Familiar versions of the international self/other dialectic, when applied to this play, risk erasing these other Englishmen's positions altogether, despite the fact that they too are important to questions of "masculine self-definition."

In addition to addressing questions about treason and English masculinity, the dialectic of sameness and difference between Stukeley and Vernon encourages critical reflection about English heroic enterprise itself, asking audiences to reconsider the necessity of violent action for avowedly patriotic ends. Vernon's status as a "proximate self" delimits Stukeley's ambition and opens it to critique. After all, his reservations about military action and his suspicion of Philip's motives turn out to be correct – what Stukeley sees as excessive deliberation actually uncovers the limits of heroic ambition and the realities of international politics, where a sovereign's noble station does not necessarily guarantee noble intent. The play's interest in exploring the limits of heroic discourse becomes evident also in Ireland, where the native rebels display too much masculine bravado, thus making them incorrigibly wild and unruly. Harbert exclaims: "Who would have thought these naked savages, / These northern Irish durst have been so bold / T'have given assault unto a warlike town?" (11.3–5). Although Harbert ascribes unruliness to the Irish, the Spanish will witness similar behaviour in Stukeley. In other words, Stukeley's rashness precludes him from adequately thinking through the implications of Philip's request. The will to heroic action, over all else, leads to his downfall and the defeat of the Christian cause in Tunis – Stukeley, for all his admirable traits, becomes a mere dupe to Spanish interests.

The play's staging in 1605 would have spoken directly to the "chivalric revival" centring on Henry, Prince of Wales – a movement that his father, the pacific King James I, attempted to defuse both inside and outside the court. The Elizabethan conflict of ideals between Essex the soldier and Cecil the temperate civilian prefigures the movement around Prince Henry. Simpson views this conflict as central to understanding how politically minded dramatists represented Stukeley.[16] Stukeley begins to look like a knight of Prince Henry's kind, one compelling admiration while at the same time endangering the peace. Vernon's "melancholy" makes this double bind known to the audience in a way not available to the rash, unreflective Stukeley – he rhetorically limits Stukeley's daring, opens it to examination, and yet eventually shares in the disastrous fate that he predicts for his rival. Despite the functional contrast between them, the two men inhabit the same space and the same historical moment, when the naive hero falls prey to heroic nostalgia and takes with him the so-called melancholic who, ironically, had resisted him all the way.

Which man, then, ultimately poses a greater threat to England's political stability – the designated renegade or the solitary wanderer? If Stukeley's transgressions defy "the traditionally established, almost medieval, social ranks," Vernon does so from a different angle by adopting the role of the solitary traveller and eschewing the jealousy, violence, and connections that typify patriarchal bonds between men. Yet over all, both hold within them some degree of the "heat" that Burton's unquiet hotspur also carries. The play invites audiences to witness humoral types, who are in fact complex personalities, in action, making debatable choices, and acting in ways that lead audiences to question where both heroism and renegadism begin, and whether there exists any firm distinction between them after all.

What is it, then, in the cold English air that stimulates the heat of the renegade? *Famous History* does not answer this question in any definitive way, nor does any other contemporary text devoted to exploring Stukeley's character. However, by redirecting the question away from foreign contexts towards English men themselves, the play takes what contemporary travel writers and medical theorists knew – that English males were highly prone to intemperance – and applies that knowledge to the story of a legendary English renegade. In doing so, the play raises the issue of how England itself might be breeding its own renegades, men with latent tendencies that could erupt into dangerous, threatening, traitorous behaviour. The cause may lie in the way the English male body interacts with the unique English climate; it may also lie in English political culture, with its absolutist and isolationist tendencies that unsuccessfully militate against wandering, desperate action, and the influence of foreign customs and ideas. Rather than proposing a definitive cause, the play's invocation of the humours invites audience members to consider England's own role in creating its renegades and perhaps even to recognize the renegade "heat" lurking within themselves. Such questioning alone facilitates critical distance from representations such as Cecil's that purport to rhetorically manage the renegade's domestic influence by presenting him as deviant. This distancing is enough to complicate the renegade's political status as absolute enemy and allow audiences to perceive his enduring, albeit perhaps unwitting, connection to the English land and people.

A primary aim of this book is to seek connections between the renegade and the culture he rejected to complicate the simple binaries of "hero" and "traitor" that seem to dominate the political discourse surrounding these supposed outsiders. Previous scholarship has described Stukeley as ironically embodying the best "English" virtues – bravery, loyalty, and chivalry – while plotting to invade Elizabeth's territories; this irony appears to reveal how the reign of James I falls short of ideal Englishness in comparison to the putative traitor. However, this scholarly narrative fails to account for what led Stukeley to rebel (and Vernon to wander) in the first place – a feeling of revulsion towards the very land in which they were born and raised, and a wish to preserve their "heat" from the "poison" of that land. Yet this denial ultimately confirms the fact that they carry England within them, in their very blood, wherever they go. Thus, if Stukeley does indeed remain "English" to the very end, his brand of Englishness encourages less national self-flattery and more critical introspection – introspection tending in indeterminate directions, perhaps, but whose very indeterminacy itself represents a political divergence from orthodox representations of the renegade – than previous scholarly accounts indicate. *Famous History* shows this "Englishness" to reside not in heroism, but intemperance, a state that makes men prone to wandering and rebellion. And as the following chapters will show, the death of one Stukeley will not mean the death of all future English renegades – far from it.

The suggestion of common ground between the renegade and his more ordinary counterparts may have enhanced Stukeley's appeal for audiences; certainly many thrilled to his renegade adventures in drama and print. The next chapter will describe a similar phenomenon in Captain John Ward, whose notoriety generated popular writing in a range of genres. Ward shares with Stukeley the aspirational streak that propels all the English renegades in this book. For Ward, however, the renegade's identity as a "low" figure plays a larger role; while Stukeley seeks majesty and adventure, Ward seeks liberty and autonomy. This time, resistance to domestic practices of labour discipline and the experience of economic desperation, not humoral imbalance, fuels the renegade's story. Exit – for now – the unquiet hotspur, and enter the runagate corsair.

Chapter Two

"We Are of the Sea!": Masterless Identity and Transnational Context in *A Christian Turned Turk*

In the previous chapter, we witnessed how William Cecil, the queen's chief administrator and panoptic eye, viewed Thomas Stukeley as a "faithlesse beast" whose danger resided largely in his ability to inspire others to follow his lead – that is, to "run away." By connecting Stukeley to two political threats – Catholicism and vagrancy – Cecil presents this "runagate" as a composite figure who marshals anxieties both international and domestic. The central figure of the present chapter – the pirate John Ward – more clearly demonstrates the renegade's basis in discourses of class disruption. Here I will describe a man who was born in an occupation deemed "masterless," who ran away from the navy that conscripted him, and who, like Stukeley, remained on the run until the end of his days. But in the case of Ward, the renegade – cut off from his nation, disconnected from its people, and radically out of bounds – remains tied to England not through his humoral profile but through the marginalizing social discourses that made him a renegade in the first place.

While Stukeley aligned himself with foreign powers by adopting the role of the Catholic crusader, the corsair Ward made himself even more monstrous by converting to Islam, in an apparent attempt to attain a level of wealth and autonomy unavailable to him at home. Historian Michael Questier demonstrates that, despite the association that late Tudor administrators drew between Catholicism and treason, movement between the English and Roman churches was common among English subjects. Conversions, frequent in number, were not reducible to the polarities of the submissive conformist and the zealous heretic, nor could reasons for conversion be reduced to a cynical bid for self-preservation or material gain, despite the assumptions that writings by

Cecil and other nationalists make about recusants' motives.[1] As Lockey has shown, many English Catholics still considered themselves *English* – that is, faithful to their queen and her realm, despite differences in doctrinal beliefs and political ideals (1–91). Conversion to Islam, however, located a subject even further outside the discursive boundaries of obedient Englishness and more fully into the realm of what Patricia Parker calls the "preposterous" – the backward, the perverse, and the inverted "in family, state, and 'minde'" (1).

The convert to Islam shares this "preposterous" condition with the pirate, also widely represented as a figure outside of the human community and thus irrecoverable by nation or religion. These two renegade types merge in John Ward. As Matthew Dimmock demonstrates, the English convert to Islam commits a singular act of betrayal by subscribing to an "oath" that causes him to "lose all vestiges of [his] identity, epitomized in the breakdown of family ties and of all national and religious allegiance," thus removing him "'from the authority of English law'" (100). Likewise, the pirate – operating on the lawless seas – lurks beyond the bounds of national community, indeed beyond humanity itself, and outside the mutual obligations that hold civil society together. Peter Lamborn Wilson notes that Europeans held Christian apostates to be "human scum" whose "motives for conversion were the lowest imaginable: greed, resentment, revenge" (13). Pirates too, in their allegedly animalistic greed and rapaciousness, were seen as voluntarily rendering themselves subhuman and thus inviting extraordinary punishment in return.

Yet, as Daniel Heller-Roazen argues, this discursive banishment of the pirate from humanity not only confirms his origins in the community of the lawful, but it also invites that community to either extend its moral code to include those outsiders or violate that code by recognizing an exception and pursuing justice in ways that run counter to that code (13–27). This particular challenge to early modern ideas of civil society, I suggest, extends beyond those whom the nation's laws identify as pirates to include English renegades more generally, whose enduring connections to their homeland disrupt their codification as monstrous outsiders. In the case of Stukeley, this disruption takes the form of the renegade's humoral temperament, a predisposition nurtured by the English "air" that links him back to England, however far he strays. In the case of Ward, the disruption occurs in the form of an explicit social critique that acknowledges England's role in creating this notorious Mediterranean pirate.

This critique of domestic practices, which draws on the injustices done to England's vagrant poor, can appear even in texts that seem to make the renegade the sole author of his difficulties, as I will show in the case of Robert Daborne's *A Christian Turned Turk*. Daborne's primary interest, according to his prologue, is to investigate "Ward turned Turk," and, by focusing on economic context in this chapter, I do not wish to ignore the theological implications explored by other critics. However, by attending more closely to the pre-conversion social identity of Ward and his men, I aim to show that the play presents their "low" identity as integral to Ward's apostasy and, as such, invites audiences to consider the role of domestic conditions in nurturing renegadism. Like the "rituals of return" for Muslim converts seeking reintegration into the Christian community,[2] this social critique recovers Ward from the symbolic hinterlands of the national community and brings his story back to England, the home country that has condemned him since his career in piracy began.

Moreover, while Daborne's play heavily incorporates standard moral condemnations of renegade conduct, I view the play as reaching beyond this condemnation towards another conversation – one that considers the benefits, drawbacks, and hindrances of capitalist freedoms for commoners. In his seminal study *Worlds Apart*, Jean-Christophe Agnew describes the early modern English theatre as a "laboratory" in which plays explored capitalism's transformative effects on social relations (43). While I agree with Agnew's premise, I also concur with critics who see in Agnew's model – and much of the later "economic" criticism it inspired[3] – a reification of "exchange" that fails to account for the changes in labour and social policy that materially underwrote such exchanges.[4] Daborne's play, I argue, pays sustained attention to exactly those changes and incorporates them into the story of a lowly fisherman who renders himself, at least for a time, "free." As such, the play enacts a powerful dialectic of sovereignty and dispossession, one that pays heed to debilitating social realities while at the same time allowing its audiences to imagine the kinds of freedom that the renegade seizes for himself.

Among the many colourful subjects treated by early modern England's popular writers, Captain John Ward was a favourite. A Kent fisherman turned high-seas criminal, Ward raided merchant ships, sold captives in slave markets, and, most notoriously of all, converted to Islam. Robert Daborne dramatizes this history in *A Christian Turned Turk* (pub. 1612), which draws on two prose accounts: former shipmaster Andrew Barker's *True and Certain Report of the Beginning, Proceedings, Overthrows, and now present Estate of Captaine Ward and Dansiker* and the anonymous *Newes from Sea, of Two Notorious Pirates, Ward ... and Dansiker*, both published in 1609. Daborne's play has recently attracted much interest, reflecting early modern literary studies' attention to global contexts as depicted in adventure plays, "Turk" plays, and mercantile-colonial romance. The maritime setting of these plays, which were written during a period of economic expansion abroad, stages the English subject in confrontation with foreign cultures, customs, and religions. Typically, the plays that appear in these discussions – such as John Fletcher's *The Island Princess* (c. 1620), Philip Massinger's *The Renegado* (pub. 1630), and Thomas Heywood's *The Fair Maid of the West* (pub. 1631) – possess a tragicomic arc that rewards risk and redeems losses, ultimately affirming Christian virtue in the form of the plucky adventurism and savvy business sense of a Christian protagonist.[5]

Although *A Christian Turned Turk* often appears in the same discussions as the tragicomedies mentioned above, I aim to show that it differs significantly from them in that it places an unredeemed criminal at the centre of the tale, rather than at its margins, making his tragic comeuppance – culminating in Ward's shameful death, alone on foreign shores, betrayed by his own allies – the main focus. In analysing this difference, I will argue that the play challenges tragicomic convention by raising provocative questions about self-determination and economic independence with respect to the play's criminal characters, figures who typically function as mere plot devices. While early seventeenth-century English tragicomedies tend to portray risk rewarded by redemption – even the profane pirate Grimaldi, the titular subject of *The Renegado*, eventually repents and helps the Christian protagonists escape – Daborne's play tells a fatally *non*-redemptive story in which the protagonist perishes at the end, regretting his own efforts to secure wealth and status abroad. The play, while it appears to assign due justice to the pirate, in fact investigates the very questions at which contemporaneous tragicomedies merely glance. These questions concern *what kind* of English subject may gain wealth from overseas adventuring and *how*. The notorious figure of John Ward provocatively tests the discursive distinctions between the greedy pirate and the patriotic privateer, the lowly criminal and the plucky English hero. Moreover, the play shifts the period's well-documented anxieties about social mobility from domestic concerns about vagrancy to a Mediterranean setting – a setting whose specific geographic, social, and economic conditions raised new possibilities of social mobility and economic participation for the lowliest English subjects, such as John Ward and his men.

The play's sustained treatment of the life of a doomed criminal and his overseas exploits represents a significant departure from the ways in which genre and class typically align in the period. "Tragedy and comedy were not forms," writes Stephen Orgel. "They were shared assumptions." By "shared assumptions," Orgel means the ways in which genre confers value judgments on a play, with tragedy in particular seeming to have a particular dignity to it, as opposed to the everydayness of comedy, with its more lowly·subjects and characters (123). Robert Ornstein too associates tragedy with cultural privilege, whereby tragedy appears suited only for the most exalted language and subjects: "our discussions of tragedy tend to be solemn and high-sounding, intoned, not merely set down. For us great tragedies are the supreme artistic expression and the hallmark of great civilizations" (260). Even later studies that stress the tragic subject's antagonistic relationship to the social order – an emphasis surely exemplified by Ward – nonetheless attend mainly to characters of higher status.[6] By these standards, which encode genre with assumptions about class and culture,[7] the story of a fisherman-turned-pirate appears distinctly unworthy of serious dramatic treatment. Yet not only does Daborne make the pirate into a reflective, morally conflicted, and ultimately tragic figure, he does so knowing the real fate of Captain Ward who, far from meeting the tragic end imagined by Daborne, continued to live, as Barker reports, "in a most princely and magnificent state" in Tunis, wearing "curious and costly" clothing and eating "sumptuous" food. Barker declares, "I do not know any Peere in England that beares up his post in more dignitie, nor hath his Attendants more obsequious unto him" (C2ᵛ).

Why the sharp discrepancy between Ward's reported success and the tragic ending Daborne provides for him? Critics have taken Ward's end to be necessary, given pirates' widespread cultural status as villains. Barbara Fuchs describes Ward's "pitiful" end as "a kind of textual retribution for the pirate's cultural duplicity" (*Mimesis* 125); Nabil Matar similarly concludes, "There was no redeeming quality in Ward […] the renegade pirate met with a violent and fully deserved death – torn to pieces and thrown into the sea" (494–95). Ward's tragedy makes his story a morality tale, sounding a warning for those who might similarly transgress, leading Lois Potter to read the play as evoking "what the renegade loses" but not "the real attractions of what he gains" (136). Daborne's conclusion also confirms the early modern era's reigning orthodoxy by casting pirates as "hostis humanis generis" – enemies of all humankind – an attitude that intensified during the reign of James I.[8]

Yet, audiences would have known about the lack of retribution in Ward's *actual* life. Moreover, some contemporaneous texts – particularly ballads – complicated the "hostis" discourse by casting Ward as a figure of masculine bravado, even a hero.[9] As a mariner witnessing the precarious state of the English fishing industry, not to mention the end of privateering after James made peace with Spain, Ward found himself among the swelling class of the "masterless" and was soon pressed into naval service.[10] By breaking away from his ship and traversing from England to the open seas, he transformed his landed status as one of the working poor into a position of opportunity, first using his talents as a privateer with England's sanction, then going criminal as a pirate, and finally selling his talents to the Muslim "other" by becoming a Barbary corsair.[11] Even the texts that condemn Ward express awe at his deeds. For example, the front matter of *Newes* features illustrations of two ships (see Figure 2.1): one of "Wards Skiffe When He Was a Fisherman," portraying two scruffy men rowing and netting, and a second depicting a massive English ship, the *Charity*, that he took not once but "twice" (A1ᵛ). The visual contrast between the two boats mixes disdain at Ward's upbringing with admiration at how far he came, pointing towards a contradiction in the way contemporaries regarded pirates; the boats also reference Ward's status as a border creature by pointing in opposite directions, suggesting a homeward bound boat in the first illustration and an outward bound ship, setting out for foreign shores, in the second.

Likewise, while the message of Daborne's conclusion is clear enough, the discrepancy between Ward's successful transgression and what Gerald MacLean calls the play's "moral-nationalist scheme" (226) condoning Ward's destruction is apparent in the admixture of outrage and empathy in the play. That is to say, the gap between the imagined (and deserved) downfall of Ward in Daborne and Barker's original report of Ward's success allows other views – views more sympathetic to Ward and his men – to emerge within the binary. Philip Sidney – the influential courtier, poet, and critic, who famously disdained "mingling kings and clowns" (n.p.) on stage – viewed poverty and lowliness as

Figure 2.1. *Newes from Sea*. London, 1609, A1ᵛ. STC (2nd ed.) 25022.5. Used by permission of the Folger Shakespeare Library under a Creative Commons Attribution-ShareAlike 4.0 International License.

beneath the dignity of tragedy, as did many of his contemporaries. By seeming to defy the widespread generic prejudices reflected in Sidney's remarks, *A Christian Turned Turk* allows for the possibility that a purported villain, and a poor one at that, can become a subject inspiring sympathy, and even empathy, rather than comic scorn.

Details on Ward's real life are sparse, but we do have a broad outline of his progress from the fisheries of southeastern England to piracy and privateering in the Mediterranean and to retirement as a Muslim convert. Born around 1553, Ward spent the early part of his life as a fisherman in Faversham, Kent; during the 1590s, he worked as a privateer, plundering Spanish ships under a licence granted by Elizabeth I. With the ascension of James I, expectations for an end to the prolonged Spanish conflict led Ward to attempt to return to the fisheries, this time in Plymouth, but he was pressed into the navy in 1603. His piracy began when he and a large group of sailors deserted their ship, absconded with another ship, and began attacking foreign merchants. Democratically elected captain of his ship, Ward soon established himself as one of the most feared pirates. In 1606, he reached an agreement with local ruler Uthman Dey to set up a base of operations in Tunis and work for him as a Barbary corsair – a privateer on behalf of the Ottoman Empire. After accumulating a vast fortune abroad, Ward petitioned James I for amnesty. When the king denied his request, Ward returned to Tunis and converted to Islam. In 1612, while Ward lived a reportedly lavish lifestyle abroad, Daborne's play appeared.

The play opens on a scene of trickery and high risk, as Ward and his men play cards and dice with a group of French merchants. Soon they take the Frenchmen captive, expressing delight in outsmarting them at "the language of the sea" (1.15),[12] suggesting a special "language" of risk, encapsulated in gambling, that is endemic to the ocean setting. Heady with his own success, Ward becomes increasingly high-handed and alienates his men; when several important crew members desert the ship in response, Ward joins forces with another pirate captain, Francisco, and sails to Tunis to sell his captives. Because Ward stands to contribute much to the Tunisian coffers, the viceroy of Tunis tries to lure him into converting to Islam. Ward resists these attempts until he meets the powerful janissary leader's sister, Voada, who immediately charms Ward into conversion. Voada soon reveals her duplicity, and

Ward's new alliances quickly unravel. He dies, full of remorse, and his epitaph makes the lesson clear: "Ward sold his country, turned Turk, and died a slave" (16.326) – a terse summation of his life and a warning for all who would emulate his path.

Daborne's focus on Ward marks the play's crucial difference from the contemporary tragicomedies mentioned above. In her analysis of *The Island Princess*, for example, Valerie Forman writes that tragicomic outcomes – happy endings in the form of moral "profit" – obscure the labour that went into their production; as "narratives of unrelenting progress," these plots advance some subjects while leaving others behind (*Tragicomic Redemptions* 24).[13] Jean Howard's observation that "genre provides a site for the consolidation of a given class's interests in antagonistic relation to those of other classes" ("Shakespeare" 310) suggests an explanation for this occlusion. The subordinated class helps the "dominant" class accrue profit, and then the subordinated class, being incidental to the narrative, disappears.[14] The tragedy of an overreaching pirate like Ward, however, questions this element of tragicomedy. Daborne alters the pirate's typical role as a plot device for the protagonists' happy ending. In that sense, he picks up the residual tragedy within tragicomedy – that is, the demise of the play's seemingly dispensable characters – and expands that plot element into a dramatic plot in its own right. In doing so, he makes poverty and social marginalization into a subject for tragedy, even as the play seems primarily interested in condemning Ward's individual choices.

To be sure, the hardships of global capitalism's lowliest labourers – whether on land or at sea – do not suggest happy endings, and, in the early modern period, audiences considered those who resisted the conditions of their labour to be in defiance of their rightful place. This belief about lower-class resistance reflects a specifically early modern response to seamen as "masterless" workers; it is a view that aligns seafaring, once a widespread pursuit among different strata of society, with social unrest, treasonous behaviour, and political instability.[15] Historian Marcus Rediker argues that the ocean was the first setting for global labour as well as an incubator for radical, profane "others" who consciously lived differently from landed communities. While not all seamen felt the need for a radical break – many maintained ties to their landed communities, as I will describe in chapter 3 – radical ideas about religion and liberty grew in the culture of seafaring. Piracy was a form of social resistance against not only oppression on land but also the slave-like conditions of the navy and on merchant ships, the only legal alternative the state had left to seamen.[16] Indeed, historian G.V. Scammell has demonstrated that a large number of those who took up piracy, including captives and other Englishmen abroad, did so as a deliberate reaction against social marginalization at home.[17] Evidence implicates state action as well: seamen considered the state appropriation of their labour a violation of their traditional rights. The common seaman's experience was rooted in physical and psychic estrangement from home, the loss of autonomy, and daily hardship.[18]

On the one hand, seamen's hardship resembles the kinds of poverty and dislocation that commoners experienced on land. On the other hand, their experience differs in that it reflects early modern notions of the ocean as "other," a space defined by its radical alterity from land. This alterity can render the ocean a menace; a mysterious, godlike force inspiring humility and awe; or, as in the case of Shakespeare's *The Tempest* and other romance plays, a space that holds vast potential for redemption.[19] All three of these aspects, but most particularly the last, account for the ocean's role in facilitating the transformation of a humble fisherman into a notorious corsair – the ocean, as a function of its difference from land, becomes a blank space for the social imaginary and thus affords physical, and consequently psychological, mobility.[20] Here the noted "multicultural" aspect of the Mediterranean, where most travel took place for the purposes of trade, becomes key to understanding Ward's situation. Alberto Tenenti observes that the early modern Mediterranean witnessed a major change in that "the new organization of pirate warfare [...] had now become systematic plunder transcending religious barriers" (86); I would add that it transcended other kinds of social barriers as well. English contact with the Ottoman Empire and its surrounding lands meant regular exposure to foreign religions, ethnicities, languages, and customs. While English writing typically represents such differences as threatening, contact with the Ottomans also presented opportunities for English seamen chafing against socio-economic hierarchy at home. Captivity narratives, such as Richard Hasleton's *Strange and Wonderful Things* (1595) and John Rawlins's *The Famous and Wonderful Recovery of a Ship of Bristol* (1622), suggest that captors tended to privilege merit over blood as criteria for captives' advancement. Furthermore, English seamen as well as slaves pressed into harsh conditions by Ottoman captors could achieve liberation through conversion to Islam. Peter Lamborn Wilson suggests that a seventeenth-century working-class seaman might be drawn to Islam and its cultures for reasons apart from pirate gold – for example, Islam's anti-clericalism would certainly appeal to an anti-establishment Christian mindset (17, 20). The emergence of such motives seems to be a particularly early modern development. While piracy had been around as long as maritime commerce itself, the political nature of organized piracy began to emerge in the seventeenth century, with groups of pirates forming democratic communities or even "quasi-states" that challenged ways of organizing politics and society on land (Thomson 45–6).[21] The infamous "pirate utopias" of the late seventeenth and eighteenth centuries, such as those documented by Wilson and Scammell, represent an extreme expression of the liberty English subjects claimed for themselves at sea.

These enabling forms of mobility existed alongside punishing forms as well. Poorer captives who converted to Islam simply because their families could not ransom them did not undertake an ambitious betrayal; rather they achieved survival by the means available. Captives from Catholic nations might look to religious orders for their ransom, but seamen from Protestant England had no such hope. Indeed, English authorities put many of their "alien" and "unruly" underclass at risk of such capture by removing them from England altogether.[22]

This context would have provided the social and material conditions surrounding the lives of Ward and his crew. It seems certain that Ward's disenfranchisement initially drove him to piracy, but no one can account entirely for his reasons for continuing in this course of life, becoming a Barbary corsair, and converting to Islam. The play and its sources suggest that poverty, ambition, and unorthodox liberty played a role; they do so by using these themes as a vocabulary for telling the story of Ward's transgressions. According to the *Oxford English Dictionary*, the word "runagate" itself – an earlier version of "renegade" – encodes the link between apostasy and masterlessness, in that it could mean either "a person who renounces his or her faith" or "a vagabond, a wanderer; a restless roving person." The etymology suggests a causal relationship between apostasy and a prior state of social dislocation; *A Christian Turned Turk* and its sources assume and develop this relationship. Claire Jowitt argues that the play operates paradoxically, as both a confirmation of orthodoxy and an oppositional text critiquing the conduct and policies of James I (*Culture of Piracy* 141–6). I would add, however, that the play – as a work of drama for the public stage – engages commoners' more immediate experiences as well by calling attention to "economic, interpersonal, and spatial mobility" (Fumerton, *Unsettled*

50) wrought by physical dislocation and economic hardship, and casting the experience of mobility in a transnational setting.[23]

⁓

MacLean attributes Ward's "turning Turk" to the "seductive temptations" of "pursuing Eastern promise" of wealth and liberty rather than to any aspect of his status as "English fisherman turned pirate" (234). Yet Daborne's own prologue suggests otherwise. There, the "low"-er class condition of the English fisherman comprises a major part of the discourse on his treason:

> Our subject's *low*, yet to your eyes presents
> Deeds high in blood, in blood of innocents:
> Transcends them *low*, and your invention calls
> To name the sin beyond this black deed falls.
> What heretofore set others' pens awork
> Was Ward turned pirate; ours is Ward turned Turk.
> Their trivial scenes might best afford to show
> *The baseness of his birth*, how *from below*
> *Ambition oft takes root*, makes men forsake the
> The good they enjoy, yet know not. (Prologue 11.3–12, emphasis added)

The prologue introduces the play's central incident – "Ward turned Turk" – by contextualizing it as "low" (iterated twice in three lines). This invocation of "low" experience correlates Ward's story with the "low" literary forms – ballad literature and popular pamphlets – in which it had previously appeared.[24] These formats do not automatically signify a strictly lower-class readership, however; as Bernard Capp reminds us, "works aimed primarily at the poor were not confined exclusively to them. In the sixteenth century, and to some extent later, the upper and lower classes shared overlapping tastes in literature and humour" (198). The possibility that a socially diverse audience encountered these "low" stories about Ward may in part account for Daborne's decision to translate his tale, however problematically, into the language of tragedy. Whether that lowly "subject" is Ward himself or his story – the term hints at "subject" in the sense of a person answerable to a higher authority, a political position that encapsulates the *agon* that cultural materialists assign to tragic subjects confronting society[25] – the "baseness of his birth" conditions Ward's tale, here summarized as one in which baseness leads to "ambition." Ward's two endings – his real one in Tunis and his tragic one on the London stage – have at least one thing in common: each links apostasy to lowly ambition. Only the outcome differs: in Daborne's version, it leads to despair and death; in Ward's actual life, it leads to wealth and relative freedom, a subversive message in and of itself.

Correspondingly, contemporaries who write about Ward contrast his colourful legend with his humble past, highlighting his common origins, rough manners, and lower-class ressentiment. Like Daborne's prologue, *Newes from Sea* describes him as "base in Birth as bad in condition [... H]is parentage was but meane, his estate lowe, and his hope lesse" (A4ᵛ, B). Barker echoes this description in his account of Ward's beginnings: "poore, base, and of no esteeme, one as tattered in cloathes, as he was ragged in conditions" (A3ᵛ). According to Barker, Ward "lived as a poore fisherman" in Faversham and supposedly kept a house, "although I have never heard that he paid his rent, all the day you should hardly faile but finde him in an alehouse: but bee sure to have him drunke at home at night" (A3). By alluding to his continual presence in the alehouse, Barker identifies Ward with the "masterless," a vagrant class of men who were known to inhabit drinking establishments in lieu of keeping an actual "home."[26] The uncertainty surrounding Ward's real home – does he inhabit an authentic house of his own, or is his "home" in fact the alehouse, as was the case for many of England's itinerant poor – reflects not just Ward's low social and economic station but his suspect character. Drunkenness, sloth, and railing characterize him both early and later in life. An Italian source describes him as

> very short, with little hair, and that quite white, bald in front; swarthy face and beard. Speaks little, and almost always swearing. Drunk from morn till night. Most prodigal and plucky. Sleeps a great deal, and often on board when in port. The habits of a thorough "salt." A fool and an idiot *out of his trade*. (Qtd in Ewen 8, emphasis added)

Among this writer's descriptions of Ward's alleged incivility, the phrase "out of his trade" is particularly curious. On the one hand, it may suggest that his profession as pirate reflects a refusal to inhabit his true station as "fool." On the other hand, if the crude and callous Ward truly possesses the "habits of a thorough 'salt,'" then the "trade" of a pirate would seem to suit him well. Either reading suggests a dangerous character. The author of this excerpt hints at Ward's desire not only to plunder ships and amass riches but also, and far more significantly so, to subvert the determinative power of his lowly origins.

Further depictions of Ward's character confirm the presence of such desire. *Newes from Sea* tells of how the "proud" Ward dreams beyond his place, seeing in the ocean a way out of his limitations: "His profession was a fisherman of Feversham in Kent, though his pride at last would be confinde to no limits, nor any thing would serve him but the wide Ocean to walke in" (B). Barker describes a bitter man who disdains his own lot and grumbles at the fortunes of others: "Othes were almost as ordinarie with him as words, so that hee seldome spake a sentence [... H]ee would sit melancholy, speake doggedly, curse the time, repine at other mens good fortunes, and complaine of the hard crosses attended his owne" (A3^v–A4). As Barker elaborates, Ward cannot settle for what other common men want; he lives "persisting as before, in his melancholy disposition, not contented, with that good and honest meanes [that] was allowed him, and [that] satisfied farre better men, to defend themselves and the necessitie of their charge" (A4). Of course, these reports represent strategic reconstructions of Ward's past – Barker and the anonymous writer of *Newes* intended to satisfy popular fascination with a well-known contemporary figure. In turn, these textual reconstructions of a malcontent dreaming above his station help rationalize the man that Ward would become in their narratives – a man who subverts limits. Thus, the ideological work of these texts becomes a matter of emphasis – and a colourful imagination. Ward is not an indigent responding to the demise of English fishing and privateering; he is a man predisposed to dangerous thinking, refusing to be content with the purportedly God-given conditions of his birth, opting for the limitless ocean where he can become his own master.

This defiance of orthodoxies of "place" has always been the basis of pirates' appeal to audiences seeking vicarious adventure. *A General History of the Pyrates* (1724), commonly attributed to Daniel Defoe,[27] tells of how a rogue priest persuades one Captain Misson to adopt deist beliefs; these new-found convictions move the captain to start a commonwealth of his own, a communist utopia called Libertalia (xxxviii). Although Libertalia ultimately fails, the writer allows these two characters to voice condemnations of penury, slavery, and widespread abuses by arrogant governors. Misson's priestly mentor, Caraccioli, preaches on such subjects regularly to inspire Misson's men to "shake off the Yoak" rather than "yield to the Tyranny" that others suffer at the hands of proud rulers (393). Under the control of Captain Misson and the influence of Caraccioli, the sea voyage becomes an opportunity to enact fantasies of social levelling and to imagine their effects at home as well.

Defoe wrote in the eighteenth century, but the Tudor writer Thomas Lodge depicts pirates similarly. In a short piece printed with *The Life and Death of William Long Beard* (1593), Lodge details the villainy of pirates who flout authority even when caught. One account tells of a captured pirate named Dionides, who is brought before Alexander the Great. When Alexander interrogates him, Dionides asserts that the only difference between a monarch and a pirate is the size of their armies:

Tell me DIONIDES, whie hast thou troubled all the Seas? to whome he thus replied: Tell me ALEXANDER, whie hast thou overrun the whole worlde, and robbed the whole sea? ALEXANDER answered him: bicause I am a king, and thou art a Pirat: trulie (replied DIONIDES) O ALEXANDER, both thou and I are of one nature, and the selfe same office: the onelie difference is that I am called a Pyrat for that I assault other men with a little armie, and thou art called a prince, because thou subdues and signiorest with a mightie hoast: But if the Gods would be at peace with me, and Fortune should shewe her selfe perverse towards thee, in such sort as DIONIDES mighte be Alexander and Alexander DIONIDES, perhaps I should be a better price then thou art, and thou a worser Pyrat than I am. (2:38)

In her study of vagrancy, Linda Woodbridge notices in coney-catching pamphlets a persistent concern with the resemblance between con men and "legitimate" beggars, merchants, and officials: these "shadow structure[s]," Woodbridge suggests, provoke anxiety in coney-catching writers by blurring the difference between legitimate and illegitimate activity (6).[28] Similarly, the seaborne criminal Dionides exploits the resemblance between his activities and those of the king. Noting the role of social orthodoxy in legitimating or criminalizing aggression, Dionides questions the existence of any essential distinction between the king and himself. More dangerously still, the passage shows Dionides himself to possess leadership qualities in abundance – he demonstrates courage, rhetorical aptitude, and a strong will, matching or even exceeding those attributes in the actual king. Indeed, the anti-heroes in each tale share similar characteristics: pride, ambition, and a talent for leadership that invites comparison with those actually entitled to lead. Dionides, like Ward and other pirates, represents a class of otherwise worthy and talented men who put their abilities to their own uses, rather than those of the monarch or the state.

Jowitt makes this point with respect to Ward, who is "an example of a serviceable and potentially useful Englishman gone wrong" (*Voyage Drama* 63). But she is primarily interested in reading Daborne's portrayal allegorically, as an indictment of James I. Yet, Ward's experience as a commoner should be emphasized as well. One ballad treating Ward's legendary defiance illustrates this specific point: that a pirate can become "king" of his own domain, erecting the sea as a parallel kingdom to the land and practising his considerable martial acumen there: "A Famous Sea-Fight Between Captain Ward and the Rainbow" (original date unknown, but printed ca. 1700)[29] depicts Ward in direct confrontation with the king's ship the *Rainbow*. The king doesn't trust Ward, as Ward has already deceived France and Spain; a traitor in one place, reasons the king, is a traitor in every place. Moreover, Ward professes sympathy for the notorious second Earl of Essex, proclaiming, "If I had known your King but one two [*sic*] years before, / I would have sav'd brave Essex life, whose death did greve me sore" (n.p.). This invocation of Essex, in and of itself, signals a critique of the present regime – in particular, it invokes a brand of neo-chivalric heroism that translates into a direct challenge to the monarch's authority.[30] Aligning himself with a famous Elizabethan traitor, Ward challenges the king's authority by erecting a land/sea parallel: "Go tell the King of England, / go tell him thus from me, / If he reign King of all the Land, / I will reign King at Sea" (n.p.). Ward's fantasy of a sea-based kingdom permits him to imagine himself as an equal of the king, one whose power rivals the monarch's. As Jowitt notes, Ward co-opts the "traditional political power of the monarchy" while at the same time "claiming maritime alterity" – a contradiction that in this case doubles his threat to the Crown's authority (*Culture of Piracy* 2).

As the ballad illustrates, the sea represents a place in which traditional modes of authority meet the alterity of the sea, with its promise of physical and psychic mobility. The "freedom of the seas" debates of the early seventeenth century represent just such a negotiation between the monarch's jurisdiction and the unbounded space of the sea. These textual debates – which Ernest Nys calls the "hundred-year book war" (qtd in Schmitt 178) – explored the extent to which a navigable body of water could and should be governed by landed estates; the spectrum of opinion ranged from Hugo Grotius's embrace of the seas as "common to all and proper to none" (in *Mare liberum*, pub. 1609; qtd in Warren

186) to John Selden's conviction that the seas could be appropriated as much as any landed territory (*Mare clausum*, pub. 1635). Whatever a particular writer's position, the debate itself testifies to the challenge that seafaring posed to terrestrial sovereignty; in Bradin Cormack's words, "the mapping of the ocean's contestable space was as fluid as the ocean itself" (257).[31] The implications of this fluidity for the social mobility of seaborne labourers and travellers merits further comment. Early modern texts that purport to manage lower-class ambition rarely account for a simple fact: that many commoners who travelled and trafficked on the seas did so out of social and economic necessity, perhaps even as a result of punishment. Yet, ironically, this expulsion from land merely made the "masterless" elements more ungovernable as they assumed new seaborne identities.

Even when *A Christian Turned Turk* appears to scorn the pirates, it still pays heed to piracy's roots in domestic poverty and subsequent criminal behaviour. Davy, a French shipmaster, describes Ward's crew members as an "infection" that corrupts the very air of their country:

Whence, being vomited, they strive with poisonous breath
To infect the general air. Creatures that stand
So far from what is man they know no good,
But in their prey, not for necessity
But for mere hate to virtue, pursuing vice,
And being down themselves, would have none rise. (2.46–51)

Davy also recalls the expulsion of the criminalized subjects when he describes the English pirates as a "race of thieves, bankrupts that have lain / Upon their country's stomach like a surfeit" (2.44–5): pirates are castoffs and undesirables, and Europe's governments let their inherent lawlessness loose on the seas. Notably, the language of "infection" appears also in coney-catching literature that detailed the lives and professions of crafty vagrants, a fact that supports Davy's representation of the pirates as lowly vagabonds.[32] Finally, the link between low social status and criminal tendencies echoes the words of Captain John Smith, who, during the reign of James I, identified hardship as the cause of piracy, noting that "those that were poore and had nothing but from hand to mouth, turned Pirats" (qtd in Jowitt, *Voyage Drama* 132). Davy's remark identifies a major point of tension. On the one hand, the policing of England's "masterless" class necessitated the expulsion of that class to the seas and beyond. On the other hand, that same expulsion created the problem of illegal maritime economies, where some of England's masterless assumed new forms as international criminals.

The play, therefore, draws on two points of view – that which criminalizes pirates as the "bankrupt" outcasts of their own country and that which sympathizes with pirates as economically desperate men. Davy, expressing the former, presents an opposing viewpoint to Smith's apparently sympathetic one, which is more in line with the latter perspective. The question is whether the play suggests that Daborne agrees with Davy or Smith. Mark Hutchings suggests that Daborne's play confirms the kind of view espoused by Davy: "Robert Daborne had little interest in exploring the complex issues that lead men to abandon their country and their god" (103). Hutchings and other critics who see Daborne's ending as inevitable argue that the playwright could not afford to alienate his audience with anything other than a deserved unhappy ending for Ward, and that Daborne could not afford to offend the king, who by this time had placed Ward at the centre of his war on pirates, having turned down his application for a pardon.[33] Ward's biographer Greg Bak disputes this view, arguing that Daborne "was one man who attempted to understand what might have made Captain John Ward defect to Islam," and that the play's singularity in this regard led to the almost immediate downturn in Daborne's professional fortunes after *A Christian Turned Turk* appeared: "Daborne's troubles arose not because his play was a failure, but on account of its success" (183). Bak's assertion rests on a distinction between how *A Christian Turned Turk* played in the theatre – apparently quite successfully – and the offence his insight into the lives of pirates gave to James and his courtiers. Bak's argument is valid. Daborne indeed has a keen interest in the "complex issues" – cultural, social, and economic – that created pirates, and this interest manifests as a dialogue between existing anxieties about masterlessness and the opportunities newly opening up for Englishmen on the seas.

The etymology of "runagate," as noted previously, contains an internal contradiction in its double association with apostasy and masterlessness. After all, if the runagate has no home or master to begin with, who or what exactly is he "turning" against when he changes his religion or social status? Daborne's play repeatedly alludes to pirates' lowly backgrounds, reiterating Ward's low birth again and again, as when Francisco taunts him for his past as a "[p]oor fisher's brat, that never didst aspire / Above a mussel boat" (4.103–4). While the play never explicitly states that Ward plunders out of economic necessity, other characters reinforce the relationship between poverty and piracy. These characters report on their *own* experience, countering the prologue's moralistic filter. For example, when the Dutch pirate Dansiker (also a historical figure, one often paired and contrasted with Ward) plots to secure a pardon from the French king, he asserts that "[w]ant of employment, not of virtue, forced / Our former act of spoil and rapine" (5.17–18).While Dansiker may not speak truthfully, he regards this argument as a plausible defence likely to be received sympathetically by the French. Later, when two sailors attempt to rob Benwash, one of the sailors excuses their actions as the result of a poor upbringing in an uncaring country: "We were born in a country that had the charity to whip begging out of us when we were young," he recalls, concluding, "You know what must necessarily follow" (10.47–9). In other words, criminal activity "follows" punitive penury. As Dansiker suggests, such desperation need not signal a "lack" of "virtue." Even the captive French gentleman Lemot acknowledges the role of poverty in making his captors who they are:

> think that you see
> Even all the miseries despised poverty
> Can throw on men, that by this one hour's valor
> We only can redeem ourselves from death. (2.65–8)

Lemot, even as he condemns the pirates' barbarity, acknowledges the reality of "despised poverty" leading men to their "miseries."

These expressions of hardship may not elicit the audience's sympathy in and of themselves. However, Daborne takes the mariners' awareness of their own indigence a step further by directing it to explicit criticism of the home country. The captured French mariners beg Ward to "deprive us not of our fair home, our country" (1.30), but Ward mocks the very idea, invoking glaringly unjust social practices of "home." He mocks the French mariners' devotion to their own homeland, which he takes as evidence of their inability to "look further" beyond the conditions of their birth:

> Is't not a shame
> Men of your qualities and personage

Should live as cankers, eating up the soil
That gave you being (like beasts that ne'er look further
Than where they first took food)? That men call "home"
Which gives them means equal unto their minds,
Puts them in action. (1.33–9)

This scathing and eloquent assessment questions the affective claims of the nation as "home." In Ward's view, "home" is not necessarily the place where one is born; rather, it is a place that allows men to thrive according to their ambitions, with "means equal unto their minds." Accordingly, Ward and his men routinely refuse affiliation with England; rather, when Davy inquires about his captors' origins, Ward's officer Gismund replies, "We are of the Sea!" (2.35). "The Sea," as international highway for illicit trafficking, makes the pirates what they are as economic agents by intermittently freeing them from hierarchies of dependency and making them into acting agents in their own right – that is, giving them "means equal unto their minds." In a similar vein, Ward tells the governor of Tunis that "I know no country I can call home" (7.13), confirming his status as an estranged English subject disengaged from his native land in favour of opportunities elsewhere. His statement appears to confirm the pure logic of capitalist subjectivity, whereby estrangement becomes the nominal basis for an independent identity that acts according to its own self-interest.

The moral status of such self-interest is complicated by the historical context in which Ward operates. Commentators on early modern piracy regularly note the slippage between the designations "privateer" and "pirate," with the former acting with state sanction and the latter without it. By definition, the early modern privateer plunders with state permission – for example, in the case of the "sea dogs" employed by Elizabeth I in the war against Spain – while the pirate plunders without it.[34] However, although the state stood to benefit by harnessing the talents of the privateer, that same privateer could – and frequently did – turn against the authority sanctioning his activities. At the same time, the breakdown in the formal distinction between pirate and privateer also could go the other way, with pirates indirectly advancing the interests of the state.[35] Citing this instability of the legal distinction in practice, Thomas W. Gallant examines pirates within the context of capitalist formation and the development of modern nation states, showing how pirates created and perpetuated markets for stolen goods and required states to expand their territorial reach in order to regulate them.[36] But in the texts under discussion here, the rhetorical "othering" of the pirate simplifies the murkiness of these categories by imposing a moral binary that makes national citizenship and piracy mutually exclusive. We first encounter Dansiker when he plans to give up piracy in order to obtain a pardon from France. Dansiker describes the agreement with France as a tradeoff in which national membership cannot coexist with piracy:

> [S]ince the breach of laws
> Of nations, civil society, justly entitles us
> With the hateful style of robbers, let's redeem our honor
> And not return into our country with the names
> Of pardoned thieves, but by some worthy deed,
> Daring attempt, make good into the world. (5.11–16)

Dansiker understands that recovering his ability to "make good" requires reintegration into the national body – the realm of "laws," "nations," and "civil society." As pirates, Dansiker and his men have been operating outside the social body and thus outside the possibility of "good"; their repentance restores this "goodness." Furthermore, the former pirates must *actively* redeem the nation's economic damage by striking out against other pirates, as we learn when Dansiker vows to destroy them all by "the same weapon we may / Our country cure, with which we wounded her" (7.24–5). Paradoxically, they must atone for their piracy through more piracy, but render the profits to the Crown. It is not enough to merely repent; the former pirate must make his repentance visible through patriotic action. Dansiker's plan for pardon draws a line between the civic-minded member of the national body and the individualistic renegade of the maritime sphere. He will foreswear piracy on his own behalf for "privateering" on behalf of the state, and thereby abandon the extreme of capitalist subjectivity, in which as a pirate, and thus a fully autonomous economic agent, he severed all loyalties except for the one to his own self-interest.

On the surface, this disengagement from communal identity in favour of individual advancement makes low-born pirates available for free and equal agency on their own behalf. Yet in the world Daborne portrays, a world in which oppression and poverty rather than freedom and equality reign, we witness tension between social reality and democratic ideals that the pirates articulate and espouse in theory, but cannot fully realize in practice; thus the purported "individualism" of the renegade is revealed as problematic. As I have described, democratic experiments frequently occurred on early modern pirate ships in the Mediterranean and the Atlantic; on these ships, pirates elected their own leaders and made decisions as a large group; such organization also carried the expectation that all men aboard shared in all kinds of work. The men on Ward's ship seemed to hold such democratic ideals. In the play, when Ward responds magisterially to Gismund's unsolicited advice regarding a raid, Gismund retorts, "I am a gentleman / Equal unto your self" (4.29–30). Later, when Gismund and his shipmate Gallop divide some plundered gold between them, Gismund reminds Gallop: "Your fellows expect their equal shares" (6.104–5). The community of pirates operates by a code of apparent equality. Given Gismund's sharp awareness of injustice at home, this code might even be called reactionary: rather than replicate the oppressive social structure of "home," the pirates embrace the idea of a fellowship among theoretical equals, united in their desire for gain.

Ward betrays this code by developing a grandiose sense of himself, one that employs the displaced language of majesty and honour in service of his own ambition. The languages of orthodoxy and alterity clash rather than support one another, a dynamic evident in other writings on pirates. While some pirates conceived of their enterprise as a democratic experiment, others went in the opposite direction, setting themselves up as kings, of a sort, in new territories.[37] Foreign locations combine with masculine bravado to make princes out of pirates, as when Ward declares, "The sway of things / Belongs to him that dares most. Such should be kings, / And such am I" (4. 83–5). Francisco channels Ward's pretensions when he greets Ward in a manner that invokes the ancient custom of the duel: "Give a charge there. Say your prayers, knight! Doomsday is nigh" (5.123–4). Undoubtedly, Francisco is ironic when he calls the low-born Ward "knight"; nonetheless by using the specific term, he confuses the boundaries between a duel among pirates and one among chivalric men. Similarly, when Benwash asks his servant Rabshake to "fetch me three hundred ducats for this gentleman," meaning Gallop, Rabshake asks, "This newcome thief, sir?" and Benwash corrects him: "Gentleman, slave!" The juxtaposition of the terms "gentleman" and "slave" renders the distinction between the two categories ambiguous. Rabshake immediately quips, "your thief is a gentleman," a statement that again challenges the binary between gentleman and thief (6.56–9).

Ward's appropriation of gentlemanly status sets him up for a fall, adding a distinct class-based dimension to his demise. For all the play's attention to the role of domestic injustice in the creation of the international rogue, the central figure dies with a warning to all subjects whose ambition outweighs their station: "Who will soar high / First lesson that he learns must be to die" (16.293–4). Ward employs the language of divine judgment in the service of social orthodoxy:

> Ambition and swift riot run when mean content
> Sits low, yet happy; and when their day is spent
> All that they get is labor and unrest,
> A hateful grave, and worst, a troubled breast. (13.119–22)

Essentially, Ward concludes his own story by cautioning audiences to remain content ("low, yet happy") in their stations and resist temptations to advance through new economic frontiers – he does so ironically, for he cautions them from pursuing the successful path of the "real" Captain John Ward.

In the play's moralistic vein, pride would seem to be the sole motivator for Ward's actions. Nonetheless, the character's lament contains one final mention of the fears that haunt him throughout the play – poverty and starvation:

> Should I bear up,
> Outlook my crimes, I want means to support me.
> [. . .] Live, I cannot: famine threats,
> And that the worst of poverty – contempt and scorn.
> Never on man Fate cast so black a frown.
> Up I am denied to fly, unpitied down. (13.110–11, 113–16)

Ward alludes to the very qualities – the ability to "bear up," as in to maintain his strength and spirit, and to "outlook," meaning to stare down and outlast – that helped him attain notoriety as a successful pirate. Yet, ironically, those same qualities that lifted him out of destitution now prove ineffectual against it. Up until the very end of the play, the realities of starvation, poverty, and marginalization trouble the assignment of moral responsibility to Ward alone, leaving the culpability of the state and its social practices unanswered and unresolved, yet very much visible.

While *A Christian Turned Turk* begins and ends with a conventional enough proposition – that "turning" from English Christianity towards Islam will surely end in damnation – it complicates its own message by attending to the ways that poverty and marginalization structure the experience of commoners abroad, and even how these adverse factors provoke renunciation of national loyalty. Ward's lowly beginnings, Gismund's outrage, and the desperation of other sailors all find room for expression in this unhappy tale, raising questions of how, exactly, "runagates" are made and what domestic conditions might have to do with the choice to turn to piracy and even apostasy. In this way, the play reorients perceptions of the renegade as wilful "other" towards an investigation of his "Englishness" – that is, the role of England in creating him.

In its address to English audiences, Daborne's *A Christian Turned Turk* offers a glimpse of the pressures that economic exchange placed on occupation and class distinction in the period. As such, the general thrust of the play exemplifies Agnew's description of the theatre as a "laboratory" for imagining the social effects of capitalism.[38] Yet as I have shown, the play's attention to the social bases of capitalist production calls for an expanded set of contexts beyond "exchange" itself. These contexts reveal the socio-economic exigencies accompanying Ward's "turning" or conversion, showing that action to be not solely a religious betrayal of England but an extreme expression of his own desires for self-sovereignty. The play concludes with a conventional kind of damning commentary on such desire. But it also poignantly suggests that hardship at home and at sea shapes pirates' conduct. Thus, the play cycles through a dialectic between sovereignty and dispossession, settling on the demise of Ward while leaving the questions of justice he represents conspicuously absent from the final scene.

By exploring these themes of poverty and disenfranchisement, Daborne complicates the moral impact of his own conclusion, and this is where he differs from his sources as well as much of the reigning discourse about pirates as radical, criminal "others." He presents his audience with multiple reasons for "turning," reasons beyond the possession of a certain wayward personality type. During this period when matters of religious faith and national loyalty continually intermingle, Daborne shows not only the penultimate act of Ward's betrayal – the play's controversial conversion scene – but the fears, fantasies, and sense of estrangement that condition that choice. In short, not all traitors "turn" from the same thing, for the same reasons, and not all regard the "home" from which they turn in the same way. By calling attention to the social and economic condition of men who turn, the play destabilizes "Englishness" as a measure for virtue by introducing a variety of English experiences into the equation.

When we attend to the domestic social struggles inherent in the story of a renegade, it becomes much more difficult to take the rhetorical distancing of the renegade as "hostis" at face value. Despite the "moral-nationalist" tenor of *A Christian Turned Turk*, Daborne's tragic version of Ward belies the ruthless, uncivil, and faithless version imparted in texts such as *Newes from Sea* and Barker's account. The play's attention to poverty, dislocation, and the expulsion of the masterless lends its morality-tale veneer a surprising element of national self-reflection, rendered as an invitation to English audiences to consider the social doctrines of their own nation and the consequences of those doctrines. In doing so, the play opens Ward up to the kinds of sympathetic and emphatic responses typically seen in tragedy, a genre purportedly above the life of a lowly pirate. While the state and much popular print condemn Ward as a rogue villain, the play counteracts this orthodoxy by asking audiences – themselves likely to be socially mixed, with experiences similar to those of the poor English seaman – to reconsider whether or not this image rings true.

In chapter 3, we will consider again how a socially mixed audience might trouble a play's generic occlusion of the poor. This time the test case is Heywood and Rowley's *Fortune by Land and Sea*, a Jacobean tragicomedy that portrays the execution of two real-life Tudor pirates, Purser and Clinton. Previous critics have noted that the play's hero – the plucky Young Forrest – and the pirate villains are closer together on the moral spectrum than the play – and the political condemnations of pirates on which it draws – seems to suggest. However, I will lend these discussions – which tend to dwell on class as a rhetorical phenomenon – a missing economic and material dimension by examining the ways in which pirates, formally enemies of the state, also sustained English communities with an influx of money and goods. On the level of the ballads, chronicle history, and drama that treat the lives of Purser and Clinton, this economic interdependence is performed in an emotional register that signals the bonds between pirates and their English neighbours. The story of Purser and Clinton, which I will analyse intertextually by reading these genres side by side, will demonstrate another way in which the radically disconnected renegade is, in fact, a creature deeply rooted in England itself.

Chapter Three

"Lend Us Your Lament": Purser and Clinton on the Scaffold

In chapter 2, we witnessed in the example of John Ward how writers drew on doctrines of class and occupation to represent renegades as dangerous lone wolves, exploiters of commercial opportunity abroad who ruthlessly betrayed their country. Texts that portray the renegade in these terms, such as Barker's *True and Certaine Report* and the anonymous *Newes from Sea*, participate in a polarizing discourse of "insiders" and "outsiders" whereby the English renegade deliberately – and monstrously – converts himself from one of the former into one of the latter. In Ward's case, this process of self-estrangement originates as resistance to his lowly social and occupational place, which itself signifies an unruly disposition; this resistance culminates in his dramatic revolt against his conscription as he breaks away from the navy and declares himself head of a band of "free" men on the open seas. The setting of the early modern Mediterranean, as a highway of licit and illicit commercial exchange, allows Ward to thrive in his criminal ambition, at once reaching over his social entitlements *and* abandoning the affective claims of English Christianity. As pirate and apostate, Ward evinces the imagined horrors that the "masterless" man can commit when not only outside authority's reach, but empowered by a new setting – and in this case, with a ship, a crew with little to lose, some navigational know-how, and substantial backing from a foreign enemy.

When seen in these terms, Ward's story at first seems to anticipate Marx's famous description of the market as a sphere of exchange between theoretically equal individuals isolated in their own self-interest. Marx describes the process of self-interested exchange as social disconnection masquerading as individual "freedom" (245). "Hostis humanis generis," the legal term for pirates, conveys the widespread cultural disapproval of such "freedom" taken too far and supports the prevailing sense of the renegade as a purely calculating creature of the market, a selfish individual detached from any sense of fellow feeling. However, as I have suggested in the previous two chapters, the early modern renegade's situation is more complex than this paradigm of the individualistic agent would seem to suggest. While the renegade indeed exploited opportunities to liberate and benefit himself, this opportunism did not necessarily rule out affective bonds with other people. In fact, this chapter will show that outlaw activity could sometimes be undertaken in the service of those bonds and in explicit defiance of state policies that attempted to regulate who could profit from overseas markets and how.

Purser and Clinton, Elizabethan pirates who operated off the southern English coast, are best known today as minor villains in Thomas Heywood and William Rowley's tragicomedy *Fortune by Land and Sea* (c. 1607–9). Between the late sixteenth and early seventeenth centuries, their story attracted the attention of not only dramatists, but writers of chronicles, ballads, and popular prose. A ballad collection commemorating their execution, *Clinton, Purser, & Arnold to Their Countreymen Wheresoever*, appeared in print in 1583, the same year as their deaths, as did two other ballads, now lost. The antiquarian John Stow followed with a description of the execution in the last edition of his *Annales* (pub. 1605); this passage copied part of a description in the 1587 edition of Holinshed's *Chronicles*, to which Stow contributed. *Fortune* appeared on the London stage several years later. Then, in 1639, another pamphlet appeared in two parts to elaborate once more on the lives and deaths of Purser and Clinton. This publication history suggests that, as in the cases of Ward and Stukeley, the story of these two pirates intrigued audiences long after the men had perished.

Fortune brings a well-known story to the popular stage, but it also shrinks that story's protagonists to fit within another story, one centring on the fortunes of two families, the Forrests and the Hardings. The kind but impoverished Old Forrest has two sons (Frank and Young Forrest) and a daughter (Susan); the rich and greedy Old Harding has three sons (Phillip, William, and John) and a new, much younger, wife. After a gentleman named Rainsford kills Frank Forrest in a quarrel, Young Forrest retaliates by killing Rainsford. Mrs Harding secretly helps Young Forrest escape the law by sending him to her merchant brother, who allows him on board one of his ships. At the same time, Old Harding discovers that his son Philip has married the penniless

Susan Forrest, and he responds by forcing the pair into domestic servitude. But the fate of the two families begins to improve with the appearance of Purser and Clinton, who have captured a ship belonging to Mrs Harding's brother, taking the merchant captive. In London, Old Harding, who had invested in the merchant's voyage, faints at the news of his capture. But Young Forrest, having been elected the captain of his ship after a successful attack on Spanish shipping, defeats Purser and Clinton and liberates the merchant, restoring the pirated goods; Purser and Clinton are apprehended and executed by hanging at Wapping Dock, London. Meanwhile, Old Harding, who had been poised to disinherit Philip permanently, dies before signing the will. As a result, Philip inherits his father's estate. Young Forrest, whose heroic defeat of the pirates earns him a pardon for murdering Rainsford, immediately proposes marriage to the widowed Mrs Harding, and all ends well.

In this tale of bourgeois English virtue rewarded, Purser and Clinton stand out as villains who are wilfully, stubbornly apart from England, operating as rogue agents answering only to themselves. This putative disconnection sharply contrasts the pirates with the play's two virtuous brothers, who seem to conduct their affairs with an eye towards the good of others, not just themselves. This ethic of mutual benefit represented, in early modern terms, the morally upright approach to economic life. Craig Muldrew has demonstrated that early modern market exchange was the opposite of individualistic and rational – it was, rather, tied to a perceived need to trust one's neighbours and thus was social and communicative in nature. Characterizing sixteenth-century market relations as "interpersonal and emotive," Muldrew describes the market as "not only a structure through which people exchanged material goods" but also "a way in which social trust was communicated." This trust, Muldrew elaborates, "was interpreted in terms as emotive as other forms of human interaction such as neighbourliness, friendship and marriage" (3, 5, 125). The Purser and Clinton of *Fortune* seem to deliberately exempt themselves from this sort of trustworthiness as they act rapaciously on the high seas and attack ships flying the English flag.

Yet the real Purser and Clinton operated in a way much truer to the historical truth of the early modern marketplace described by Muldrew. Earlier accounts of these men – namely, the ballads commemorating their 1583 execution and Stow's description of the same episode in the 1605 *Annales* – portray them not simply as defiant rebels, but also as vulnerable men who remained deeply tied to their local communities until the very end. While Heywood and Rowley describe Purser and Clinton as traitors to vertical, hierarchical order, the texts of 1583 and 1605 attend to the men's place within horizontal economic networks that pirates in general regularly infused with money and goods. For Heywood and Rowley, the drama of Purser and Clinton exists in their transgression; for the earlier writers, however, the drama takes place on the scaffold in an exchange between the condemned and their witnesses, who represent the friends and neighbours for whom the pirates strove to provide. This history infuses the play's representation of Purser and Clinton with a subtle critique of the state's judgment, lending the pirates a sympathetic dimension that belies their formal status as wilful transgressors deserving punishment.

At first, the play appears to work against such a reading. Like the other seventeenth-century tragicomedies I describe in chapter 2, *Fortune* depicts a cycle of risk and redemption in which the bourgeois protagonists accrue material and emotional rewards after a period of trial. Recent criticism correlates the generic pattern of tragicomedy with contemporaneous arguments about capitalist investment abroad that seek to justify investing English money in foreign commercial endeavours.[1] Tragicomedy, in parallel fashion to the ventures promoted by mercantilist writers, justifies temporary suffering with a happy ending in which the bounty invested returns to the protagonists, with interest. Plays like *Fortune*, which positively portray the gain of wealth on the high seas, particularly speak to this development.[2]

Yet, even as such plays affirm one kind of economic experience, they occlude others, for tragicomedy's elevation of the plucky bourgeois hero excludes the labourers – slaves, servants, and other low-paid workers at home and abroad – whose work generates the wealth that rewards the hero. Happy endings in the form of "profit," Valerie Forman notes, obscure the labour that went into these material rewards; thus, these "narratives of unrelenting progress" advance some agents while leaving others behind (*Tragicomic* 24).[3] *Fortune* follows the same pattern insofar as it mirrors social reality by rewarding the bourgeois merchant and punishing the pirates; the play embraces, in Mark Netzloff's terms, "the prospect of the expulsion of England's poor and recuperation of national wealth" (*England's Internal Colonies* 57). Tragicomedy, in valorizing profit at the expense of other narratives, performs its own "expulsion" of those lowly elements. Presumably, it would violate tragicomic convention to give these "others" – common labourers and, often, the criminals who originate from their ranks – a voice beyond their status as mere plot devices.

Recent criticism recognizes this gap by revealing problems in the play's superficial affirmation of bourgeois virtue. According to these accounts, the characters of Purser and Clinton encourage a subtle, but potent, critique of state policy. Noting Elizabeth I's dependence on piracy for empire building, Barbara Fuchs examines the pirates alongside Young Forrest to note the conceptual permeability between the pirate and the plucky English entrepreneur. By destroying Purser and Clinton, she argues, the play reasserts the class boundaries that the resemblance between the common pirate and the gentleman privateer threatens to erase ("Faithless" 65). While Fuchs sees *Fortune* as a critique of English expansionism, Claire Jowitt reads its treatment of piracy as nostalgia for the Elizabethan privateer, an enterprising and masculine figure who stands in stark contrast to the widely perceived passivity and effeminacy of James's reign. The minor differences between Young Forrest and the pirates point to, in Jowitt's words, "a coded, yet growing, dissatisfaction with the king" ("Piracy and Politics" 218), particularly the *Rex Pacifica* that formally eliminated the state's reliance on privateers as an instrument of war.

I agree that we should not take the play's destruction of Purser and Clinton at face value, and, indeed, this chapter and the previous one depend a great deal on the important insights that emerge from the work of Fuchs, Jowitt, and other commentators on the play. However, I wish to shift the focus of these analyses, which dwell on the play as a critique of state policy, to address an element that gets lost in that focus – that is, the agency of the play's audience and, particularly, its capacity to regard the pirates in a different light. While previous criticism valuably uncovers the political and social anxieties surrounding empire building, such works often assume that these same anxieties are shared by members of the theatre audience, who, in reality, may not feel invested in – or even fully aware of – the state's struggle against piracy.[4] Jean Howard describes the early modern theatre as a "popular institution" that attracted "diverse social groups," including "women as well as men, sailors, tradesmen, merchants, as well as courtiers and gentry" (*Stage and Social Struggle* 13). Thus, if the play indeed expresses a "dissatisfaction with the king," I would push that suggestion further to ask precisely *whose* dissatisfaction the play addresses – Heywood and Rowley's, the theatre audience's, or the nation's as a whole.

To answer this question, this chapter will argue that the texts that served as *Fortune's* sources suggest a different kind of conflict than the ones previously suggested, a conflict nonetheless key to understanding how the play handles questions of class and economic participation. Specifically, I will show that these texts reveal the pirates' ultimate concern to be not their agon with the state, but the potential rift between them and the communities that benefited from their activities. Drawing my impetus from what Stephen Greenblatt calls "the problematic relation in the Renaissance between genre and historical experience" (1), I will examine the non-dramatic accounts of Purser and Clinton, which include a broader range of perspectives on pirates and piracy itself than can be found either in tragicomic drama or in other forms of moralistic discourse about pirates. These texts push against representational norms – norms that confer "enemy of the state" status on pirates – by conferring empathy on Purser and Clinton, men whose connection with audiences typically gets occluded by the villainization of pirates as monstrous renegades. The 1583 ballads and Stow's account, in particular, counter the "othering" moves of moralistic discourse by portraying the interdependence between pirates and landed communities, a relationship that exposes the English economy's dependence on piracy itself. While previous critics and historians have noted, to various ends, pirates' embeddedness in their communities, I will apply these observations in a new direction – towards popular literary representations of crime and punishment that expose the commonality between the condemned and the public, a commonality that poses a counterdiscourse to portrayals of pirates as "enemies of all humankind."

Historians characterize Elizabeth I's policy on piracy as slippery and inexact – if "policy" is even an appropriate term for a strategy that seemed contingent on the state's immediate ambitions. The conflict with Spain, as well as the drive towards empire building, made Elizabeth turn a blind eye to the activities of adventurers such as Martin Frobisher, Francis Drake, and Walter Raleigh, who plundered Spanish ships and seized riches under patriotic guises.[5] However, as we learned in chapter 2, the end of the Anglo-Spanish conflict under James I led to a change in foreign policy that culminated in a "war against the pirates," with the king taking an active interest in apprehending English subjects engaging in seaborne crime.[6]

This shift provides important context for Heywood and Rowley's play, as well as for the 1583 ballads, Stow's chronicle, and the 1639 *True Relation, of the Lives and Deaths of the Two Most Famous English Pyrats, Purser, and Clinton*. However, a focus on state policy, valuable as it is, does not tell the entire story about Purser and Clinton's cultural, political, and, above all, economic significance. Scholars applying Michel Foucault's analysis of "theatres of punishment" to early modern England have found that the state, despite its aims to inscribe its ideology on the body of the condemned, does not necessarily have the last word; public executions can just as well become scenes of "carnivalesque" inversion in which the condemned and the crowd show resistance.[7] As I note above, existing scholarly readings recognize the potential for subversive critique in textual representations of Purser and Clinton's execution, but these readings do not address the critical role of the crowd that, in interaction with the condemned, makes new meaning out of the state's judgment. Peter Lake and Michael Questier note the "variously constituted popular audience" present at early modern English executions; such a diverse crowd plays a key role in creating the "unexpungible air of dialogue [that] hung over the proceedings" (66, 76). The history of Purser and Clinton in print shows the dialogue between the condemned and the crowd to be at least as important as the relationship between the condemned and the state. Moreover, this dialogue matters because it scripts the link between the pirates' market activity and its embeddedness in the communities that Purser and Clinton do not abandon – as anti-renegade discourse might suggest – but in fact sustain.

The execution scene from Stow, which only Jowitt analyses in detail, illustrates this dynamic. John Stow – Londoner, "citizen historian," and tailor by trade – spent his life chronicling the history and geography of England, particularly his beloved metropolis. Among the plethora of early modern English chronicle writers – such as Raphael Holinshed,[8] Francis Bacon, William Camden, Samuel Daniel, John Hayward, and Walter Raleigh, all university-educated movers in elite circles – Stow was a historian without a university education, a man whose background led one contemporary to contrast his work to that of William Lambarde, whose "'labours are feasts for scholars, not [like Stow's works] daily fare for common people'" (qtd in Beer 18). This commentator mistakenly characterizes Stow's readership as exclusively "common." However, Stow's modern readers note his enduring interest in the experience of ordinary Londoners over the intrigues of court and parliament and especially his tendency to praise elites who helped the poor and thus demonstrated a traditional ethic of charity that he saw fading in the Elizabethan period. Throughout his chronicles, he continually acknowledges the plight of the poor and recognizes great men who practised the paternalistic ideal of "good lordship."[9] Although Stow wisely refrains from calling out less charitable men by name, his critique reveals deep concern about a perceived shift from an economics of mutual help, where market activities serve social ends, to a competitive landscape in which each person benefits himself and erodes civil society in the process.

The Purser and Clinton episode of the 1605 edition, however, offers an intriguing variation on the theme of noblesse oblige. Here Stow depicts not the largesse of great men, but rather the largesse of criminals *impersonating* great men:

> Walton [Purser] as he went toward the gallows rent his venetian breeches of crinoline taffeta, and distributed the same to such his old acquaintance as stood about him, but [Clinton] Atkinson had before given his murrvey velvet doublet with great gold buttons, & his like coloured velvet venetians laid with great gold lace apparel too sumptuous for sea rovers, which he had wonne at the seas, and wherein he was brought up Prisoner from Corse castell in the isle of Porbeck to London unto such friends as pleased him. (2: 1175)

The rich "venetian breeches" and "velvet doublet" worn by the two pirates attest to status acquired – indeed, *stolen* – rather than status ascribed. Stow calls the clothing "too sumptuous for sea rovers," yet, as Jowitt reminds us, many Elizabethan rovers were courtly men nominally entitled to sumptuous clothing. Because swashbuckling favourites such as Drake and Raleigh would have worn such fashions, Purser and Clinton's clothing embodies a "mimetic relationship to court fashion" that points towards the unstable class distinction between pirates from privateers (*Culture of Piracy* 22). Jowitt notes further that the distribution of costly apparel serves as a *memento mori* of shared resistance between the pirates and their "old acquaintance" and "friends." The gesture exemplifies Ann Rosalind Jones and Peter Stallybrass's sense of "the animatedness of clothes, their ability to 'pick up' subjects, to mould and shape them both physically and socially, to constitute subjects through their power as material memories" (2).

Certainly, the episode testifies powerfully to the pirates' seizure not only of "sumptuous" goods, but of the status meant to accompany those goods. If we read the episode in isolation from Stow's other writings, which exhibit a strong preoccupation with charity, then a reading that casts the clothes as *memento mori* makes sense. But given the enduring concern for the poor that Stow demonstrates throughout his writing,[10] it is worth pausing further over his choice to include an episode portraying the "distribution" of the garments to "old acquaintance" and "friends" in the third edition of his popular chronicle. While Jones and Stallybrass are primarily interested in the "fetishism" of clothes as objects, they also acknowledge that early modern fetishism coexisted with the development of commodity logic as the latter emerged increasingly within the international trade of goods that occupied seafarers (11). Jones and Stallybrass seek to reclaim the idea of "fetishism" from the denigrations of colonialist discourse; inversely, I see Stow's Purser and Clinton episode presenting commodity logic in a positive light. That is to say, the pirates' gesture is both affective *and* practical, for costly clothing can also be sold for a sum of money to shops, pawnbrokers, or other buyers, thus providing resources for commoners who struggled with daily survival. Giving away the clothing indeed flaunts the pirates' success; but the same gesture also suggests a desire to continue caring for people on land.

This alternative reading gains support from the fact that, as historian C.M. Senior reports, many pirates remained tied to their landed communities, even benefiting these communities by providing a steady supply of wealth and cheap goods (39). While the suppression of piracy might have meant greater social and economic security for the English state, that same suppression disadvantaged the lower orders. Within this economic context, money and goods not only were commodities trafficked by calculating, self-interested agents, they also represented efforts to sustain localities that had affective claims on the love and loyalty of those same economic agents. Thus, despite the formal binary of the commodity's "use value" and the fetish's "symbolic value," Stow's portrayal of the pirates' actions leaves intact the garments' affective power to seal bonds of friendship and "old acquaintance." The distribution of clothing represents a last attempt to care for those left behind, men and women who will no longer materially benefit from the infusion of plundered money and goods into their communities.

Furthermore, the fact that people frequently pirated goods out of economic desperation – rather than illicit, self-serving desire – complicates the chutzpah that Jowitt finds in Stow's representation. Common mariners who lacked access to the capital necessary to become legitimate merchants had few options apart from naval service, which contemporaries such as Raleigh and Sir Henry Mainwaring, former pirate and later admiralty official, likened to "slavery."[11] As noted above, the shift in status and earning power cost those who relied on the influx of wealth from piracy. But pirates' occupational itinerary, as well as their enduring local ties, also troubles the "othering" on which much legal and popular discourse relied – the same kind of "othering," that is, that discursively created the renegade, a creature radically apart from the rest of humanity.[12] For all the scintillating representations of flamboyant criminals we find in texts such as Thomas Lodge's *The Life and Death of William Longbeard, the Most Famous and Witty English Traitor* (published in 1593 with a rogue's gallery of notorious pirates), the anonymous *Newes from Sea,* and Barker's *True and Certain Report,* many mariners drifted between piracy and legitimate employment, in the Newfoundland fisheries, for example, or in coal shipping in Newcastle. Furthermore, according to Admiralty court records from the first four decades of the seventeenth century, 73 per cent of pirates were listed as mariners by profession.[13] Thus the meaning of "pirate" varied in the period, making it not so much an ontological identity, an expression of extreme otherness or social rebellion, as one that could be easily slipped on or off according to opportunity or necessity;[14] as Christopher Harding insists, "we need to view the piratical identity itself as less stable and neatly defined compared to that presented in later images" (38). This historical evidence uncovers a social reality different from the assumptions behind "hostis humanis generis," pointing instead to a class of men who not only practised care for others, but whose daily experience can be characterized as one of poverty, itinerary, and dislocation. The "economic, spatial, and psychic mobility" that Patricia Fumerton finds in early modern commoners' daily lives, and especially in the lives of seamen, supports a reading of Stow's episode that considers the shared experience of the spectator *and* the condemned (*Unsettled* 50).

Thus, given the pirates' dubious characterization as "others," it becomes difficult to imagine that spectators' responses to their execution fit neatly with the moralizing "hostis" discourse prevalent in legal and popular texts. This difficulty leads to the question of why, near the end of his life, Stow chose to include the execution of Purser and Clinton, by then a twenty-two-year-old incident, in his final edition of the *Annales.* While it may be impossible to say for certain, I suggest that

Stow was captivated by this ironic articulation of the medieval charity – a one-time mechanism of social bonding through economic relations – that he so widely praised. Furthermore, if "nostalgia" is present in this text, it is not for the Elizabethan privateers, but for an ethics of mutual interdependence that Stow associated with earlier times.[15] It seems that charity, which Stow regards as shamefully absent from the "new men" populating the capital and privatizing their wealth,[16] still exists – among men deemed criminals.

To be sure, Stow does not comment explicitly on state policy, but he typically refrained from such discussions.[17] Notably, apart from the aside about clothing "too sumptuous for sea rovers," he also stays silent on the subject of the pirates' social origins. His restraint towards – or perhaps lack of interest in – Purser and Clinton's class identity contrasts sharply with Holinshed's treatment of the execution. After an account that matches Stow's later one virtually word for word, Holinshed then reports at length that Clinton – here identified by his surname, Atkinson – was "a personable fellow, tall of stature and well proportioned, of acceptable behaviour when he kept shop for himselfe, being a free man of London, and like enough to doo well if he had taken good waies."[18] But Clinton is not merely a respectable bourgeois merchant, for Holinshed shares further that he "had his name of the late earl of Lincolne now deceased, who christened him being an infant, & by whose speciall meanes (being growne a proper man) he was not long before saved." In contrast to Stow, who shows the pirates sharing one fate and bonding with their fellows in the audience, Holinshed seems interested in Clinton's *difference* from this company of men, as though his lineage, onetime occupational stability, and formerly "acceptable behaviour" make him an exception to his fellows and a curious anomaly among pirates. The scandal of Clinton, for Holinshed, stems from the fact that he was once settled, with a legitimate occupation and a title, and not – unlike the lowly Ward, the son of a fisherman – prone to masterless conduct.

For Holinshed, Clinton Atkinson's turn to piracy represents a "fall," the personal tragedy of a man who "forsook his owne native countrie" and the upbringing of his "honest parents" to join in "bad companie and libertie, the verie spoile of many a one that otherwise might liue & thriue." This take on Clinton exemplifies Netzloff's observation that "Jacobean texts on piracy elide its political ramifications and economic origins in favor of an emphasis on piracy as personal drama" (*England's Internal Colonies* 62). By contrast, on the moral significance of Atkinson's

fall from respectability into criminality, Stow – himself an earlier con-
tributor to Holinshed's *Chronicles* – offers nothing in his own *Annales*.
His silence signals a departure from the conventional "personal drama"
to a narrative with more broadly social and economic implications. His
use of the Purser and Clinton episode, as well as the special attention
to acts of charity paid throughout his *oeuvre*, invites a broader inquiry
into Purser and Clinton's social roles as men who destroyed some, but
supported other, economies and ways of life.

John Stow is known chiefly as a Tudor figure, but by 1605 he was a Jacobean writer who looked back on Tudor history while retaining medievalist longings. When he adds the Purser and Clinton episode to his
1605 *Annales*, then, he integrates a new reign and its attendant political
changes into his understanding of Londoners and their lives, which,
after all, were his primary interest. The state appears uninvolved in
the execution – its work of apprehension, judgment, and sentencing is
done – leaving us to view the pirates interacting with their "friends"
and "old acquaintance" at the last. The episode demonstrates a notable
contrast to what Stow regularly reports – selfish individuals accruing
all the wealth to themselves. In giving expensive clothing away, the
pirates counter such behaviour with a display of mutual care. Unlike
newly great men or elites shirking their moral and spiritual duty, the
pirates pass their bounty along.

Stow's description of the execution complicates pirates' juridical status as "enemies of all humankind" by showing Purser and Clinton to
be mindful of their legacy as providers. The "hanging ballads" of 1583
show Purser and Clinton's alleged renegade activities to be not only
communal in nature, but, in Muldrew's term, "emotive" as well. The
connection between market participation and emotional bonding is
encapsulated in the early modern idea of "compassion," a word used
in the ballads. In her brief genealogy of the term, Marjorie Garber reads
"compassion" in sixteenth-century context as describing "both *suffering together with one another*, or 'fellow feeling,' and an emotion felt *on
behalf of another who suffers*" (20, italics in original). This "fellow feeling"
captures a sense of compassion not yet defined by the attitude of con-
descension that emerged as a primary association in later periods. The
Good Samaritan parable depicts the compassionate subject as the good
neighbour, the "helpful passerby, who does not cross the road to avoid

involvement" in another's distress (Garber 22). To exhibit compassion, in this sense, is to recognize one's connection to another person by coming to his or her aid.

Although this notion of compassion evokes medieval standards of Christian charity – waning standards, in Stow's view – it can also pose a threat to political order, particularly in violent contexts such as executions. As Bridget Escolme observes, the early modern passions in general represented "a potential threat to social stability," as they were associated with subjects being "moved," as opposed to remaining passive. Compassion, like other passions, holds the potential for "political as well as somatic turbulence and movement" (xxii). Emotion is somatic, seated in the body, and thus moves the body to act. As Michael Schoenfeldt's work on the early modern humours has shown and as the account in chapter 1 of Thomas Stukeley's rebellious "heat" illustrates, this politically disruptive aspect of embodiment suggests a major reason why Renaissance commentators affirmed the stabilizing effects of reason over the tremors of emotion (15–16). Historian Evelyn Berckman, in her reading of Admiralty court records from the period, describes those hearings in ways that exemplify emotion's capacity to create political instability. Trials for accused pirates were "intensely emotional affairs" characterized by "a clamour of voices and presences alive and harsh, possessed by the injury they have suffered, by accusation, or by equal extremity of denying accusation; all these incandescent with hate or fogged with lies, evasions, contradictions, anything that gives the least hope of escape" (6). Such extremes carried forward to the execution sites, where crowds displayed "their gleeful ferocity of appetite for the spectacle, their deafening cheers, shrieks and catcalls as the cart with the condemned was fighting its way towards the gallows, the senseless violence ready to explode into attempts to rescue the prisoners" (11–12). Given the emotional charge inherent in pirate arraignments, authorities justifiably worried about disorder at the scaffold.

Scholarly analyses of emotions typically focus on affect – that is, the way that the observer experiences emotion and how that experience registers in the body. Notable studies of compassion, from philosopher Martha Nussbaum's work on compassion as "social bridge" to Lauren Berlant's more sceptical view of compassion as political quietism, also maintain a focus on the observer, the would-be "ameliorative actor" affected by sentimental scenes in film, literature, and political life.[19] The 1583 ballads, however, offer a different perspective – they depict the sufferer himself seeking emotional response – in this case, compassion.

While first-person displays of repentance and remorse typify the genre of the "hanging ballad" popular in late Tudor England (Capp 224), the 1583 ballads treat this convention in an almost perfunctory way, instead focusing on Purser and Clinton's explaining their story to the audience and seeking "compassion" as a sign that the pirates do not die for nothing. While the potential for the spectators to be "moved" in a way that threatens the state may still exist, I find that the pirates' emotional outreach sidesteps the question of state policy – the focus of previous scholarly readings – to focus instead on the emotive economic relation between the condemned pirates and their public.

Before turning to the ballads, I will describe as a point of contrast the 1639 pamphlet *A True Relation, of the Lives and Deaths of the Two Most Famous English Pyrats, Purser, and Clinton*, a text that seems to deliberately work against emotional identification with the pirates. The identity of the pamphlet's author and its connection to *Fortune by Land and Sea* are unclear. Although *Early English Books Online* attributes the pamphlet to Heywood, nothing in the text itself specifically identifies Heywood as author. Netzloff assumes that Heywood wrote the pamphlet as a way to fill in details unaddressed in *Fortune*, while Jowitt refers to the work as "anonymous."[20] Whether Heywood or someone else wrote *A True Relation*, the text resembles *Fortune* in that, while it may supply more detail on the pirates, it packages this detail mainly as entertainment that looks back on two notorious Elizabethans from the vantage point of 1639.

A True Relation leads with a clear moral agenda – "Chap. 1. Of the Power of Justice," "Chap. 2. Wherefore the Lawes Were Made," and "Chap. 3. All Ill Actions Ought to Be Awarded" – that sets the terms for its ensuing treatment of two "malefactors" deserving punishment (A3–A5). Yet this seriousness is everywhere undermined by an imperative to entertain readers with romantic, heroic, and salacious tales. The title page promises a slice of colourful history through these two figures from "the Reigne of Queene Elizabeth." Punning on "Their Takings, and Undertakings," the title page further promises "Other Pleasant Passages Which Hapned before Their Surprizall Worth the Observing." Yet readers do not encounter Purser and Clinton until the two men meet each other in chapter 5. Until then, the text frontloads their story with reflections on the righteousness of law and order – and then, in chapter 4, the text abruptly shifts to a rogue's gallery of famous pirates. The prose is integrated with a ballad stanza that links the heretofore sententious text to more ephemeral forms of popular entertainment:

Sextus, of *Pompey* who was cald the great,
Th'unworthy son; banishd his native feate
To the *Syllean* Seas: did triumph there,
A famous Pirate; such as had no Peere, & c. (A5)

Chapter 4 digresses into the historically and culturally remote – Roman times, the reign of King Edgar, and the reign of Edward III, for example – before turning to matters "more domestick" (A5) and closer to the present. This quick history casts piracy as a transhistorical phenomenon rather than the product of specific historical moments. The pirates become the mere subjects of "pleasant" yarns enjoyed throughout the centuries.

From the perspective of state policy, *A True Relation* may indeed make "larger political points" about the pacifism of James I and Charles I, as Jowitt argues; other critics analyse the text in a similar vein, focusing on its critique of the present reign through "a nostalgic expression of nationalism" or on the irony in the fact that these criminals possess skills valuable to the state.[21] But from the overlooked perspective of popular readership, the text indulges its audience – most likely men and women who had little knowledge of or involvement in state policy – in a portrayal of pirates as frightening, but still interesting and frequently amusing in their defiance. Readers learn of how Clinton "utterly abandon[s]" his apprenticeship to pursue a seafaring life as a navigator (A5). The text suggests that this abandonment was driven not by temporary desperation, but by a compulsion to break out of a structure of obedience, for both men are described as "haughty and ambitious spirits" who rail against their places aboard merchant ships:

> that in regard of their experience and skill in Navigation, what basenesse it was in them to bee no better than servants, who had both the Judgement, and ability to command, and to bee onely Imployed to benefit and inrich others, whilst they in the Interim wanted themselves: They further reasoned that service was no heritage, and that in regard they had eyther of them beene more than a prentiship to learne their Art, it was now high time to be freemen of the Sea, and set up for themselves. (A8–A8ᵛ)

"Setting up for themselves" means, in this context, detaching from labour hierarchies aboard merchant ships to become illicitly self-determining makers of their own fortune – that is, "freemen" operating on the ocean. Once they rob their first vessel, a Spanish ship, they begin to deem themselves "halfe Lords at the Sea," imagining a form of social distinction that works for them better than the occupational hierarchies that kept them in "service" (B2ᵛ). To be sure, this defiance largely reflects the legacy of James's anti-piratical policies, when the pirate became an enemy of the state and thus discursively isolated in a criminal identity that textual representations intensified. But it also signals to the pamphlet's audience the pirates' distance from the supposed good order of normative social life.

Purser and Clinton's rebellion leads all the way to a confrontation with Elizabeth herself in Part II. After sending the Admiralty after the pirates, the queen, in her "clemency," offers them "a large promise upon her Royall word, and under her broad Seale of their imployment in her owne Navy, so they would prove themselves true and Loyall subjects" (B6ᵛ). The text presents this offer as a gift, yet given the widely known slave-like conditions of the queen's navy, it is hardly so – rather, it reads as an offer to make use of the men's skill by reining them back into the same oppressive structure they escaped. After deliberating while "sitting in Counsell, where they kept a great state, and were attended as if they had beene no lesse than two Princes, and rival Commanders of the maine Ocean" (B7), Purser and Clinton reject the queen's offer. Their refusal of Elizabeth's "clemency" links them to the figure of the "runagate," that early version of the "renegade" that rebels against labour discipline by running away from service or refusing to work. Worse still, the men claim ersatz titles for themselves – "halfe Lords at the Sea" – that reflect their newfound independence. Their pride, their "Prince"-like demeanour held in "great state," sets them up for their fall.

As in Stow's *Annales*, Purser and Clinton give their clothing away to "private friends" at the execution site. But while Stow merely implies the reasoning behind this action, the 1639 writer makes it clear that the clothing is strictly a memento, a set of objects that cement the memory of these men so "brave in habite" and "bold in spirite" (C5ᵛ). The men seem to face their deaths alone, without any further interaction with the crowd. They also receive a Christian burial because, after all, they openly repent: "desiring first, pardon of all men whom they had wronged, and then remission of their sinnes from God, whom they had most heinously offended" (C5ᵛ). The scene presents the conventional "personal drama" and tragic fall. Here again, however, the author seems conflicted on what the audience should take away from the episode. Indeed, the men die resolutely and a formidable set of skills dies with them. Yet at the beginning of the pamphlet, the writer denies the possibility of sympathy by encouraging derision instead: "I conclude with *Solon*; Wretched and most infortunate is that man, whose life the people mourne and lament; and at whose death they Clappe their hands and rejoice" (A4ᵛ–A5). On the one hand, the pirates are would-be heroes whose loss is unfortunate, albeit clearly their own fault. On the other hand, their fall is presented as a farce encouraging readers to "[c]lappe their hands" at the delivery of much-deserved justice. Audiences may identify, or agree with, a political critique if it is present in the text. But the entertainment agenda cuts them off emotionally from the pirates, depicting them as monsters outside of community and state. The "clapping" prompted by the author puts the period on the men's disconnection from the English public.

If the 1639 pamphlet indeed is Heywood's, it may justly be seen to continue the treatment that Purser and Clinton receive in *Fortune*, supplying more detail with the similar goal of entertaining a paying audience. Regardless of its authorship, however, the text packages these Elizabethan swashbucklers as colourful yet aberrant figures; moreover, audiences are encouraged to view them as getting their just deserts. The 1583 collection of ballads, in contrast, provides a perspective more immediate to the actual execution date. It also introduces a new factor into the spectacle – compassion, in this case an expression of the connection between the condemned and their audience. The ballads, drawing on the kinship between public execution and theatre encapsulated in the term "scaffold," exemplify Lake and Questier's observation that "throughout the period some people who came simply to see the show went away emotionally or religiously affected or even 'converted' by the experience" (104). The ballads' voices of the condemned mine the potential for the spectators to be "emotionally or religiously affected" – in fact, the men's attempts at stoking emotional connection become a major part of their farewell. To borrow terms from Berlant, the execution becomes a politicized "scene of emotional contestation" between the condemned and an "affective public" ("Epistemology" 47) – a public whose emotional response correlates with its economic reliance on the pirates and even subverts the logic of the state that isolates and punishes them.

At first glance, these hanging ballads appear concerned only with affirming the righteousness of the pirates' punishment. The title exhibits something that historian J.A. Sharpe regards as a Tudor phenomenon: the performance of penitence. The title promises "unfeigned penitence," "patience in welcoming their death," and "dutiful minds towards her most excellent majesty," which places it in the company of other Tudor gallows literature that is, in Sharpe's words, "didactic and normative in its intent" (148). By portraying the condemned confessing their sins and showing remorse, the pamphlet does the political work of displaying the queen's justice and showing the grisly consequences of breaking her laws. It also singles out the men from the rest of society. This exclusion is expressed poignantly in their standing on the scaffold, on display, facing directly against the mass of spectators representing the aggrieved public.

An unexamined aspect of these ballads, however, emerges in the men's direct address to the spectators at the foot of the scaffold. After offering the conventional expressions of penitence, the pirates strive to engage the spectators in the details of their experience, as if it is crucial – outside of the mechanisms of state justice – that the spectators understand for themselves what happened and what it means. The suggestions of prideful, rebellious personality that we see in 1639 do not exist here; instead, we find men who describe their arrival at the scaffold as a culmination of unfortunate accidents and failures of chance. The men are, all the way to the end, obedient: unlike the wilful transgressors of 1639, Purser of 1583 asserts that "I ever wisht my Queene and country well" (A2) and that he backed off after inadvertently attacking an English ship. Yet, while still owning his faults, he nonetheless ascribes his capture to Fortune's fickleness:

> I held a haplesse Shippe,
> precisely riggd, and furnish for the nones;
> Whome nothing craz'd, till Fortune gan to trippe,
> and dasht my state so stiffly gainst the stones,
> as brake my barke, and brused all my bones:
> But if I say my sinne deserv'd the same,
> In telling truth I merite meaner blame. (A1ᵛ)

Purser admits that his "sinne deserv'd" his ill luck, but that Fortune nonetheless arbitrarily "gan to trippe" and hasten his demise. Moreover, it seems that Fortune "dash[ed]" the men despite the good they claim to have done for others. For example, grim irony pervades their comrade Arnold's own account of helping some French mariners repair their boat and then receiving "a tunne of coales" for his effort. Arnold puns on the ultimate result: "These coales by law the jury did convart / To such a case cooles me at the hart" (A4). Fortune punishes bad deeds, as Purser relates; yet, as Arnold counters, Fortune (in the form of a jury) punishes good deeds as well, a fact that suggests mystifying randomness in the distribution of divine and earthly justice. By helping the French mariners, Arnold attempted to enact an ideal of neighbourly behaviour on the seas; the ill fortune he sustains, which he connects in ironic fashion to his willingness to help, suggests a betrayal of the trust – in God, and in one's fellows – meant to hold such a system together.

This unlucky state becomes the basis for an appeal to the spectators' emotions. The condemned men describe themselves as pawns of fate and, therefore, as victims who seek "some compassion" from the spectators gathered at the scaffold. Purser concludes his speech:

Onely the manner of my losse of breath
is cause that I for some compassion cry:
my soule is sav'd where ere my body lie.
This makes me sigh, that faith unto my frend
Hath brought me thus to this untimely end. (A2ᵛ)

Stemming from the traditional Christian duty of relieving another's suffering, "compassion" in sixteenth-century usage also signifies "[s]uffering together with another, participation in suffering; fellow-feeling, sympathy." The idea of suffering *with another* links the sufferer to a shared experience with a "fellow," enacting the exact opposite of the kind of schadenfreude that would encourage, as the 1639 pamphlet would have it, smiling or rejoicing over a fellow human being's death. Purser's appeal to decency castigates anyone who responds in the way later encouraged by the 1639 text: "'Tis foule," Purser of 1583 protests, "to triumph in an others fall." He asks the crowd instead to "lend us your lament" and bond with him in his suffering (A2).

This appeal to compassionate "fellow-feeling" takes on a self-consciously dramatic dimension when Arnold begins to speak. He asks the spectators to apply their imaginations to the scaffold scene:

[S]uppose that you in presence see
an aged man, of no great personage,
Yet of a minde, as many others bee,
more nobly bent then seemed by mine age:
who mongst the thickest thrust unto the stage,
To breath abroad from my constrained brest
The smoaky reekes of mine extreame unrest. (A3)

In this speech, Arnold assumes a dual dramatic role as the doomed, suffering hero *and* the chorus commenting on the suffering. *He* is the "aged man, of no great personage" undergoing "extreame unrest" on the "stage"; at the same time, he explicitly guides the audience into "suppose[ing]" him as such, in similar fashion to the chorus of *Henry V*: "Work, work your thoughts" (3.0.25). And although Arnold pleads poverty as his motive for turning pirate, he informs the crowd that he is, in fact, "by birth a gentleman / of honest parents" (A3ᵛ). Arnold's original status as gentleman further enhances the sense that he has fallen from great heights, as does the (typically noble, in the influential Aristotelean formulation) tragic hero suffering a reversal of fortune.[22]

Arnold's speech suggests that this particular execution exhibits more than just the Tudor performance of penitence identified by Sharpe. The scene also employs conventions of *de casibus* tragedy, with its traditional emphasis on calamities of Fortune. The appeal to "compassion," then, also recalls the Aristotelian "pity and fear" model still current in early modern England.[23] Although he occupies the role of common criminal, Arnold's tale and that of his comrades reads like a staging of tragic irony, one deserving tragic response rather than condemnation, because, in the realm of "pity and fear," condemnation is beside the point. In fact, as Clinton sees it, condemnation represents a failure of tragic response that indicates not only a lack of compassion but also a shameful forgetfulness regarding the benefits that the pirates have conferred on individual English men and women, including perhaps the spectators themselves. Clinton, charging the spectators to "mourne with me" (B), pleads for pity while reminding Londoners of the risks he took "when others tooke their rest":

> Poore I, that fought to pleasure each opprest,
> poore I that sought to cure anothers paine,
> Poore I, that watcht when others tooke their rest,
> poore I, that did my countries cause maintaine,
> poore I that sav'd must now my selfe be slaine;
> Poore I, that wisht my Queene and countries welth,
> Am now supprest, but hope upholdes my helth. (B2)

Clinton's lament quickly turns into a direct indictment of these same Londoners – not necessarily for failing to keep him from punishment but, strikingly, for their failure to respond to his present suffering as a doomed man. The anaphora – "poore I" – stresses Clinton's desperate state (and perhaps, in the beginning of his pirate adventures, material impoverishment) as a man in need of help or, at least, compassionate acknowledgment. Yet he finds his expectation of help unfulfilled:

[T]hough they stand like stockes and sensles stones,
whome I have holpe whilst I in hap did live,
and sooner might have fild an emptie five:
The time hath bene when they to please me prest,
But now they dare not, cause I am distrest. (B2)

Rather than being moved by the spectacle of Clinton's punishment – a spectacle that, drawing on tragic convention, should invoke "compassion" – the Londoners stand dumb, "like stockes and sensles stones." It is a response no better than the "triumph" that Purser castigates in the earlier stanzas, for both responses deny the economic and emotional connections binding the audience and the condemned. Just as Fortune failed him, so do his neighbours, Clinton finds. The system of mutual help – expressed in terms of economic exchange but involving emotional ties to family, friends, and community – has fallen apart, finally leaving Clinton standing alone as the single criminalized author of his own deserved fate.

Given that these sentiments spring from the mouths of criminals, some might object that the pirates' words do not signify sincere lamentations but disingenuous protests at perceived unfair treatment. To be sure, these pirates would not be the first, or the last, apprehended criminals to blame their fate on someone or something else. But it is crucial to remember that these speeches were written for a wide public of ballad readers and singers and also that they were written in a way that departs from the conventional kinds of penitence expressed in hanging ballads as well as the entertaining "bad guy" conventions employed in the 1639 pamphlet. If the voices of 1583 portray criminal minds manipulating their audiences merely to make excuses for themselves, then that manipulation is subtle indeed. The stanzas' repeated efforts to engage the sympathies of the public ring much stronger; moreover, the economic and emotive relationships they describe resonate with the experiences of the very audiences reading, singing, or hearing these ballads. The fact that the ballads allow sympathy for the pirates at all poses a level of nuance not typically found in popular representations of pirates. This sustained exploration of fate's bitter ironies indicates something far deeper than a winking acknowledgment of criminal duplicity.

These ballads reveal more than an ideologically motivated, Tudor-style performance of penitence. Furthermore, unlike the 1639 pamphlet, the ballads do not dramatize the pirates' disobedience, nor do they make it into the subject of derisive entertainment. Instead, they drama-tize not only the pirates' remorse, but their relationship with the public, a public that is concretized as the crowd present at the execution. Jowitt reads the pirates' self-justification as "powerfully describ[ing] a climate of betrayal" on the seas (*Culture of Piracy* 28), but I would extend this theme of betrayal to England's landed communities as well. Clinton in particular calls his audience to account, reminding them of how much they have benefited from the influx of plundered wealth and goods – and, even if one were to read the rest of Clinton's remarks as deluded or insincere, it is fundamentally true that the audience *has* benefited. The men and women who now turn their backs on him, standing silent and "senseless," deny the connection in their refusal to "lend" their "lament." Their lack of response shows them as Clinton now finds them: bad neighbours who betray the bonds that previously sustained them all.

The surviving copy of the 1583 ballads appears to have been cheaply made and cheaply sold, written in ballad style and presented in black letter script. Like the 1639 pamphlet, it is popular entertainment, but not the kind that dehumanizes the pirates as monstrous, albeit fascinat-ing, rebels. Instead, the ballads invite the audience to share in the men's plight via tragic response – "compassion." They enact a conversation with a community of observers because, by this point in the saga, the struggle with the state is over, as indicated by the pirates' conventional "obedience to queen and country" (Netzloff, *England's Internal Colonies* 66). For this reason, the conversation between the pirates and the spec-tators matters a great deal to our understanding of pirates' significance in the period, because it uncouples the interests of the state from the diversity of interests embodied in consumers and audiences. This fact indicates that "England" represents not one state-approved agenda but a collection of disparate and even contradictory views of piracy and pirates. It also reveals the dependence of these communities on illicit systems of exchange that seem to have succeeded better in providing for the destitute than the state – a distant abstraction – ever did.

After reading the range of stories surrounding Purser and Clinton, *Fortune*'s tragicomic reward of bourgeois virtue at the expense of "others" becomes more visible yet, at the same time, more difficult to explain away in generic terms. Editor Herman Doh speculates that Heywood and Rowley later assigned the names "Purser and Clinton" to a generic pirate subplot constructed to help the play's hero, Young Forrest, achieve victory. The fact that the play makes only one allusion to the early lives of Purser and Clinton supports this suggestion (Doh 27–9). Yet this single allusion matters because, as the captured merchant recognizes Clinton and names him, he mentions Clinton's "skill" as a sailor and, particularly, his usefulness as part of the labour hierarchy aboard merchant ships: "Clinton I know thee, and have us'd thy skill, / Ere now in a good vessel of my own, / Before thou tookest this desperate course of life" (1620–3).[24] Young Forrest, in contrast, openly acknowledges his own status as an "unexperienc'd Gentleman" (1671) aboard a merchant ship: "So weak is my ability and knowledge / In navigation and exploits at sea" (1668–9). Yet he is a "Gentleman" nonetheless, however inexperienced, and thus enjoys "special favors" and the loyalty of the crew. The juxtaposition of Clinton's "skill" with Young Forrest's privilege underscores the play's devaluation of skilled maritime labour; this devaluation becomes most visible when the "unexperienc'd" Young Forrest wins in battle against the experienced Purser and Clinton, seizes their booty for himself, and sends the pirates home to hang. Hierarchies of labour and class thus are encoded in the pirates' demise and the bourgeois protagonist's happy ending. The 1639 pamphlet thought to be Heywood's does nothing to trouble this assumed ideology – that Purser and Clinton may be colourful and fun, but ultimately rebels who deserve punishment, not wealth.

The overarching moral frames of *Fortune* and the 1639 pamphlet clearly centre on the "right" way to acquire wealth abroad, with Purser and Clinton serving as foils to the protagonist. In contrast, Stow's *Annales* and the 1583 ballads render the pirates' story with more ambiguity and add an important element – an audience *within* the text itself, there to witness the men die. These witnesses interact with the condemned in a way that highlights pirates' deep involvement with English communities, an involvement expressed as a bond both economic and emotional. Stow's treatment hints at the relationships of interdependence that many English people had with pirates. The ballads amplify these relationships by having the pirates explicitly address the crowd and the readers, underscoring that interdependence explicitly (in the case of Clinton's accusations of betrayal) and implicitly (by asking the audience to identify with them by sharing their grief). This connection, performed for readers, makes the pirates into more sympathetic figures and, possibly, men that audiences recognize from their own lives.

While *Fortune* possesses an ostensibly different moral agenda, the emphasis on compassion in its sources nonetheless invites us to re-examine the play with an eye towards the fissures in Purser and Clinton's apparent wilfulness. Purser and Clinton initially appear to deny their Englishness, thus marking themselves clearly as the villains of the play. Yet I would argue that "Englishness," in this context, begs for a more precise definition. To be sure, Purser and Clinton attack ships flying English flags, a practice they justify to themselves: "Nay since our country have proclaim'd us pyrats, / And cut us off from any claim in England, / We'l be no longer now call'd English men" (1618–20). But although Fuchs quotes this line to show that Purser "wants nothing of English nationality" ("Faithless Empires" 53), the line could also be read as a simple statement of fact: it is the state, not Purser and Clinton themselves, that declare them to be pirates, without "claim in England," and thus no longer "English men." In this sense, Purser places the original responsibility for this new non-English identity on the state, not on himself.

If we understand the line in this way – that is, as describing a series of punitive events leading to the men's disengagement from England – then the much-discussed scene depicting a "pursevant" and a clown can be read differently as well. Before Purser and Clinton appear on stage, the pursevant delivers a proclamation against Purser and Clinton to the clown, who echoes each line back with a bungling, perhaps deliberate, twist. Following on Jacques Lezra's reading of a similar scene in the 1639 pamphlet, both Fuchs and Jowitt describe the clown's responses in *Fortune* as mangling the queen's commands and thus undermining the power of royal authority.[25] Indeed, some of the clown's answers are merely ridiculous and do make the proclamation into a mockery: for example, "Pyecrusts or Sheeps-heads" for "Pirates Ships or Heads" (1560–1). Other responses, however, seem to rewrite the words of the proclamation as a counterrnarrative, hinting at an interpretation that is more sympathetic to Purser and Clinton. For example, the pursevant's iteration of "Purser and Clinton," when translated by the clown, "Lost their purses at the Clink," a line that refers to the notorious debtors' prison in which poor prisoners, who had to pay fees for their paltry maintenance, languished for life because they could never buy themselves out (1544–5).[26] Likewise, the pursevant's "If a condemned man liberty" becomes the clown's "If a man at liberty condemned," alluding to the criminalization, and perhaps the incarceration, of a man otherwise at "liberty" on land or at sea (1566–7). Such has been the plight of what the pursevant calls the "banishd man" who took on a rogue identity only once he was, in the clown's words, "banish[ed] his country" (1564–5). The clown's responses translate the words of the proclamation into the pirate's point of view, which is that his country acted upon *him* before he ever acted upon *it*.

If the play does voice the pirates' perspective in this way, Purser and Clinton can be understood as rejecting not "England" writ large, but merely *one* version of Englishness – the punitive version, originating from state authority, signified by the English flag. Instead of embracing the behavioural ideal promoted by the very state that punishes them, they opt for an alternative sense of "Englishness," one formed in explicit reaction to the state's oppression of them and their kind. While Jowitt describes Purser and Clinton's ship as mirroring England and thus creating a parallel state ("Piracy and Politics" 221), the pirates' practices in fact critique England in one notable way – they distribute their bounty equally, while also remaining open to input from those who might feel slighted: "In equal shares, and not the meanest of any / But by the custom of the sea may challenge / According to his place, rights in the spoyl" (1582–4). Young Forrest also promises to split the bounty with his crew, but with a crucial difference: "in equal shares, / To every mans desart, *estate*, and place" (1850–2, emphasis added).The similarity in language between the two statements, with the notable addition of "estate" in the latter, makes the pirates appear more civic-minded and more in line with true fellowship than the play's nominal hero, who considers a man's social rank when distributing supposedly "equal" shares. Purser and Clinton's approach to sharing the wealth is even farther removed from that of their social superiors on land, represented by the callous Old Harding – who dies while trying to write his own son out of his will – and the gentlemen who refuse to help the destitute Philip when they realize he cannot reward them in return (1985–2019, 1506–25). Such differences lead one to ask which set of characters – the rogues, the English merchants, or the landed gentry – is truly guilty of betrayal, particularly when we shift "England" away from its association with the signs of state power towards a vision like Stow's, one that equates good Englishness with civically responsible economic behaviour.

These multiple representations of Purser and Clinton offer a specific angle on the subject of this book – renegade behaviour and its representations in early modern English literature – by bringing intersections of community and economy to bear on the renegade's discursive status as a figure radically apart. Just as, in the ballads, Purser, Clinton, and Arnold invite dialogue with the crowd, so do these texts themselves invite dialogue with their audiences. Arnold asks the crowd to remember its role as the material beneficiaries of the risky behaviour for which he now suffers; the text itself – as a product for consumption, also subject to regulation and seizure – testifies to the circulation of licit and illicit commodities and the reader's role as a purchaser in that network. Moreover, just as the scaffold can become the site of drama beyond the reach of the state, so do print products allow for a range of unscripted responses outside of their original purpose. The "haughty and ambitious" Purser and Clinton thus appear less as renegades – conscious, rebellious English others – and more as members of a network of dependencies, extracted from their landed and seaborne communities and "thrust unto the stage" for making their participation too visible. "Poore I," cries Clinton, as if anticipating the coming generations who will be urged to "[c]lappe" their "hands" at his death.

Chapter Four

"Extravagant Thoughts": The Sherley Brothers and the Future of Renegade England

We have witnessed to this point different ways in which literary representations of renegades both portrayed flamboyantly deviant behaviour and yet also suggested that such behaviour might not be so deviant after all. When plays, ballads, and prose revisit the story of a particular renegade again and again – even long after his death or disappearance – these texts do not merely entertain audiences with ripping good tales; they entertain in a way that awakens these audiences to their own capacity for resistance and, quite possibly, renegade behaviour of their own. In doing so, these texts invite an element of shared experience – shared, that is, across a range of classes, thus mirroring the diversity of audiences for the popular print market and the public stage – into renegade tales' reception. By inviting audiences to see their country's social practices, and even themselves, reflected in the story, these texts complicate and ultimately dispute the common view of the renegade as an alien dramatically estranged from his homeland and its people. In telling of one individual, renegade tales address an entire nation; in telling of otherness, they direct attention to England itself.

Continuing to trace this interplay between the exemplary and the exceptional, we now arrive at Thomas (1564–c.1634), Anthony (1565–1635), and Robert Sherley (c. 1581–1628) (variously spelled "Shirley"). Biographer D.W. Davies describes these three brothers – born to Sir Thomas Sherley of Sussex and Anne Kempe, daughter of Sir Thomas Kempe – as "gentlemen on the make" – that is, as part of a species of minor gentry who sought profit and adventure outside the formal dispensations of royal patent, charter, or diplomatic assignment (1). Although the brothers indeed may have been recognizable as a certain roguish "type," their deeds both fascinated and repulsed their contemporaries. The oldest, Thomas, began his career in military service but soon turned privateer, motivated in part by his spendthrift family's financial distress. The second brother, Anthony, acquired a lowly knighthood from the French king Henri IV that, although relatively meaningless in the French court, nonetheless got him thrown into prison in England, where he was forced to recant his oath of loyalty to the bemused Henri. Anthony is best known for serving as "ambassador" to European Christendom on behalf of the Persian Shah 'Abbas I. The youngest brother, Robert, accompanied Anthony to Persia in 1598. After Anthony abandoned his Persian embassy to pursue new opportunities in Spain, Robert married a Circassian woman rumoured to be the shah's niece. He also is noted for turning up at the English court in a turban to argue for enhanced trade arrangements between Persia and England.[1]

To be sure, such adventures make the Sherleys curious specimens even in an age full of rogues – they may even be, as biographer Boies Penrose offers, "one of the most picturesque families in the annals of the human race" (4).[2] Nonetheless, recent scholarly treatments attempt to tease out the Sherleys' cultural and political significance beyond these eccentricities. Such commentary attends largely to the brothers' status as travellers, since travellers themselves represented a suspect group in early modern England.[3] Worse still, the Sherleys were travellers who overreached their social entitlements, insinuating themselves into circles where they did not belong. Jonathan P.A. Sell writes that Anthony, in particular, "constantly challenged legitimacy and the social and political consensus, into whose upper echelons Sherley attempted to introduce himself" (105) in France, in Persia, and finally in Spain, embarrassing himself and his country along the way. Other critics extend the particulars of Anthony's travels towards a broader examination of tensions between political ideals of sovereignty and transgressive individual actions. Following M.T. Nezam-Mafi, Bernadette Andrea employs the term "Sherleian discourse" to argue for Anthony as a figure who "simultaneously exemplifies and complicates Edward Said's mapping of Orientalism as representative not of the Eastern Other, but of the Western Self" (281). As such, Anthony becomes a liminal kind of self-fashioning Renaissance man, a creature both English and other, and a subject powered by self-interest in an age that demanded absolute loyalty to one sovereign. The fluidity that Anthony exemplifies, Sanjay Subrahmanyam argues, exposes the inadequacy of early modern ideas of sovereignty that assumed a single unitary state, not a state coexisting with other states (77) – and, I would add, not the large number of English subjects who experienced cultural and geographical mobility as a matter of course.[4]

Widespread mobility among the English populace notwithstanding, the Sherleys stood out not simply as wanderers, but as wanderers with a special talent for presumption – that is, they combined the stigma of the traveller with other potent stigmas around social overreaching and acting without royal sanction. As a result, the Sherleys incurred much damage to their reputation at home, prompting them to launch what Jonathan Burton calls a "public relations campaign" ("Shah's Two Ambassadors" 33) in the form of commissioned pamphlets and one play, *The Travels of the Three English Brothers* (1607), co-written by John Day, William Rowley, and George Wilkins. Echoing Burton's assessment, other scholars view these texts as strained attempts to rescue the Sherley reputation. Julia Schleck, for example, reads a version of their story that appeared in the second edition of Hakluyt's *Principall Navigations* (1599) as a "propagandistic" attempt to redeem the family from its "great disgrace" (786, 790), while Laurence Publicover reads *Travels* as seeking "directly to influence public opinion" concerning Anthony's "controversial political programme" (695).

I do not aim to controvert these arguments, but rather to expand their import in ways that account more fully for the role of English audiences in constructing the Sherley story, a role suggested in previous scholars' recognition of the family's efforts to reconcile itself with the English public. I propose that the Sherleys represent more than such contemporary phenomena as "gentlemen on the make," illicit self-advancement, or suspect travel – they symptomatize, in fact, a larger conversation about England's future. This conversation adjusts the brothers' reputation at the time as faithless wanderers in a more positive direction; concomitantly it orients audience members' vision of themselves towards their own potential for adventure, enterprise, and wealth. In her recent book, *Untold Futures*, J.K. Barret offers a useful heuristic for plotting this transition. She finds in early modern English texts "an artistic generativity and experimentation particularly focused on uncertainty, flexibility, and possibility" (3). These imaginative acts, she elaborates, anticipate a future that is neither impossible nor inevitable, thus providing us with "avenues for understanding approaches to the future not already bounded by our own categories and assumptions" (6). In the case of the Sherleys, those binding "categories and assumptions" reside in the labels and judgments that cast the brothers as "runagates" – men supposedly headed for prison, the gallows, or eternal perdition. However, I argue that the pro-Sherley texts addressed in this chapter controvert that narrative. By linking the Sherleys' aspirations to a more open-ended, potentially prosperous future – one in which other English subjects, inspired by the Sherleys' boldness, might also contribute – these texts reframe the brothers' seamy ethical status in a more collective, more hopeful, and indeed more patriotic way.

The history of the Persian Empire supplies important context for this reframing. As Jane Grogan demonstrates, that empire occupied an important place in the historical imaginary of Renaissance humanists who studied the deeds of Xerxes and Cyrus as moral and political *exempla*. Even in the less illustrious contemporary Persia, the memory of a glorious ancient empire nonetheless persisted and fertilized new imperial desires, clearing the way for the East India Company to collaborate with Persia to take the island of Ormuz back from the Portuguese (Grogan 1–11, 180–4).[5] Between these two historical poles – the ancient empire and the liberal trading empire, which functioned in similar ways to a state – exists an attempt, borne out by company men as well as political philosophers, to reconcile the twin corruptions of ancient empire and Asiatic trade with aspirations towards civic virtue and the pursuit of wealth as public service.[6]

Texts written in support of the Sherleys – which variously describe the brothers in terms of their old-fashioned "honour" as well as their Machiavellian savvy – exhibit this tension, as Grogan shows in her illuminating reading of *Travels* and Anthony's own prose account of his Persian embassy (1613) (150–79). However, I will demonstrate that these texts do more than reveal the contours of the inchoate trading empire – they present the story of these anti-establishment figures in a way that attempts to plant the seeds of imperial thinking among audiences, imbuing those audiences with an adventurous and aspirational mindset that reconciles the individual pursuit of glory with the pursuit of national wealth and prestige. As several examples will show, the pamphlets yoke the brothers' attempt to wrest their personal quest for "honour" away from accusations of self-interest and towards the anticipation of a larger national project. *Travels* tries to advance this project by using theatrical space to encourage audiences to imagine *themselves* in new territories, undertaking bold new endeavours through social and economic risk. In short, *Travels* prompts audiences to envision – dangerously, daringly – a future of empire. While Richard Brome's satirical comedy *The Antipodes* (c. 1640) represents peripatetic desires in a conventional way by cautioning its audience against "extravagant thoughts" (1.1.148),[7] *The Travels of the Three English Brothers* actually encourages such thoughts. In doing so, it shows the excursive Englishman not as a venal "gentleman on the make," but as an empowering harbinger of national prosperity – but only if others dare, as he does, to see their country and themselves through renegade eyes.

After years of debt, imprisonment, shifting loyalties, and outlandish political presumption, the Sherleys sorely needed a "public relations campaign." The European public viewed Anthony in particular as a man who followed the money and hatched schemes that never came to fruition; these behaviours earned him such descriptors as "inconstant," "a man of inventions," "a man with no religion," and "a man who comes running whenever there is an offer of money" (qtd in Subrahmanyam 91, 91, 95, 95). His association with other notorious figures did not help matters. For instance, he counted himself a favourite of the second Earl of Essex, whom he served in the Low Countries and on voyages against Spanish possessions in the Caribbean; Anthony later identified the controversial late nobleman as "the patterne of my civil life" and "a worthy model for all my actions" (*His Travels into Persia* B1ᵛ). Having married Essex's cousin Frances Verney in 1594, Anthony saw himself as one of the family and, by the time he travelled to Italy at the end of the sixteenth century, he still operated under Essex's patronage. Anthony associated with troublemakers at the lower end of the social scale as well, including Captain John Ward, our subject in chapter 2. According to Samuel C. Chew, Anthony attempted to collaborate with Ward on attacking the Ottoman Porte (289–90), although the anonymous 1609 pamphlet *Newes from Sea* reports that Anthony also appealed to Ward, as a countryman and a Christian, to abandon his "detestable life" (C).[8]

In addition to these real-life associations, Anthony's suspect activities imaginatively connected him to another renegade he likely never met: the mercenary and recusant Thomas Stukeley, the subject of chapter 1.[9] Anthony Nixon addresses this resemblance in the commissioned pamphlet *The Three English Brothers* (1607):

I am drawne into an admiration, that Sir Anthony Sherley, having so
slender beginnings, should nevethelesse continue that state, countenance,
and reckoning, as hee hath done ever since his departure out of England,

even in the Courts of the greatest Princes, in, and out of Christendome: so farre exceeding Stukeley, that I am afraid to be tared [?] of an impartiall, and rash judgement, but to intimate a comparison between them, there being so great difference, both in the manner of their travels, the nature of their imployments, and the ende of their intendments. The one having his desire upon a luxurious, and libidinous life: The other having principally before him, the project of honour: which, not in treacherous designes as Stukeley attempted in the behalfe of the Pope, against his Countrie) he hath impaired, or crazed: But contrariwise hath so inlarged, and enhanced the fame, that his fame and renowne is knowne, and made glorious to the world, by his honourable plots and imployments, against the enemie of Christendome [...] (G1ᵛ)

Musing on Anthony's modest origins, Nixon expresses "admiration" at the "state" Anthony has achieved "in the Courts of the greatest Princes"; he implies also that this international prestige validates Anthony's "departure out of England" and thus exempts him from "runagate" status. The trajectory still resembles Stukeley's own. But the difference between the two men, according to Nixon, rests in "the nature" of their business, the "manner" in which they travel, and ultimately in their "intendments." In this schema, Stukeley "intended" only the pursuit of "a luxurious, and libidinous life," and his counterpoint is Anthony, whose "principal" aim is "the project of honour." Stukeley's designs, which served only to gratify himself, led him to collude with the pope against his own queen. In contrast, Sherley's "intendments" include only "honourable plots and imployments" against the "enemie of Christendome." Nixon leaves this "enemie" unspecified, and for good reason, given that, although at one time Anthony tried to rally Persia and European Christendom against the Turk, he later abandoned this project to ally himself with England's traditional "enemie," Spain. But according to Nixon, the "intendments," not necessarily the outcomes, definitively distinguish Anthony from the infamous Stukeley. Anthony's overarching "project of honour," we are told, overrides any resemblance to the Stukeley story.[10]

Of course, the rather strained way in which Nixon distinguishes the two men implicitly acknowledges their resemblance as much as it explicitly argues for their difference. Nonetheless, the term "honour," used repeatedly by Nixon, represents a major pillar of the Sherley defence in this text and others. On the one hand, "honour" evokes medievalist modes of international crusading, an association that squares with

Anthony's devotion to Essex and Anthony's later association with the militant Protestant circle of Prince Henry, King James I's oldest son. Yet this nostalgic mode, like all forms of nostalgia, evinces a clear awareness of the present[11] – not only the political orientation of England in the world, but the conversation about the Sherleys in England.

Another concept cited by Nixon – "fame" – functions in a similar way. According to the *OED*, "fame" – often personified in late medieval and early modern literature as a swiftly flying figure – consists in public talk or report, ideally of a positive nature, but not always, as the term could also signify notoriety or infamy. Similarly, "fame" signifies "reputation" on a wide scale, the social capital accrued in what others say about a person's deeds or character. In this sense, Nixon deploys the word to counteract the negative kind of "fame" surrounding the Sherleys in England – their vainglory, their alleged treachery, and their roving natures. "Honour," in turn, indicates the positive kind of fame that the Sherleys desire instead – respect, esteem, and reverence from the public, all testifying to the "nobility of mind and spirit" that Nixon claims for Anthony. Thus, Nixon's use of the term "honour" signifies an attempt to direct public attention – manifest as "fame" – away from the obvious resemblance to Stukeley's outward actions and towards a discussion of inward character.

Crucially, the twin concepts of "honour" and "fame" recognize the essential role of the public in constructing the Sherley story. Julius R. Ruff offers a succinct definition of "honour" that well captures Nixon's own use of the term: "Honor embraces the value one places on oneself, but *even more importantly* it also represents the esteem in which society holds one" (75, emphasis added).[12] This view of honour as residing in the "esteem" of "society" orients traditional aristocratic notions of honour towards public opinion – that is, towards the men and women who read popular prose and attended public theatres. Of course, this subjection to popular opinion carries both benefits and potential risks. As Jeffrey S. Doty demonstrates in his work on the early modern concept of "popularity," public esteem can enhance the power of an individual figure (by providing validation) or detract from that figure's power (by tainting him or her with the putatively inferior judgments of the vulgar rabble).[13] Like popularity, "fame" also signifies the presence of "political content in the public sphere," an arena in which various "communicative acts" "subjected political matters to the scrutiny of 'the people'" (Doty, *Richard II* 189). This very subjection expands and diversifies the range of perceptions beyond the court into the realm of the commons, a direction that by definition challenges the privilege of elites who controlled public access to political information. According to Paul Yachnin, the early modern theatre in particular exemplifies this expansion of "social and political imagining," a cultural movement that "exploits the nature and accessibility of public space, speech, and action" to create a politically aware public (87). This public represents an early articulation, one among many, of what Jürgen Habermas would later identify as the "bourgeois public sphere."[14]

I agree that the theatre possesses unique advantages for the creation and galvanization of a critical public; I will return to this point in my discussion of the Sherley play. However, in line with Habermas's original attention to print culture, I find that the pro-Sherley prose in its own way constructs a pro-Sherley public and appeals to that public to promote a revised view of these erstwhile faithless wanderers. This effort challenges the idea of Anthony as alien, radically disengaged from his homeland by self-serving pursuits. The 1602 *A True Discourse, of the Late Voyage Made by the Right Worshipfull Sir Thomas Sherley the Yonger* pushes further against common perception by elaborating on Thomas's "honour" in a way that includes all of England in the Sherley "project." This account, written by an anonymous "gentleman that was in the voyage," describes a successful raid on three Spanish towns, a castle, and a priory. The same manly "heat" we saw in Stukeley arises also in Thomas's blood when one town refuses to yield: "our Admirall (not a little moved) returned him with a scornefull and sterne visage instead of an answere, and then (after we had carried aboard such provision as we thought good, and suffered our men to pillage what they could) we began to fire the Towne" (B1ᵛ). Yet this fiery raid is no mere self-glorifying exercise, as Stukeley would have performed it, because the glory therein does not redound only to Sherley, but to his country; the title page insists that these deeds were "no lesse famous and honourable to his Country, then to him selfe glorious and commendable" (A2). As if to answer the Sherleys' reputation as "gentlemen on the make," the pamphlet frames Thomas's raid in a way that attempts to correct any perceived separation between what is "glorious" to Thomas and "honourable" to his country. This raid, as part of a "project of honour," achieves both.

In justifying Thomas's actions, this particular iteration of personal and national honour both looks back and looks forward. This yoking together of nostalgia and anticipation exemplifies a trait that Bronwen Wilson and Paul Yachnin find in early modern publics more generally:

"early modern public making was harnessed to the traditions, authorities, and forms of behavior of the past as it also initiated some of the lineaments to which future forms and expressions of public life were to become tethered" ("Introduction" 9). As for the past, the account draws inspiration from the illustrious example of Francis Drake, who waged a private war against Spain with the queen's consent. Essex's 1596 raid on Cadiz provides another historical template for Thomas's voyage and, as such, the 1602 pamphlet strategically applies the blurred distinction between hero and rebel to Thomas himself. Compared to these figures, the gentlemanly amateur Thomas proceeded with far less expertise and resources, not to mention a lack of formal dispensation. But by assigning Thomas a place in the Elizabethan privateering tradition, the pamphlet positions its hero's exploits as ultimately beneficial to England and, in this sense, anticipates the future as well. As John C. Appleby shows, England came relatively late to the European race for colonial expansion, and, as a result, it relied on privateering to wage war against Iberian enemies who already held powerful land empires (56). Yet, although maritime conflict "remained in the hands of private adventurers who pursued their own interests with little effective control" (67), this loose and contingent strategy nonetheless signified a serious and ultimately effective program of aggressive expansion into new territories. Fernand Braudel calls the practice of seaborne plunder a "sign of arrival" in the early modern colonial world – that is, a sign that a new and upstart power is challenging an older, more established empire (2:865–91). As other historians of early modern empire have shown, these smaller aggressions undertaken by non-state agents played a major role in opening up the kinds of imaginative and territorial spaces that would make English colonization possible in the next two centuries.[15]

Compared with the achievements of such figures as Drake and Essex, it is unlikely that Thomas Sherley's adventure played a pivotal role in this historical process. However, the 1602 account makes its case for Thomas's excursion by borrowing heavily from the nationalistic discourses of heroism, religious crusading, and economic competition that shaped the contributions of more famous privateers. Further, it incorporates into this strategy a suggestion that, by inheriting a place in this tradition, Thomas will continue to advance his country's prosperity and reputation. For example, his service to his country's "honour" does not merely entail the abstract glory of conquest; it also involves the seizure of booty that his men bring home to England. The conquest of Tavaredo, reports the eyewitness narrator, yielded "great store of wheate, wine & fish" (A4ᵛ), which Sherley's men took for their own provision, underscoring the fact that privateering posed a more cost-effective option than a navy for England's notoriously parsimonious queen. Reiterating the message of material bounty, the pamphlet's con-clusion reports that "the ships arrived at Hampton the 10 day of June, 1602, not without good boote and pillage gotten by the Mariners and souldiers" (B3). This "boote and pillage" adds material and economic benefit to Thomas's personal "glory," thus arguing for his actions as nurturing not only himself, but also his nation's reputation, its religion, and its people all at once. But, most crucially, the success of this pro-gram depends on the future participation of others beyond the Sherley family. The narrator writes with an eye towards the "encouraging of other Gentlemen, desirous to honour their country with their travailes, and to win perpetuall fame and credit to themselves, by shewing their valour upon the common enemy of God, and their Country, and on such as are the Generall disturbers of all tranquility and peace in Chris-tendome" (A3). By erecting Thomas as *exemplum*, the pamphlet invites others to seek opportunities to advance themselves *and* their nation through courageous – even if not officially sanctioned – action.

This alignment of personal "honour" and national benefit echoes in *A True Report of Sir Anthony Shierlies Journey Overland to Venice* (1600), but with a somewhat different emphasis – this account by Anthony more explicitly notes the perils endured by him and his men for the sake of their journey. While the 1602 story of Thomas's Spanish adventure describes the "travailes" of a "tedious" voyage (A3, B3), the story of Anthony's initial trip to Venice insists on the great trouble – here again, "travail," a word suggesting both travel and difficult labour (A3)[16] – undertaken by Anthony and his men. Such gestures assure the audience that the Sherley excursions are not mere junkets, but serious endeav-ours performed at great risk. The title page itself conveys the vast geo-graphical expanse that Anthony covers: first Venice and "from thence by sea to Antioch, Aleppo, and Babilon, and soe to Casbine in Persia." The 1613 account of Anthony's journey to Persia, written, like the account of the Venice adventure, by Anthony himself, also continually mentions the trip's hazards; even the Persian counsellors who dislike Anthony appreciate that he has made a journey "so full of dangers and expences" (M2). Likewise, a member of Sherley's entourage, William Parry, stresses in his own 1601 account the dangers the men incurred as they travelled home: "we were continually tossed and tumbled with contrary Windes: and once had beene like to have beene utterly cast away, so that wee all were overwhelmed in despayre" (F2). The end of all such effort, as the 1600 title page proclaims, is "[p]riviledg obtained of the great Sophie" – that is, safe passage for English trade throughout the Middle East. The pamphlet concludes with a letter from the shah to Christian princes that asserts that only Anthony has achieved peace between them and made it possible for them to communicate. Like the account of Thomas's Spanish adventure, this narrative asks its audience to recognize that the Sherleys court considerable danger to bring benefits – free travel for trade, valuable booty, and conquest of the Spanish menace – to England.

This is not to say, however, that these tales ignore the Sherleys' "runagate" reputation. Anthony's 1613 account acknowledges the stigma of his special brand of travel and, in one scene, even makes it the subject of debate, one that begins to destabilize distinctions between criminal adventuring and visionary bravery. The subversion inherent in this kind of conversation will register most explicitly in the theatre, as I will show; the prose, however, intimates it while hedging explicit subversion. Early in the story, Anthony assures his audience that he is no ordinary, ignorant traveller, but "a Gentleman bred up in such experience, which hath made me somewhat capable to penetrate into the perfection or imperfection of the forme of the State, and into the good and ill Orders by which it is governed" (C1ᵛ). This "experience" testifies to a gentleman's humanist education, one steeped in exploring questions of virtue and good governance. Such a background, Anthony maintains, makes his observations more valuable than those of the common traveller. Non-courtly readers can expect to glean insight into "the forme of the State" from Anthony, whose class and education afford him both access to the inner circles of power and a lens by which to observe how those circles work.

The defensive tone of this assertion, however, also reflects an awareness of his transgression. It is a defence, in short, against the suspicion of being an opportunistic striver evading trouble at home; it argues instead for Anthony's bravery in pursuing and enacting Christian ideals. This acknowledgment of the unstable line between commendable bravery and runagate imposition surfaces in questions raised by Persian royal counsellors, who argue against Anthony's advice to the shah. Much of the counsellors' argument hinges on Anthony's murky origins. "For what likely-hood was there," the counsellors wonder, "that a Gentleman of quality, without some great disaster fallen him, should take such a voyage, so full of dangers and expences, upon a fame of a Prince, spread by ordinary Merchants?" (M2). They view Anthony's devotion to the shah as strange and question his true intent, which may be to benefit himself: "why should hee not give time to the growing of his better fortunes, by your Majesties Munificencies and favours" (M2)? They predict that, after leading the shah astray, Anthony will abandon him and then "relye upon those, to whom hee oweth greater obedience, for more permanent benefits" (M2), which can mean either a return to England or a change in allegiance to the next power – perhaps even the Turk – with "more permanent benefits" to offer. Even a courtier who supports Sherley's position admits that "I cannot discerne his reason," but this courtier chooses to give him the benefit of the doubt by arguing that Anthony's ability to counsel the shah towards heroic and virtuous action would increase Anthony's reputation at home – if, that is, "his condition be good in his owne Countrie" (O).

The counsellors' discussion makes explicit to the English audience one crucial fact: that to pursue "honour" abroad is to hazard the "runagate" label. Anthony's Persian involvement thus becomes the occasion for evaluating his motives, which the courtiers take to be an extension of his suspect social and political status at home. In other words, Anthony becomes a runagate – with all the term's implications about illicit aspiration and criminality – in the moment he oversteps his social and geographical bounds. This moment reveals the highly relational and discursive nature of class in the early modern period: the gentleman of a respectable Sussex family overreaches, and therefore becomes potentially a lowly turncoat, when he stretches beyond his social entitlements and seeks to influence the affairs not only of his betters, but of his betters far from home. "Though of a well-established family," D.W. Davies writes of the Sherleys, "they refused to remain established" (1), suggesting that the brothers' excursive pursuits damaged, or even cancelled out, the legitimating power of their gentlemanly birth.

Given these prose accounts' obvious investment in vindicating the Sherleys, the accounts cannot be relied upon to reveal any stable "truth" about the brothers' activities or their motives. They do, however, reveal the binary terms of a conversation heavily laden with cultural anxieties about social and geographical mobility. Anthony is either consistent in his allegiances or he changes them according to opportunity. He either acts forthrightly with the shah, for the good of the shah himself as well as Christendom, or he acts according to his own desires. He either is a man of transparency, stability, and good reputation at home, or he is a "gentleman on the make" whose self-seeking agenda undercuts whatever "gentleman" status he may formally possess. Anthony's 1613 account displays these binaries, yet, by acknowledging them, the account also articulates the misconceptions an ambitious English gentleman must overcome to do good on his country's behalf and, at the same time, attempts to repair the misconceptions that have damaged the Sherley reputation.

In short, the message of these prose texts – albeit couched in neo-chivalric, vainglorious and overblown rhetoric – is that the Sherley travels provide great benefit for England, and they do so at great sacrifice to the Sherleys themselves. Of course, the actual significance of these achievements – relative to the previous successes of English privateers, diplomats, and merchants – is questionable. But this fact does not necessarily negate the power of the Sherley narratives as *imaginative* exercises in envisioning the military, entrepreneurial, and diplomatic capabilities of the English gentleman of "slender beginnings." *The Travels of the Three English Brothers*, performed in the public theatre during the early years of James I's reign, stages these possibilities for an economically active and socially restive audience just beginning to apprehend England's place on a world stage. The play's narrative is the Sherleys', but the larger implications of that narrative are England's own.

◦◦◦

Among the Sherley texts, *The Travels of the Three English Brothers* plays a special role in the campaign to recuperate the family reputation. The play, which portrays all three brothers but focuses mainly on Anthony and Robert, represents the "project of honour" in a way that lends the immediacy and excitement of theatre to events previously reported in prose – the Persian embassy, the marriage of Robert to the shah's niece, and the splendour of the Persian court. In doing so, it brings an experience of courtly life into the popular realm and, in a manner following the process of public making discussed above, subjects that court to the judgment of its social inferiors.[17] It also initiates, against the background of the Sherleys' tarnished reputation, a public conversation about the brothers' countervailing virtues. The playwrights, writing on the Sherleys' behalf, cannot fully control the outcome of this conversation, but they can and do strive to direct it in ways that not only reframe the brothers in positive terms, but also stoke excitement about future possibilities for English glory.

The play begins in the ancient capital of Qasvin, where Anthony and Robert meet the "Sophy" (Shah 'Abbas I). They dazzle him – and the English audience – with a demonstration of English combat, of guns and gunpowder (which the play suggests, incorrectly, had never before been seen or used on Persian soil), and of their mercy in sparing the lives of their prisoners rather than, as the Persians do, mounting the prisoners' heads on spikes. So taken is the Sophy with these displays that two of his courtiers, Calimath and Halibeck, grow jealous and vow to ruin the brothers. Meanwhile, Halibeck and Anthony begin their mission to the Christian world. First in Russia and later before the pope, Halibeck's attempts at discrediting Anthony backfire; meanwhile, back in Persia, the Sophy's niece (the play gives her no proper name) falls in love with Robert, despite Calimath's efforts to woo her on Halibeck's behalf. As for Thomas, the Turks take him prisoner during a raid in Greece; when Robert learns of Thomas's capture, he attempts to trade his own Turkish prisoners in exchange for his brother's life. These attempts, as well as his secret marriage to the niece, earn the Sophy's rage, which abates when Robert shows that he seeks only to redeem his brother. Indeed, the Sophy is so pleased with this latest example of honour that he agrees to baptize the child of Robert and his niece, extend toleration to all Christians in Persia, and erect a house for the religious education of Persia's Christian children. The play concludes with the three brothers and their father geographically separated and gazing at one another through a prospective glass – a tool by which to see each other, as well as the future, at great distances.

Travels conveys the excitement of the Sherley story, in large part, by speaking to the early seventeenth-century vogue for travel literature and its various subgenres. Broadly speaking, the play inhabits the general category of the "travel play," which used the popular art form of drama to give a largely insular population a glimpse of the world. English theatregoers inhabited a culture in which, Anthony Parr notes, "interest in a wider world was vigorous but largely unfulfilled" – suggesting viewers eager to travel in their imaginations, even if they were tethered to the island (3). One type of play that satisfied such curiosity was the "knight-errant drama," which drew on medieval heroic modes of crusading to portray the travels of adventurers. Knight-errant plays, while not exactly on the cutting edge in 1607, nonetheless remained popular at playhouses such as the Red Bull (where *Travels* was performed) and the Fortune.[18] The "citizen romance" genre represents a related source of influence, although it focused more on legendary Londoners and the denizens' capacity for old-fashioned virtue. Examples include Heywood's *Four Apprentices of London* and *Edward IV*, both of which incorporate ordinary men into what Lawrence Manley describes as "an inclusive, neochivalric ethic of loyalty, service, and moral nobility" (*Literature* 439). *Travels'* debt to citizen romance registers in its resemblance to *Four Apprentices*, which features three brothers who aspire to liberate Jerusalem from the "Saracens."[19]

Although these older dramatic forms retained their popularity, the success of *Travels* may also reflect its relationship to more contemporary genres that, like *Travels*, were topical in nature. The "Turk play," although also grounded in romance, flourished during a time of engagement with Muslim lands, particularly the Ottoman Empire, with whom Elizabeth I sought trading arrangements (that were, incidentally, threatened by Anthony's interference in the Ottoman-Persian conflict, thus augmenting the queen's anger at him). These plays reflect awe at the cultural sophistication and perceived monotheistic purity of Muslim nations while at the same time rehearsing stereotypes of the "Turk" as militaristic, barbarous, and cruel, perceptions no doubt enhanced by the Ottomans' actual invasions of Europe since the Middle Ages. While *Travels* applies these stereotypes most obviously to the "Great Turk" character who battles the Persians, the Persians themselves – particularly Halibeck and Calimath, but also the Sophy when angered – do not escape the "raging Turk" stereotypes that Turk plays often applied broadly to people of the Middle East and North Africa.[20] Finally, another genre that corresponds to contemporary topics, particularly issues of trade and empire, is what Ania Loomba calls the "mercantile-colonial romance" ("Break Her Will" 68). I discuss this genre, with the particular lens it offers on economic participation in international settings, more fully in chapter 2. But *Travels* too reflects the genre's influence insofar as it endows the Sherleys' residual modes of knightly self-representation with the more emergent traits possessed by successful trader-diplomats, such as business savvy and access to superior military technology.[21]

Travels shares with these genres a keen interest in exploring the possibility of English expansion into the larger world. Yet among these plays, *Travels* stands out for its strategic use of audience and theatrical space to achieve two interrelated objectives: one, to vindicate the reputation of a still living family by directly involving audience members as social actors; and two, by using that family's story to awaken the audience's sense of its own potential for adventure. This dual strategy begins with the prologue, when a chorus enters "attired like Fame." As "Fame," the chorus echoes a primary objective of pro-Sherley prose literature, which, as we have seen, seeks to restore "honour" to the family and to involve a wide audience in that restoration. The script stops short of offering further detail on the chorus's costume. To be "attired like Fame" might mean that the chorus wears wings, although it was also conventional in pageants and emblem literature for Fame to appear in "a robe 'thickly set with open Eyes, and Tongues'."[22] If this chorus wears something similar to the latter example, then that costume calls special attention to two things that play a crucial role in spreading "fame" – public curiosity ("open Eyes") and the human tendency to report what one sees ("Tongues"). Both eyes and tongues, such a costume would visually suggest, play an essential role in the construction of reputation, or "fame."

Thus the play would immediately enlist the audience as participants in its articulation of the Sherley story. If the spectators first experience the chorus with eyes facing back at them from its robes, such a visual directly involves the audience in the spectacle before the chorus even utters a word – that is, the audience does not merely see the play in linear fashion; rather, that audience exists in reciprocal relationship to the play. The audience, in other words, is "seen" in return. Even if the chorus's costume does not feature eyes, the chorus's first lines call attention to "tongues" and add another element of sensory input – the ears:

> The tranquil silence of a propitious hour
> Charm your attentions in a gentle spell,
> Whilst our endeavours get a vocal tongue
> To fill the pleasing roundure of your ears. (Prologue 1–4)

The chorus aims, conventionally enough, to "[c]harm [the] attentions" of the spectators and direct their focus to the scene. The next two lines, however, highlight two vital engines in the public construction of fame – the "vocal tongue" and the "ears." The "vocal tongue" may be that of the chorus and the other actors, filling the "ears" of the audience with their tale. Yet, soon enough it becomes evident that the audience has its own vocal role to play in this production. As it happens, the chorus needs the audiences' own "tongue" to activate the first scene: "Our scene lies speechless, active but yet dumb, / Till your expressing thoughts give it a tongue" (Prologue 30–1). This invocation of the audience's "expressing thoughts" refers most obviously to the spectators' capacity to enhance the experience through their own cheers, shouts, and other vocal signs of participation.[23] In the context of "fame," however, the image of the "vocal tongue" also reminds the spectators of their own part to play in constructing fame, whereby these spectators might speak what they take in through their eyes and their ears. Furthermore, if the audience learns something new, and refreshingly positive, about the Sherleys from the production, the articulation of that audience's "expressing thoughts" can help sustain the momentum of that message by reporting the events of the play to other people.

However, while the chorus acknowledges the theatre's potency in constructing "fame," it also acknowledges that the theatre poses certain limitations on the formation of "expressing thoughts." Those limitations stem from the inadequacies of the physical stage. Calling upon "your assists / To help the entrance of our history," the chorus commands the audience first to "see a father parting with his sons" in a dumbshow, where Thomas Junior, Anthony, and Robert take their leave of Thomas Senior. Next the audience must rely on its imagination to "see" what the stage *cannot* represent:

> Imagine now the gentle breath of heaven
> Hath on the liquid highway of the waves
> Conveyed him many thousand leagues from us.
> Think you have seen him sail by many lands;
> And now at last, arrived in Persia,
> Within the confines of the great Sophy,
> Think you have heard his courteous salute
> Speak in a peal of shot, the like till now
> Ne'er heard as Qasvin, which town's governor
> Doth kindly entertain our English knight –
> With him expect him first. (Prologue 32–42)

Unlike the parting brothers, these elements – waves, sail, and the splendour of the real Sophy – exist outside the representational possibilities of the material stage. In acknowledging that fact, the play resembles other dramas that apologize for the material constraints of the stage – most famously Shakespeare's *Henry V*, whose chorus conjures the audience to "work, work your thoughts" to bring distant Harfleur into view (3.0.25).[24] The chorus of *Travels* operates similarly, commanding the spectators to "Imagine now" and "Think you" (twice) as the scenes unfold. These commands imply not only an attempt to compensate for the stage's limitations, but a recognition that much of the audience likely has not seen such sights as "the liquid highway of the waves," "many lands" including "Persia," and the "confines of the great Sophy." Thus, in compensating for the shortcomings of the stage, the audience – largely confined to London, or even a single neighbourhood within it – at the same time must stretch its own imagination to "see" and "think" new places and people.

While such gestures appear to apologize for the stage's limitations, the play also makes use of those limitations, paradoxically, to stoke excitement about the wonders it sets out to portray. These references to the stage's material deficiencies sharply delimit the theatre as bounded space and, as such, heighten a sense of the vastness beyond it – city, nation, continent, and world. The prologue enables this traversal further with a device that assists the imagination's travels beyond bounded space, across the seas, and into Persia – and that is the "peal of shot" that makes the Sophy "speak" for the English audience. The shot introduces the theme of military conquest, a theme that plays out over the scenes to follow and to which I will return below. But in the context of the prologue, which persistently strains to command the audience's eyes, ears, and tongues, the shot assaults the ears in a way that cannot help but startle the audience to attention. If a shot were actually fired to accompany this reference, the sound would have resonated outside the open-air playhouse into the neighbourhood and the city, thus paralleling the audience's efforts to imaginatively reach outside the restricted space it inhabits. The shot also links the prologue, with its metatheatrical consciousness of spatial and imaginative restriction, to the opening scene, where Anthony and the governor of Qasvin anticipate the Sophy's arrival. Here the governor conflates the "new" (supposedly to the Persians) experience of hearing gunshot with the arresting effect of Anthony's magisterial command:

> It is the Sophy's high will and pleasure
> That you be seated here in the market-place
> To view the manner of his victories;
> Which, would you greet with your high tongues of war
> Whose thunder ne'er was heard in Persia
> Till you gave voice to them at Qasvin first […] (1.18–23)

Just as the prologue's opening shot clears space in the audience's attention, so does Anthony's "thunder" command the attention – and the awed respect – of the Persians. The governor's reference to "high tongues" repeats the chorus's own allusion to tongues, this time aligning the power of speech with the gunpowder that transforms the Persians into Anthony's rapt audience. The shot, echoing from the playhouse into the scene, thus not only transports the audience across spatial and conceptual distances, but enlists them in the "project of honour" that will play out.

Yet this project is not without its moral hazards; these hazards remind audiences of the negative possibilities inherent in the concept of "fame." Just as the prose narratives frequently incorporate the Sherleys' unsavoury reputation into their argument, so must the play also deal with that reputation, which no doubt exists in the minds of the same audience it attempts to transport, figuratively speaking, into Anthony's world. The play signals this attempt, as well as its strategy, in the prologue's final lines, where the chorus hopes that the play will inspire Anthony's "native country" to treat him with "courtesy," since, as the play will show, "foreign strangers" have found it within themselves to be "kind" (Prologue 43–6). Theatrical representation of "foreign strangers" – their personalities and customs, as well as their dramatic actions and reactions to the brothers – will argue the case for the family's "honour." But the role of these "foreign strangers" in building that argument will be a complicated one, because those strangers will exhibit a range of opinion, not all of it "kind," concerning their English visitors. On the one hand, the incredulous Sophy, witnessing the brothers' military conduct and their expressions of fidelity, is moved to hyperbolic expressions of respect, as is the niece when she hears of the brothers' exploits in a battle with the Ottomans. On the other hand, Halibeck and Calimath become actively malicious versions of the sceptical courtiers described in Anthony's 1613 account, men who spread doubt about the brothers' true status and intentions. For example, in a confrontation at the Russian court, Halibeck calls out Anthony as a "fugitive, / A Christian spy, a pirate and a thief" (4.21–2). These lines explicitly echo the kinds of epithets – accusations the audience would have recognized – attached to the Sherleys at home. After all, Anthony had left England in 1598 and would never return, and in the play Anthony admits to being a mercenary (5.80). In keeping with Halibeck's hope, the Russians pause at these allegations, although later Anthony is vindicated at the Russian court, where "after question of his life and birth / They found him sprung from honourable stock, / And that his country hopes in time to come / To see him great, though envied of some" (5.13–16).

Such an interlude indicates the play's acknowledgment that it must, and will, grapple with the Sherley reputation and that it will attempt do so to the Sherleys' ultimate benefit. One strategy is to portray the brothers dramatically triumphing over their detractors, as we see in the scenes with Halibeck. Another, more explicitly theatrical, strategy emerges in the play's use of foils to help delineate the Sherleys' virtues. These foils represent extreme "runagate" types recognizable from contemporaneous English drama. For example, when the Sophy rages at Robert, he likens Robert to a "low and mean-bred Saraber" (11.96) – that is, a "Saracen," one of that race of desert marauders who overran Persia in the eighth century. In metatheatrical context, the Sophy's comparison would have immediately recalled Christopher Marlowe's bold, overreaching, and spectacularly violent "Scythian" Tamburlaine, the title character of two plays that still attracted enthusiastic audiences in 1607.[25] In the context of international politics, the "Saraber" recalls Persia's historical vulnerability to invasion and, at the same time, vindicates Robert as someone with no such intentions. The "Saraber" is a "low and mean-bred" figure whose nomadic lifestyle makes him an especially dangerous brand of runagate, one invoked to highlight Robert's relative mildness, faithfulness, and integrity. But at the same time, the comparison also suggests the valiant and militaristic Robert's potential to conquer if he chooses to do so. The Sophy, for lack of further information, is alarmed for good reason.

By using the "Saraber" as a foil, the play advances its larger intention to vindicate the Sherleys' honour, although this approach succeeds only partially, given that it reveals the Sherleys' resemblance to, as well as their distinction from, runagate types. The same interplay of similarity and difference appears in Anthony's encounters with an assortment of wandering "others," including a money-lending Venetian Jew named Zariph, a harlequin, and the harlequin's wife, who turns tricks for customers. These minor figures, represented in hyperbolic and stereotypical terms, serve to define Anthony's difference from more suspect travellers, even if they call attention to some resemblance.

However, the play also invokes itinerant types whose behaviour, for English audiences, is more difficult to stigmatize. In the subplot involving Robert, a blurring of distinctions between patriotic hero and faithless runagate occurs in reference to a much-admired figure in English culture – Aeneas, founder of Troy and mythological founder of Britain. After Robert leaves the besotted niece's chamber, she and her maid wonder about the consequences of falling in love with such a man.

Specifically, they ponder the example of Aeneas, who "played false play" with Dido (3.122) by abandoning the queen of Carthage to pursue his destiny. This time, the comparison raises the question of the difference between running *away* from something – in this case, the trappings of domesticity – and running *towards* something greater. That is, the women's discussion prompts the audience to consider why Aeneas himself is not a runagate, but a visionary founder and epic hero. Such a discussion naturally also applies to Robert, who shares his brothers' reputation as a fugitive and a rogue. As it turns out, the line between manfully pursuing one's vision and adhering to the norms of domesticity is indistinct. The example of Aeneas, and the classical authority conferred on him by humanist learning, suggests that the story of the Sherleys might too be written from the perspective of the future, a perspective very different from the present one that holds the brothers in suspicion. The play's reference to Aeneas indicates one possible reason why *Travels* highlights, rather than de-emphasizes, the brothers' status as travellers – to be a traveller is not necessarily to be a faithless migrant, but to be a man of destiny.

Thus, the play interrogates the brothers' resemblance to the "runagate" by placing them alongside different iterations of the wanderer and comparing the brothers in ways that acknowledge the power, as well as the liability, of wandering. By acknowledging the ways in which the brothers differ from *and* resemble other travellers, the play resists restoring any kind of reassuring "English" domesticity to the Sherleys, opting instead to endow them with a bolder ideal. While the play takes care to differentiate the brothers from the worst aspects of the Saracen raider, the wandering Jew, the strolling player, and the prostitute, the Sherleys still act in ways that seriously challenge social languages that restrict ordinary subjects from extraordinary visions and actions. For example, when the Sophy, fascinated with Anthony's relation of England and its queen, asks "what's the difference 'twixt us and you?" (1.162), Anthony answers that there *are* no differences, only *constructions* of difference:

All that makes up this earthly edifice
By which we are called men is all alike.
Each may be the other's anatomy;
Our nerves, our arteries, our pipes of life,
The motives of our senses all do move
As of one axletree, our shapes alike.

> One workman made us all, and all offend
> That maker, all taste of interdicted sin.
> Only art in a peculiar change
> Each country shapes as she best can piece them. (1.164–73)

Anthony implies two things in this speech. First, he maintains that there is only one god, "[o]ne workman," who created all humans in "shapes alike." This argument erodes political claims of absolute difference – or, as Daniel Carey terms them, fictions of "incommensurability"[26] – that designated one nation, one religion, and one authority as superior to, and therefore radically different from, others. Second, Anthony asserts that "[o]nly art" accounts for such differences and that, moreover, "[e]ach country" embraces the form of "art" that best serves its purposes.[27] The implication, again, is that there are no essential differences – even on the level of "anatomy" – between the people of different nations who worship their god under different names. Anthony's statements also raise the question of essential differences among commoners and nobility. Throughout the play, Halibeck and Calimath chafe at the Sherleys' presumption, but never more so than when the Sophy seems to reward such aspiration by elevating the brothers beyond what the Persian counsellors feel to be their station. Yet, evidently the Sophy is not offended by Anthony's suggestion that he and Anthony – and members of all nations – are fundamentally alike.

Thus, although Anthony fashions himself as a Christian crusader – it is at least the stated cause that propels his adventuring – he espouses a distinctly secularist outlook, disclaiming the existence of any divinely ordained hierarchy among nations and people. Anthony does not acknowledge one truth, mandated by one national identity and history. Rather, he observes multicultural correspondences among forms of worship and culture that erode nationalistic notions of uniqueness or specialness. Another episode echoes the point: when Zariph asserts that "sweet music" was "first revealed to Tubal Cain / Good Hebrew" (10.69–71), Anthony counters by debunking this claim for the mythological Hebrew smith:

> So much the Hebrew writ doth testify,
> Yet there are different to that opinion:
> The Grecians do allow Pythagoras,
> The Thracians give it to their Orpheus
> As first inventors of the harmony. (10.72–6)

To this, the less worldly Zariph merely replies, "All errors; Tubal, Tubal, Hebrew Tubal" (10.77) in a display of cultural insularity. By desacralizing the sacred in general, Anthony challenges the "great chain of being" and other familiar early modern theories of social organization that endowed some subjects and groups with more grace – that is, higher status – than others. The signs and symbols of particular cultures and religions become empty and interchangeable signifiers, as we see at the start of the war with the Turks when Robert enters the stage wearing both a turban *and* the old red cross badge of England (7.sd.6). National costume, in Sherley hands, becomes something to be put on, taken off, or combined with other items according to circumstance, thus severing any presumed relationship between the costume and the true identity of its wearer.

Robert's mixed attire testifies to the newly established partnership between England and Persia. Yet the figure of the crusading knight also signals that, although Anthony's theory of difference could be interpreted as pacifistic, the Sherley vision in fact incorporates violent conquest – and lends to it an element of hard-nosed business strategy. It bears remembering that the play opens with Anthony and Robert instructing the Persians in the art of war, with Anthony and Robert demonstrating their style of battle for the Sophy. The Persian ruler shows particular interest in why the English take their prisoners alive instead of killing them. Anthony responds:

> In this I show the nature of our wars.
> It is our clemency in victory
> To shed no blood upon a yielding foe.
> Sometimes we buy our friend's life with our foe's;
> Sometimes for gold, and that hardens valour
> When he that wins the honour gets the spoil.
> Sometimes for torment we give weary life:
> Our foes are such that they had rather die
> Than to have life in our captivity. (1.102–10)

Impressed by these words, the Sophy exclaims, "We never heard of honour until now" (1.111). This "clemency" represents a show of "honour" that is supposedly new to Persian culture, one that demonstrates superior Christian morality in war. Yet, in truth, this proclaimed "clemency" rests on the fact that killing a prisoner wastes valuable resources. By saving one foe's life, "we buy our friend's life" in return, as Robert will do when he ceases killing Turkish prisoners to trade the rest for Thomas. Alternatively, he might hold prisoners in exchange "for gold," a practice that implicates Anthony in the ransom market for Mediterranean captives, a market in which pirates also thrived.[28] If he cannot cash in on his prisoners, then Anthony relishes the "honour" that he feels accrues to him when holding a captive who "had rather die / Than to have life in our captivity." Thus, upon closer examination, Anthony's approach to his prisoners begins to look less like "clemency" and more like callous disregard for a captive's humanity. It reveals a calculating entrepreneurial mindset by which a human captive becomes an asset to be traded or sold.

Anthony's valuation of his prisoners takes the Sherley "honour" beyond its initial resemblance to medieval crusading into the present realm of international business and politics, a realm dominated by the circulation of luxury goods and human commodities and defined by business arrangements forged in spite of religious or ethnic difference. Seen from this viewpoint, it is possible to view the Sherleys' activities as both rogue *and* nationalistic – undertaken for their own "honour" and without the Crown's permission but, at the same time, beneficial for England's future, as they suggest in the pamphlets discussed above. In *Travels*, the Sophy learns lessons from Anthony Sherley; but, in the 1613 relation of his travels, Sherley offers Persia as a lesson for his own compatriots. The title page promises, among other details, "a True Relation of the Great Magnificence, Valour, Prudence, Justice, Temperance, and Other Manifold Virtues of ABAS, Now King of PERSIA, with His Great Conquests, Whereby He Hath Inlarged His Dominions" (A1). This does not much clarify the relationship between the shah's virtues ("Great Magnificence, Valour, Prudence, Justice, Temperance, and Other Manifold Virtues") and the "Great Conquests" by which "He Hath Inlarged His Dominions." Whether these successful conquests stem from the shah's virtues is uncertain; what is certain, however, is that a monarch can cultivate these virtues and at the same time expand his dominions, almost as if expansion were the natural reward for practising those virtues. The shah, then, heads an example of a successful empire, one worth studying, as Sherley opines: "I doe thinke verily, That in Asia the Persian hath as great an extent of Territories, as the Turke, and better inhabited, better governed, and in better obedience, and affection" (F2ᵛ). The desirability of an empire "better governed, and in better obedience, and affection" could not have been lost on English readers, conscious as at least some of them were of England's comparatively small territorial reach – and perhaps in the view of some other readers, its inferior governance, devoid of "obedience, and affection."

To be sure, that English brand of empire would take a different shape from that of Safavid Persia, and, moreover, the process for getting there would be long and complex. The Sherley texts play a role in that process by stoking the imagination of other Englishmen – that is to say, the readers and spectators of the Sherley story. The play in particular suggests that England – and English men of "slender beginnings" – will advance in the world not by being punctilious, but by being bold. If the Sherleys had an unofficial motto, it might well have been something like our modern saying "better to ask forgiveness than permission" or, in early modern political terms, better to act without official dispensation than to stay at home where, as the raiding Thomas declares in scorn of his more domesticated countrymen, one might "die unknown, so buried and forgot" (6.41).

True to the historical record, the Anthony of *Travels* disappears after his meeting with the pope, leaving Robert alone to deal with the Persians. But Anthony's example need not be perfect to be powerfully suggestive to the play's audience. This point perhaps is most apparent in the epilogue, when the three brothers and their father invite the audience to imagine possibilities of adventure for themselves. Still in his guise as Fame, the chorus gives the four Sherleys a prospective glass through which to view each other at a distance. The Thomases Senior and Junior abide at home (where, in fact, Thomas Junior was serving out a sentence in the Tower). Anthony is in Spain, receiving the order of St Iago (after abandoning the service of Shah 'Abbas). Robert remains in Persia (where Anthony had left him). They peer at each other through the glass, maintaining their connection through what was "traditionally a magical device for seeing distant or future events," a device that functioned as a magnifying glass as well (Parr 133, n. 13.6). The prospective glass as stage prop emblematizes the expansive Sherley vision, one not restricted by the political and affective demands of the homeland, and shows how this family retains its cohesion, and its roots in England, even over great distances and in separate grand endeavours.

Given the chorus's repeated attempts to enlist the audience's "expressing thoughts" in telling the Sherley story, it is worth pausing to consider further what role the prospective glass plays in this program. Grogan views the appearance of the prospective glass as signalling a "disruption" (155). I would add that this "disruption" intervenes in norms of English "settledness" by inviting the members of the audience to "see" further and exercise their imagination, free of physical, social, and temporal limitation. The prospective glass extends the audiences' vision out of bounds in two specific ways. First, it brings distant objects into sight, thus eliminating the physical impediment of distance and allowing the viewer to take in faraway places. For the Sherley father and sons, the glass allows them to view one another's whereabouts and activities with a kind of immediacy that letter writing cannot afford. Were a member of the play's audience to look through this glass, he or she would experience new sights with that same kind of immediacy, experiencing foreign places with a level of apprehension not available simply through travel writings, which filter exotic locales through someone else's ken. By bringing distant locations within the sight of the bounded subject, the prospective glass allows the spectator to travel in his or her mind with a concrete vision. Second, the prospective glass allows *time* travel as well – specifically, a vision of the future, as mentioned in contemporaneous astrological treatises.[29] When the Sherleys peer through the glass and see each other in ways unfiltered by the moral judgments that define their current reputation, they see a legacy of adventurers, the continuation of the family line from England, where Thomas Senior dwells, into Persia, where Robert's son – with his Persian royal blood – has just been born. The future, for the audience member looking through the glass, perhaps is less distinct, but the view of new places helps fertilize a sense of possibility that might never have existed otherwise.

Travels is a play whose import exceeds that of a merely self-serving "public relations campaign." First, the play does not recuperate the brothers as domesticated, and therefore "safe," English gentlemen, but samples the characteristics of stereotypically threatening others – the "Saraber," the wandering Jew, the itinerant player – as well as culturally revered travellers such as Aeneas to put pressure on conceptual distinctions between the lowly runagate and the visionary man of action. Second, rather than representing the Sherleys in a linear and self-contained way that assumes a passive audience, the play transports that audience into a sensory experience of excursive action, ultimately suggesting that audience members consider adopting such action for themselves. Even if the play does not explicitly call the spectator – perhaps also a man of "slender beginnings" – to become a Drake, a Raleigh, or an Essex in his own right, it at least prompts him to begin courting the "extravagant thoughts" necessary to traverse the physical and conceptual boundaries of the domesticated English subject.

Thus, like the other texts explored in this book, *The Travels of the Three English Brothers* speaks to a diverse audience of readers and theatregoers, a group of individuals whose interests are not necessarily coterminous with those of the state. The discursive gap between the Sherleys' official status as troublemakers and the dramatic excitement of their example registers in the play's refusal to completely expunge renegade attributes from its heroes. The tension between the needs of the "public relations campaign" and the fascination inherent in the brothers' adventures perhaps is most apparent in the contradictions that the brothers display in *Travels*. Anthony's polished speech and courtly mannerisms are belied by his shows of military force; these displays hint at his power to brutally overrun enemies, Tamburlaine-style, who fail to yield to rhetorical persuasion. Likewise, he professes an ideal of Christian "honour" in preserving his prisoners, yet this "honour" is revealed to be a matter of rational economic calculation. Robert's later killing of his Turkish prisoners, which he ceases only for the purpose of trading the survivors for Thomas, further obstructs any clear takeaway regarding the brothers' "honour." Anthony's very reason for being in Persia was murky – possibly motivated by trade, possibly by crusading – and the idealistic pretensions of his Persian embassy were quickly abandoned for the sake of Iberian pursuits. Such contradictions reflect, in part, the conflicting agendas informing the play itself – the need to recuperate the Sherley "honour" while at the same time exciting, and inspiring, the theatre audience with topical drama that engages widespread cultural curiosity about the world and the future possibilities promised by new social and economic opportunities.

Yet these contradictions, I suggest, also adumbrate the Sherley's place in a larger historical trajectory, one characterized by a tradition of intellectual engagement with the larger significance of empire. Early modern thinkers, whether philosophers or entrepreneurs, exhibited both a preoccupation with the glories and pitfalls of ancient empires and a keen interest in how future empires might take shape. The humanist fascination with the old empires included Persia, but dwelled chiefly on Rome. The Roman ideal of the "imperial," as Anthony Pagden describes it, centred on the idea of sovereignty – that is, an emperor's dominion over his own kingdom – ensured by "extended territorial domination" achieved through "military rule" (11–15). But although the Roman imperium represents the intellectual point of origin for the political thought that underwrote later notions of Christian empire and the absolutist state, humanists nonetheless were circumspect about the viability of Rome as a positive example for nations, viewing its legendary corruption as a major cause of the militaristic imperium's fall.[30]

In the early modern period, this association of empire with corruption combined with native English insularity and traditional prohibitions on the accumulation of wealth; the result was widespread disapproval of the same trading endeavours that would import wealth into the nation and position it to compete with other European powers – particularly Spanish, Portuguese, and Dutch – on the international stage. The East India Company (EIC) in particular, which conducted trade at immense distances from the homeland, garnered such disapproving commentary; as Philip Stern explains, "For those many early modern English theorists and statesmen who regarded wealth, accumulation, and commerce with deep suspicion, the English East India Company was easily damned as the greatest of reprobates" (510). The EIC, as Stern notes further, countered this perception by espousing trade as a matter of national service intended to ensure wealth for the public good. Furthermore, the EIC played a major role in erecting the figures of the tradesman and the seaman as symbols of civic virtue and even as new kinds of gentlemen whose trading activities secured "fame, fortune, and family" as cornerstones of their "estate."[31] The EIC's concern with the moral import of its Asian endeavours, activities that admittedly courted the possibility of greed and corruption, is seen in its policing of "interlopers," Englishmen who lived on the borders of the company's cities without its permission. The interloper, who attempted to trade in foreign environments outside the legitimizing structure of the company, represents a later version of the Tudor-Jacobean renegade who sought to prosper outside legitimating state dispensations. His defiant independence attracted moral castigation but at the same time reminded the public of the potential for immorality and incivility within all wealth-building endeavours, particularly when carried out among the supposed depredations of non-Christian "others."[32]

By invoking this history, I do not claim any simple or direct relationship between the Sherleys' brand of adventuring and the non-state agents – legal, like the EIC, or illegal, like the pirates or "interlopers" who lurked on the fringes – that later hastened English commercial expansion abroad. I do, however, wish to argue for the literary representations discussed in this chapter as signs of a larger conversation that sought to reconcile virtue with the pursuit of national wealth. When the play's epilogue presents the prospective glass to its audience, it not only invites that audience to translate its curiosity into action, but it does so in a way that implicitly critiques the state's hesitancy to exploit the kinds of opportunities abroad that would ensure both wealth and national prestige in the future. Again, England came relatively late to the race for expansion among European powers; furthermore, Tudor ideals of empire were not expansionist in nature, but rather aimed at maintaining independence from the papacy and ensuring the Crown's sovereign command over British territories.[33] While English monarchs supported projects when called upon and only occasionally obstructed them, the founding of the commercial empire was not a royal achievement, but the legacy of non-state agents that, in M.N. Pearson's terms, "put political power and privileges to commercial purpose" (92).

That commercial and diplomatic opportunities abroad must be seized – with or without royal dispensation – seems to have been the Sherleys' conviction. Therefore when, in the play, Anthony complains of his "[c]old and unactive" (1.144) country, these words may express more than just frustration at James I's pacificism and his country's lack of countervailing "heat." They may also capture a mood of impatience at England's reluctance to assume a role as legitimate player on the international economic scene, a role that the brothers take into their own hands by privately attempting to negotiate trade agreements. The conflicts that ensue in the play's version of the Sherley story reflect not only the tension between old ideals of "honour" and new imperial desires, but tension between ideals of obedience to the sovereign and the visionary drives of the excursive subject.

By articulating these tensions in various ways, the play and its sources represent another way in which renegade tales of the Tudor and Jacobean period reflected as much, if not more, on England and its people as they did on the foreign worlds in which renegades roamed. Just as *The Famous History of the Life and Death of Captain Thomas Stukeley* – published and revived, incidentally, two years before *Travels'* first staging – suggests the presence of restive "heat" within all Englishmen, so do *Travels* and its sources highlight the boldness – exemplary in the Sherleys – that, if properly harnessed, advances the "project of honour" throughout the world. Like the other tales examined in this book, the Sherley texts exhibit distinct awareness of the social and political costs of such transgression; at the same time, by cultivating the corresponding aspirations of readers and audiences, they court the potential renegadism of England itself. The English army of Shakespeare's *Henry V*, full of ragtag "bastard Normans" (3.5.10), once modelled and embraced the kind of scrappy courage that would come to defeat stronger powers, making "bastardy" into a badge of national pride. The Protestant Reformation, and England's unique role in furthering it by making a radical break with the Roman Church, further established this geographically isolated island as a renegade among European nations – divergent, wilful, and somewhat of an underdog. Then, after the break with Rome, England would be ruled by a Protestant queen who refused to marry and left no heir, eventually naming a Scot to succeed her. And in time, England would maximize its position as an island nation by embracing the oceanic frontier as the basis for a maritime empire that would dominate for centuries. To get there, England would have to become somewhat of a renegade itself. Perhaps the Sherleys, by their imperfect example, helped to plant the seed.

"Skillful in Their Art": Criminal Biography and the Renegade Inheritance

By analysing literary representations of renegades from late sixteenth-
and early seventeenth-century England, this book makes a twofold
argument. First, it demonstrates that ideas about religious, social, and
economic transgression drew heavily not only on hierarchies of class,
but more specifically on the labour practices that supported those hierarchies. The term "runagate" points to this link between low socio-
economic status and the renegade behaviour of the revolted servant. At
the same time, the qualities of the runagate – treachery, faithlessness,
mobility, and illicit aspiration – emerge in representations of renegades
from a range of social positions, from a poor fisherman to minor gentry;
this fact reveals the susceptibility of class identity to discursive recon-
struction based on a subject's behaviour. Second, literary representations of renegades as a whole neither romanticize nor condemn their
subjects, but rather use colourful tales to open up conceptual space
for conversation and self-reflection among readers and spectators.
Accounts of figures such as Thomas Stukeley, John Ward, Purser and
Clinton, and the Sherley brothers brought provocative questions about
masculinity, heroism, social justice, national loyalty, economic individualism, community, enterprise, and empire to diverse audiences who,
as consumers in the markets for drama and print, encountered those
dialogues anew with each fresh representation.

Literary representations of renegades therefore function as cases
by which to test the limits of some important cultural attitudes indigenous to Tudor and Stuart England. At the same time, the renegade
has endured as an archetype well beyond that period, from the "rogue
fiction" popular in the post-Interregnum years to contemporary televi-
sion, films, and comic books, to name just a few media. A full exploration

of each subsequent historical moment lies outside of the scope of this chapter. Yet, by way of conclusion, I wish to suggest that the early modern "runagate" is an important part of that archetype's history. I will do so by noting how his characteristics reverberate in a set of texts widely believed to have heavily influenced the development of modern fiction: the criminal autobiographies of early eighteenth-century England.

The impetus for this chapter derives from Ian Watt's *The Rise of the Novel*, a text of seminal importance to the last six decades' worth of scholarship addressing early British fiction. While critics have argued with Watt from a variety of angles, I alight on a particular feature of his study – his treatment of criminal biographies as proto-novels that influenced the later fiction of Daniel Defoe, Samuel Richardson, and Henry Fielding. To cite but one example, Watt attributes to Defoe's Moll Flanders a "criminal individualism" that echoes the roguish defiance portrayed in criminal biography (111, 42). From this example and others, Watt argues that the popularization of individualistic traits in fiction signals a wider cultural movement towards the affirmation of "economic individualism" over traditional privileges of birth; thus, economic individualism also becomes "political individualism" that deeply challenges entrenched notions of class, status, and economic agency (63 passim).

While acknowledging the importance of individualism as an early modern phenomenon, I wish to suggest that criminal biographies' alleged embrace of the individual is more problematic than Watt allows. These biographies, I will show, reflect the influence of earlier Tudor and Stuart renegade tales such as those studied in this book. Renegade tales exhibit an attitude towards economic calculation that can best be described as complex. The embrace of individualism, as we might understand it today, is modified by the renegade's ties to his community, ties often figured as the relationship between the renegade tale and its audience. The later criminal biographies demonstrate a similar pattern, thus inviting a reassessment of individualism as a positive trait inherited by early British fiction.

Just as Tudor and Jacobean readers thrilled to stories of pirates, apostates, and soldiers of fortune, so did post-Interregnum readers raptly consume tales detailing the exploits of pirates, highwaymen, housebreakers, murderers, coiners of false money, smugglers, and prostitutes. Although we do not possess reliable sales figures, anecdotal evidence from publishers and printers combines with the sheer number of surviving biographies – between two and three thousand texts, according to Philip Rawlings – to show that crime indeed was "one of the principal subjects for popular literature" in the late seventeenth and early eighteenth centuries (1–2). These biographies include ordinaries' accounts (eyewitness reports from prison chaplains) and "last dying speeches" (written in the voice of the condemned, often printed and sold before the actual execution). Newspaper articles, which too played a major role in arousing public interest in a particular criminal, add to Rawlings' estimate. The genre's most notorious figures include the housebreaker and escape artist John ("Jack") Sheppard, the "thief-organizer" Jonathan Wild, the pickpocket and gang leader Jenny Diver (née Mary Young), and the highwayman James Hind. Audiences could read biographies of more criminals in compendia such as Alexander Smith's *A History of the Lives and Robberies of the Most Noted Highwaymen, Footpads, Shoplifts, and Cheats* (1714) and Charles Johnson's *Lives and Actions of the Most Noted Highwaymen* (1734).

While Tudor and Jacobean renegade tales sometimes ended in ways that departed from the renegade's real fate, the later criminal biographies focused on figures who died at the gallows. Lincoln B. Faller observes that criminals who escaped or were deported to America almost never receive attention in this genre (167). The conventional ending on the Tyburn gallows drives home the putatively inevitable consequences of an individual's fall from lawfulness, godliness, and respectability. Male criminals typically begin their careers by prematurely and even violently deserting their apprenticeships to a respectable trade. Frequently an encounter with a sinful woman hastens their fall. Although women typically figure one-dimensionally as temptations in biographies of male criminals, the ordinary's account of Jenny Diver begins in a fashion similar to those of the men – Diver, working as a seamstress, abandons the supervision of a "nurse" to pursue her own adventures in London. These biographies impart the lesson that breaking away from the stabilizing structures of service and family leads to fatal consequences. Ordinaries' accounts in particular infuse the lesson with religious significance, using the criminal's alleged repentance as an opportunity to sermonize against the violation of godly order.

This typical narrative appears to lend an overall moral purpose to a genre that otherwise merely entertains with the adventures of one charismatic rule-breaker. Noting this moral purpose, John J. Richetti has characterized criminal biographies as "mythic" accounts that portray the consequences of too much individual self-will, strive to contain that disruptive energy, and ultimately support the idea of social hierarchy as a means to ensure stability (35–9). Recently, however, critics have disputed Richetti's argument that criminal biographies ultimately contain the subversions they portray. Erin Skye Mackie, for example, sees in the genre "two major trajectories of energy and intent: one generated from the individual's deeds, and the other from the orderly containment of those deeds within an authoritative narrative." This tension between authority and transgressive self-will, Mackie argues, does not necessarily resolve itself in favour of the former, because "the more fully – and, from a rhetorical perspective, the more successfully – the criminal's circumstances, motivations, and rationales are narrated, the more completely his life seems to authorize itself, independent of and in opposition to the law" (75–6). Hal Gladfelder connects this captivating drama of the transgressive individual to biographies' audiences, whom he sees as more willing to entertain subversion than the "mythic" structure identified by Richetti allows. Citing "the long-running popularity of such morally unpretentious forms as the canting dictionary, picaresque tale, and sessions paper," Gladfelder argues:

> the pleasure of [criminal biographies] does not derive from their endlessly reiterated endorsement of the prevailing social and political orders, for this is an obligatory gesture, but from their smuggling of vividly concrete and sometimes problematic material into the traditional patterns and their consequent stirring up of the very subversive possibilities, the threats of disorder, they (presumably) set out to contain. (77)

The criminal biography, in Gladfelder's view, owes its popularity not to the apparent moral lessons it imparts, but to the opportunity it affords audiences to take vicarious "pleasure" in lawbreaking. This pleasure, Gladfelder implies, holds the potential to inspire resistance to the existing social order by "stirring up" "subversive possibilities" and "threats of disorder" perhaps otherwise not imagined.

As I have shown in the preceding chapters, subversive possibilities lurk as well in Tudor and Jacobean renegade tales, even those that appear to condemn the actions of their subjects. Throughout these tales, mentions of social injustice, suggestions of native propensities towards wandering, invitations to sympathy and empathy, and the very charisma of renegades' personalities problematize attempts to paint these figures as anti-English villains driven by callous self-will. Drawing on later criminal biographies of Jack Sheppard and Jonathan Wild as examples, I propose that the characteristics of the Tudor and Jacobean renegade tales echo in early eighteenth-century criminal narratives. I aim to suggest that these tales deserve consideration alongside other sixteenth- and seventeenth-century forms – such as the aristocratic romance, the picaresque tale, and the spiritual autobiography – currently thought to influence criminal biographies and, eventually, the early English novel.[1] If, as Nicholas Hudson argues, the novel exhibits "tension" (n.p.) between the stabilizing social order and the entrepreneurial energies of that society's non-elite members, the renegade tale portrays that tension as class conflict taking root in the late sixteenth and early seventeenth centuries.

Jack Sheppard (1702–24) was born to a poor family in the crime-ridden London neighbourhood of Spitalfields. Young Jack was apprenticed to a carpenter but left before completing his training; this decision coincided with his meeting the prostitute Elizabeth Lyon, known as "Edgeworth Bess," in one of the Drury Lane taverns he had begun to frequent. Soon he took up a life of stealing, applying his skills in carpentry to burglarizing houses. In 1724 the authorities apprehended and imprisoned him five times; four of those times he broke out of prison. Stories of his ingenious escapes circulated in print and made him famous among Londoners. The fifth imprisonment finally led to his hanging at Tyburn, an event attended by a crowd of ardent supporters who regarded him as a hero. From the first newspaper articles reporting his escape, to several contemporaneous biographies, to nineteenth-century texts such as W.T. Montcrieff's play *Jack Sheppard, the Housebreaker* (1825) and William Harrison Ainsworth's novel *Jack Sheppard* (1839), writers revisited the tale of the wily Sheppard for over a century. Indeed, Peter Linebaugh deems Sheppard "the single most well-known name from eighteenth-century England" (7).

As a thief active in London, Sheppard of course knew the "Thief-Taker General" Jonathan Wild (1682?–1725) – in fact, Wild played a role in Sheppard's final arrest, as he did in many other cases of criminals condemned to hang. Wild too was born to a poor family, in the West Midlands town of Wolverhampton, where he served as a buckle maker's apprentice. Although Wild completed his apprenticeship, soon he abandoned his trade, his wife, and their young son to move to London, where he became a servant. While serving a four-year sentence in debtors' prison, he became acquainted with both sides of London's criminal world – the criminals themselves and the justice system – and he learned to exploit them both. Having acquired familiarity with how both sides operated, upon release he became a criminal organizer who gained riches by selling his minions out to the authorities when they no longer proved useful. Wild aspired to gentlemanly status, as evidenced by his purchase of a country house and a sumptuous wardrobe, and fancied himself a public servant, an image he promoted by calling himself "Thief-Taker General." Yet, as with Sheppard, Wild's luck also eventually ran out – indicted in 1725 for stealing from a lacemaker whom he had promised to help, he was hanged at Tyburn to the jeers of the crowd. He too inspired articles and biographies during his life, and after his death he would live on in literary representations. John Gay, author of the immensely popular play *The Beggar's Opera* (1728), based the character Peachum on Wild; Henry Fielding published the novel *The Life and Death of Jonathan Wild, the Great* in 1743; and nearly two hundred years after Wild's death, Arthur Conan Doyle's Sherlock Holmes would invoke Wild to describe the villain Moriarty.[2]

These two criminals' lowly origins – and more specifically, their respective ways of defying labour hierarchies designed to manage the poor – signal the first link to the Tudor and Jacobean "runagate." According to the *Authentic Memoirs of the Life and Surprising Adventures of John Sheppard* (1724), written by one "G.E., Gentleman in Town," Sheppard abandons his apprenticeship to be more "at liberty," a sentiment he expresses to his employer (5). While Wild does complete his apprenticeship, within two years he abandons the trade for which he trained, a move that the author of *The True and Genuine Account of the Life and Actions of the Late Jonathan Wild* (1725) interprets to mean that Wild's "thoughts" lingered "above his trade" (3).[3] Whether or not these men truly possessed such independence of spirit, the biographies nonetheless assign this trait to them and then criminalize it by drawing on the conventional narrative of the revolted apprentice. William Hogarth's series of twelve engravings, *Industry and Idleness* (1747), visually depicts the dire warnings against the particular kind of revolt found in such texts as the anonymous *The Servants Calling* (1725), Samuel Richardson's *The Apprentice's Vade Mecum* (1734), and in the previous century's much-publicized story of Thomas Savage, a vintner's apprentice – one prone to "extravagancies" and fond of whorehouses – who eventually robs his master, murders a fellow servant, and hangs for his crimes.[4] Hogarth's character Tom Idle meets a similar fate after falling asleep at his loom, breaking the Sabbath to gamble, spending a period at sea after his master orders him away, taking up with a prostitute upon returning to England, and finally committing murder. Hogarth juxtaposes Idle's trajectory with that of a fellow apprentice, the diligent and devout Francis Goodchild, who marries his master's daughter, inherits his master's shop, and eventually rises to become Lord Mayor of London. *Industry and Idleness* as a whole depicts a cultural script of punishment for idleness and reward for hard work within socially approved structures. Significantly, unlike Hogarth's other series that originated as paintings, *Industry and Idleness* originated as engravings that sold for one shilling apiece, thus making them affordable for a relatively wide audience (Paulson, *Hogarth's Graphic Works* 194).

Like Tom Idle, Sheppard and Wild rendered themselves "masterless" through their own self-will. Their respective biographies further signal the men's divergence from socio-economic order in modes that recall Tudor and Jacobean "coney-catching" tales. Just as those tales purported to portray London's criminal underworld, so do the Sheppard and Wild biographies embed their subjects in the urban subculture of thieves, prostitutes, confidence men, and murderers. The anonymous pamphlet *The English Rogue Revived: Or, The Lives and Actions of Jonathan Wild, Thief-taker* (1725) describes Wild and his associates using "Cant," the "Language of the Profession," to communicate among themselves (n.p.).[5] This "language" helps to characterize Wild's world as a parallel society that resembles a legitimate "profession" with its own technical language and yet possesses its own culture of evasion and improvisation. Much of the characterization of Sheppard also derives from the Tudor coney-catching tradition. According to "G.E.," Sheppard speaks with "all Cant and Hypocrisy." He is a "gamester" at cards who revels in his liberty: "He ventures to indulge his wearied Faculties, and take a hearty Nap in a more enlarg'd Habitation; the Earth his Bed, and the Heavens his coverlet" (*Authentic Memoirs* 57, 62–3, 52). Such descriptions tantalize readers with Sheppard's lifestyle as much as they condemn it. The freedom that Jack enjoys, albeit temporarily, recalls the fantasies of liberation that playwright Richard Brome depicts in *The Jovial Crew, or the Merry Beggars* (pub. 1652), where two young couples from the rural gentry play at the beggar's life in defiance of their families' respectable and unadventurous values. Similarly, tales of Wild and Sheppard afford their audiences a vicarious thrill by giving them a glimpse into the "unsettled" life.

The "coney-catching" elements of these pamphlets thus allow audiences to experience subversive pleasures. Yet, while the vicarious enjoyment of such pleasures may seem innocuous, the biographies also offer pointed political critique that speaks directly to the arbitrary nature of class privilege. The preface to *The English Rogue* announces this intent by promising to portray "greater Stratagems and Plots form'd by Fellows without Learning or Education, than are to be met with in the greatest Statesman, who have been at the Heads of Government" (A4). While the author wastes no ink detailing Wild's despicable double-crossing, the writer invites admiration for Wild's cleverness and "skill" – skill that, the pamphlet suggests, exceeds that of men in formal positions of power. The pamphlet reinforces this comparison between Wild and the heads of government by describing the former's elaborate criminal network as a "Common-wealth" in its own right:

> To govern a Common-wealth already fix'd and establish'd, is no more than what may be done by any common Capacity; but to form and establish a Body of such lawless people into what we may call a Form of Government; to erect a Commonwealth like that of the Bees, in which there should be no Drone; and every Member was obliged to bring an Offering to him their King. (n.p.)

On the one hand, the image of Wild as "King" illustrates his foolish aspiration towards higher status. Yet at the same time, the passage highlights the impressive managerial skills necessary to rally "such lawless people" into "a Body," "a Form of Government," and "a Commonwealth like that of the Bees." The reference to bees recalls Canterbury's speech before the court in Shakespeare's *Henry V*, where he appropriates Aristotelean natural history to describe "the act of order to a peopled kingdom." "Honeybees," he states,

> [...] have a king, and officers of sorts
> Where some, like magistrates, correct at home;
> Others, like merchants, venture trade abroad;
> Others, like soldiers, armed in their stings,
> Make boot upon the summer's velvet buds,
> Which pillage they with merry march bring home
> To the tent royal of their emperor,
> Who, busied in his majesty, surveys
> The singing masons building roofs of gold . . . (1.1.187–98)

Of course, this socially conservative vision of orderly, divinely ordained "places" for all represents a political ideal, one that eluded every English monarch at least since Elizabeth, if the proliferation of rogues, vagabonds, and other English criminals at home and abroad is any testament. Yet the low-born Wild, the pamphlet suggests, has accomplished just such an organizational feat – he has assembled London's "lawless people" into order, made them serve him, and, as thief-taker, brought otherwise elusive criminals to justice. Moreover, he has achieved this feat by breaking away from his trade and his family, acquiring knowledge in debtors' prison, and applying that knowledge with success.

What Wild lacks in birth, he makes up for in skill and cunning. The same qualities help Jack Sheppard repeatedly escape confinement. As the author of *A Narrative of All the Robberies, Escapes, &c. of John Sheppard* (1724) puts it, Sheppard "makes a mere jest of the Locks and Bolts, and enter'd in, and out at Pleasure" (B2), thus mocking authority every time. Yet, although this pamphlet presents his escapades as "jests," elsewhere Sheppard adopts a serious tone when speaking about his own abilities. *The History of the Remarkable Life of Jack Sheppard* reports that, before leaving his apprenticeship, Sheppard "began to dispute with his Master, telling him that his way of Jobbing from House to House, was not sufficient to furnish him with a due Experience in his Trade; and that if he would not set out to undertake some Buildings, he would step into the World for better Information" (2–3). In this passage, which G.E. echoes in *Authentic Memoirs*, Sheppard complains that his master does not give him sufficient work experience and threatens to strike out on his own for "better Information." While it is not clear what Sheppard means by "better Information," it does become clear that he does not mean another apprenticeship – rather, he will take his existing talents as an engineer and apply them to housebreaking, a pursuit more directly beneficial to him. Sheppard's transgression thus begins not when he physically abandons his apprenticeship, but when he makes an independent assessment of his own value. The fact that he knows his worth – and is unafraid to state it – emerges in *The History of the Remarkable Life of John Sheppard* when he speculates that "had he been Master at that time of five Pounds, England should not have been the Place of his Residence, having a good Trade in his Hands to live in any populated Part of the World" (56). While prosperity abroad was in no way a guarantee – indeed, deported commoners frequently languished in indentured servitude, captivity, or even slavery – it also is true that criminals with valuable skills such as carpentry stood a good chance of receiving deportation in lieu of capital punishment.[6] In America, such skill could become the basis for a new and more empowered economic status, as was the case for the transported burglar Anthony Lamb, who applied his trade of instrument making to improve his fortunes once outside England (Moore 106). In a suggestion that echoes the renegades of the pre-Interregnum period who abandoned the state to achieve economic mobility, Jack hints at the possibility of greater prosperity for men of his class *outside* England – prosperity, that is, for men more in possession of skill than the advantages of birth. Thus, Sheppard's low status in England becomes relative and ultimately malleable.

From the various portraits of these two men, we see a cultural narrative familiar from the renegade tales of the previous two centuries: rampant individualism, accompanied by illicit aspiration and self-regard, taking the form of rogue economic agency. That agency, the narratives further suggest, takes shape as criminal activity that exhibits the "extravagant" nature of the lowly servant not content to abide in his station. But the preface to *The English Rogue* suggests another way to view the renegade's story. The author declares, "it is not a Man's Grandieur, or High Station in the World, but the strange Adventures of his Life, and his Art and Conduct in the Management of Things, which give us a curiosity of looking into this History" (A3). This passage – which, occurring in the preface, advertises the interest of a subject such as Wild – suggests that it is not the "virtue" inherent in a subject, but how that subject handles life, that makes a captivating story. Subjects such as Wild are "skillful in their art" (A4) and thus interesting to audiences; as such, "skill" becomes a new way to value a subject and the story of his life. If criminal biographies are indeed reflected in the early English novel, one way in which they do so is in their portrayal of the "skilled" person navigating unpromising beginnings and the "strange Adventures" that follow. The novels of Defoe, who possessed a lively interest in criminality, manifest this counternarrative in such protagonists as a pirate (*Colonel Jack*), a prostitute transported to Virginia (*Moll Flanders*), and an Englishman of modest origin who, like Thomas Stukeley, abandons the study of law to take up a life of adventure abroad (*Robinson Crusoe*). In each instance, "Art and Conduct in the Management of Things" becomes the meat of the story, a tale whose interest resides largely in its uncertain relationship to the moral orthodoxies of the time.

This focus on "skill" may at first seem to affirm non-elite individualism. As noted above, Watt advances a similar argument about the criminal biography and, by extension, the novel. The Tudor and Jacobean renegade tales, however, caution against such a conclusion, at least as it relates to economic agency. As chapter 3 in particular shows, the renegade's relationship to community comprises a crucial part of his textual legacy. Although Wild and Sheppard shared lowly origins, transgressive mindsets, and extraordinary "skills," the public regarded them in distinct ways. London's denizens avidly sought news of Sheppard's latest exploits; *A Narrative* reports that the labouring poor neglected their work, "all engag'd in Controversies and Wagers, about *Sheppard*" (27). Sheppard himself learns of his influence when trolling the streets in disguise. On one particular jaunt, he encounters ballad-singers entertaining crowds with tales of his escapes; later he converses with a woman in an alehouse who wishes a curse to fall on anyone who betrays him (27). A blacksmith and a joiner once help him escape, applying the tools of their trades to assist him (25–6). Working-class boys mimicked his crimes.[7] Clearly, Jack Sheppard was a popular hero, one embraced by and even subversively inspirational for his fellow working-class Londoners.

In contrast, commoners cheered the destruction of the treacherous Wild. Sheppard stole from his social betters but does not appear to have craved their esteem or done anyone serious bodily harm. Wild, on the other hand, became wealthy by exploiting the authorities *and* the criminals who worked for him. If any figure in this book truly behaved like an amoral, calculating, self-serving agent, it was Wild – and the jeers he met at the scaffold suggest the low opinion the public held of such behaviour. Most reprehensibly of all, the thieves of Wild's underground network included children whom he transformed into rogues and then condemned to hang. Reflecting on this practice, *The True and Genuine Account* assesses Wild's life as in many ways "a kind of Comedy, or a Farce" but concludes that, due to the victimization of young innocents, Wild's life became "a Tragedy at last" (33). Such a story, the pamphlet's author concludes, "is not [to be] related with an air of Banter and Ridicule" (33) – in other words, the tale should not be treated as a merry jest, but as a tale inspiring the "kind of universal rage" (39), full of execration and curses, that greeted Wild as he approached Tyburn. His reception at the scaffold suggests that Wild's career in the end did not signify a lofty notion of liberty, as did Jack Sheppard's, but rather a violation of human decency as the crowd understood it. Charles Dickens, writing *Oliver Twist* over one hundred years later, may well have shared this understanding – Fagin, Dickens's own abuser of children, closely resembles Wild.[8]

The comparison between Wild and Sheppard, therefore, indicates that audiences responded positively to forms of subversion that proposed an alternative moral code, not the *absence* of human connection, sympathy, or empathy for others. Wild, as a truly individualistic economic agent, clearly falls in line with the later. Wild's difference from criminals who achieved the status of popular heroes registers in the pamphlet *Sheppard in Egypt, or News from the Dead* (1725). Published shortly after Sheppard's execution, *Sheppard in Egypt* imagines the late burglar in the underworld, where he joins Rob Roy, the French highwayman Cartouche, the pirates Captain Kidd and Blackbeard, and other famous thieves, highwaymen, pirates, murderers, and counterfeiters. Lucifer presides over them all. The pamphlet satirizes Grub Street's posthumous exploitation of executed criminals. For example, some "Female Hawkers or News-Cryers" descend upon the underworld; they appear to be pregnant, but are in fact carrying news sheets – and several of Sheppard's own dying speeches – underneath their aprons (15). Lucifer himself demands a "journal" of Sheppard's last days, which Sheppard does not possess, but as a consolation he offers Lucifer a "narrative" left with his executor (18). Yet, although Wild kept the press just as busy as Sheppard, and Lucifer inquires after Wild "in the most tender and affectionate Manner," Wild does not yet inhabit the underworld. Instead, a "poetic epistle from Charon," published in the same volume, laments a "late Misfortune" that unexpectedly left Wild alive, disappointing the denizens of hell who prepared to welcome him "with suitable Honours" (23). The epistle states that Wild "shou'd have dy'd, / As best behov'd his Crimes, but sluggish Fate / Jogs on to [*sic*] slow, and Justice craves too late" (21). While Sheppard and other beloved figures languish in the underworld, Wild – who put many of these figures away – ironically remains at large, a fact that stokes hell's disappointment at the "lateness" of "Justice." At the same time, the pamphlet strives to reassure its audience that a special reception in hell, one fitting the special nature of his crimes, awaits Wild. Thus, even a pamphlet as merry and diverting as *Sheppard in Egypt* darkly hints at a particularly harsh comeuppance for the wily thief-taker whom fate will "take" in the end.

Within this history of renegade identities in early modern England, Wild presents a complex case with which to conclude. On the one hand, his particular brand of calculation led him to deceive and exploit everyone around him. Unlike Purser and Clinton, he seems to have looked after no one; nor did he inspire heroic epitaphs, like Stukeley; nor did he bring questions of socio-economic justice to the forefront, like Ward; nor did he, like the Sherleys, conjure his contemporaries to pursue adventures of their own. Wild was unambiguously perceived as a villain, cut off from humanity, with no romantic legacy of principled rebellion or uncompromised liberty. Yet, at the same time, as a character for the print market, he retained just as much popular appeal as the Tudor and Jacobean figures and his more beloved contemporaries such as Sheppard. This fact suggests that the fascination for socially unorthodox figures ultimately does not follow a single moral code or tight set of generic expectations. There is, in other words, no stable model of "renegade identity" unto which we can seamlessly map the popular transgressors of early modern literature. Just as class is constructed in discourse, so is renegade identity. What is clear, however, is that renegades colourfully, dramatically, and unforgettably expose the contradictions belying the norms of early modern English society – obedient service versus entrepreneurial initiative, dependence versus responsibility, heroism versus transgression – and provocatively invite audiences to consider those norms in new ways.

This is not, however, to romanticize those perspectives. While the scandalous yet tantalizing subversions of the renegade tale posed a variety of challenges to socio-economic orthodoxy, renegade activity could and often did contribute to the foundations of empire, maritime and military aggression, and types of economic development that led to new forms of poverty, oppression, and victimhood. Although Jack Sheppard did not receive transportation to America in lieu of execution, his brother and sometime accomplice Thomas, "a Sea-faring Person," did receive this supposedly more merciful sentence, as did Elizabeth Lyon shortly after Sheppard's death (*Narrative* 12, 30).[9] Neither accomplice received biographical treatment in his or her own right, so we can only wonder: did they perish in slave-like conditions in Virginia? Did they serve out a sentence and then return to England? Or did they, like the fictional Moll Flanders or the real life Anthony Lamb, find opportunities for personal reinvention and economic prosperity unavailable to them in England? Plate 1 of Hogarth's *Industry and Idleness* hints at alluring possibilities for the transported criminal: as Tom Idle snoozes away at his loom, a copy of *Moll Flanders* sits at his feet. The book's presence indicates not only that Tom prefers to spend his time absorbed in fiction rather than working, but that Moll's story of upward mobility holds special attraction for him. Moll's particular happy ending, however, sees her becoming a plantation owner who profits from the labour of others. It is only this development that allows her to eventually retire in England, repenting her criminal past. She begins as a picaresque rule-breaker, but she ends as the beneficiary of an unjust institution. If

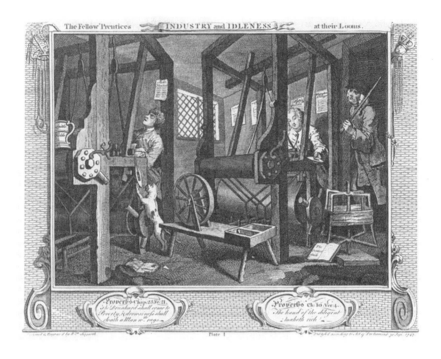

Figure 5.1. William Hogarth – *Industry and Idleness*, Plate 1; "The Fellow 'Prentices at their Looms," distributed by a Creative Commons license.

Tom Idle were to follow her script, even in a spirit of anti-establishment rebellion, he too might become a member of an oppressive establishment after all.[10]

The irony of Moll's fate mirrors the ironies of pirates who laid the foundations for empire even as they bedevilled their country's admiralty, of rogue diplomats who urged settled men and women to become imperialists, and of a treasonous mercenary who turned out to be more essentially "English" that the authorities cared to admit. Their tales prove to be subject to historical change and thus malleable in their meaning over time. But this same vulnerability to historical change also argues that the renegades of early modern England were not outliers in their world after all. Rather, they were *part* of that world, interacting with audiences as co-creators of their national story.

Notes

Introduction

1 On the masterless phenomenon see, for example, Andrew Appleby; Beier, *Masterless* and *Problem*; Hindle; and Schofield.
2 On this demographic change see Porter 28, 32, 131.
3 For reprints of such tracts, see Kinney and Judges.
4 For more detail on these attitudes see Carey, Hadfield, and Clare Howard.
5 For more on this pressure see Carey 37.
6 Hadfield cites the scriptural example of Cain as a traveller who exhibited criminality and suspect character. Notably, the civic pageants of the late Middle Ages associated Cain also with servant identity, "unfree" labour, and vagabondage; on this history see Rice and Pappano 146–59, 170–1.
7 For a fuller discussion of factors, see Sebek.
8 For more on cultural attitudes toward international merchants, see Aune.
9 On the paradox of travel as both education and moral peril, see Aune 130–3, Carey 34–7, and Haynes 32–4.
10 For a reading of the scriptures that highlights these traits, see Graeber 80–7.
11 In a recent article, Claire Norton questions the truth of alleged torture in Muslim captivity, suggesting that such motifs did not so much reflect reality as represent "a response to the wealth, power, and economic opportunities available in North Africa and the subsequent phenomena of 'mass' economic migration and conversion such opportunities engendered" (264) – in other words, descriptions of forced conversions represent a cultural attempt to deny the desirability of adopting another culture for the sake of increased social and economic opportunity. Norton is correct that North Africa afforded opportunities unavailable

to commoners in England and that captivity narratives reflected much strategic exaggeration. However, I am not prepared to dismiss entirely the reality of torture in captivity, given the flourishing of the slave and ransom markets. For an overview of "white slavery" in the Mediterranean, see Davis.

12 According to some scholars, these vulnerabilities have a uniquely English dimension. Jane Hwang Degenhardt describes England "a tiny player in an international arena of commerce and power," and self-consciously so (84). Jeffrey Knapp suggests that English literature, with its pervasive sense of national exceptionalism, was formed largely in response to "dispiriting tokens of England's weakness – its littleness, its circumscription by enemies, its female monarch" (4). See also Vitkus, *Turning*. It is beyond the scope of this book to test these arguments against other national literatures. However, I believe that English renegade tales dramatize a particularly mortifying aspect of this vulnerability insofar as renegades' very activities testify to the state's tenuous hold over its own subjects and thus reveal the limits of its sovereignty. The renegade, himself a "masterless" figure, connects England's domestic liabilities to the world outside its borders, thus exposing those liabilities to the world.

13 Parker 14.

14 Some early modernists remain wary of the term "class," preferring terms such as "degrees," "orders," "sorts," and "estates" to describe socio-economic distinctions among early modern subjects (see, e.g., Wrightson, "Estates"). I acknowledge that these terms, not "class," appear in the period's texts. However, the problem with excluding "class" from our scholarly parlance is that doing so creates an illusion of discontinuity between past and present, as if the Industrial Revolution marked an absolute break between earlier and later experience. When I use the term "class," I do so not to erase historical differences, but to gesture towards the social divides that, now as before the Industrial Revolution, led to the enduring appeal of the renegade as an expression of resistance. In this I follow the work of early modern historians and literary scholars who have argued for class as an appropriate, and indeed revelatory, category for analysis. Keith Wrightson proposes that class resides in "similarities of status, power, lifestyle and opportunities" as well as in "shared cultural characteristics and bonds of interaction" ("Social" 196); Michael J. Braddick adopts this flexible and eclectic definition to describe class not as an "exclusive consciousness," but rather as one "language of differentiation" among other languages constituting early modern society (1n.1). Within literary studies, scholars such as James Holstun (96–106)

and Mark Netzloff (*England's Internal Colonies* 14) embrace the term as a means by which to account for the various ways in which texts portray socio-economic relations of power and subjection. The nature of these relations, often suffused with racial, religious, and gendered terminology, shows class to be an intersectional term that, when explored, helps define the nature of other, less obviously economic, forms of power. For a classic example of such intersectional scholarship, see Amussen.

15 Armitage writes: "The necessity of colonisation arose from simultaneous overpopulation at home, and the contraction of English markets abroad. The manifold commodities would therefore be general and particular: general, in providing an outlet for surplus population and production, and relief from those 'very burdensome to the common wealthe'; and particular, in the provision of new materials and products for the English economy, 'the vent of the masse of our clothes and other commodities of England, and … receavinge backe of the nedefull commodities that wee nowe receave from all other places in the worlde.' The overall aim of the new colonies would be to return the economy of England itself to self-sufficiency by balancing its production, consumption and population. This could only be achieved by the export of people, and the institution of new markets, all of which would be conceived as parts of the commonwealth, albeit across an ocean, rather than new commonwealths in themselves" (*Ideological Origins* 74–5).

16 Fumerton, *Unsettled*; Bailey, chap. 4; Bartolovich.

17 See "Faithless" and chapter 5 of *Mimesis*.

18 Cited in Garcia-Arenal and Wiegers 132.

19 This view is applied to converts with particular frequency; for a critique of such views, see Rothman 18.

20 For a description of Lithgow's encounter, see Tinniswood 49–50.

21 On the ballad history of Ward as "entrepreneurial hero of old England," see MacLean 231–2.

22 For these approaches, see Lockey; Fuchs, "Faithless" and *Mimesis*; and Jowitt, *Voyage Drama* and *Culture of Piracy*.

23 For more on social diversity among early modern English audiences, see Jean Howard, *Stage*. On class diversity in particular, see Burnett.

24 The complete essay is reprinted in Hall et al., 128–38.

25 The legal category of "petty treason," which included killing a husband or master, derived from the medieval concept of betraying one's feudal lord. This idea of treason, which addresses the defiance of subordinates, relates more closely to the kinds of experiences I discuss here than does the latter category of "grand treason," which specifically concerned disloyalty to the monarch. On kinds of treason, see Dolan, "Subordinate('s) Plot" 317–18.

26 Simmel's complete essay is reprinted in Levine 143–50.
27 For a discussion of Cade in these terms see Arab's chapter 2.
28 Quoted in Ewen 8.
29 I will elaborate on the idea of early modern "publics" in chapter 4.

1. "Unquiet Hotspurs": Stukeley, Vernon, and the Renegade Humour

1 Vitkus also addresses the theme of illicit ambition, observing that "the venturing heroes and antiheroes of the London playhouses cross over into an imaginary territory that always holds the potential for contamination" ("Adventuring Heroes" 79). While Vitkus's comment poses "contamination" as a rhetorical point-of-no-return, I suggest that the renegade contains such potential for contamination within him all along.
2 See, for example, Paster 12 and Siraisi 102 for discussions of the heart as the centre of "heat" in the humoral body.
3 See Siraisi 101–2 for an elaboration of this idea.
4 Stukeley's disregard for learning – which, in the case of the Inns, includes training in the art of rhetoric and argument – connects him to another English rebel from the dramatic canon: Shakespeare's Hotspur, on whom I will elaborate in the following sections. In *Henry IV, Part 1*, Hotspur disdains the Welsh Glendower's being "trained up in the English court," where Glendower boasts of having learned the art of poetry and rhetorical persuasion. Hotspur replies: "I had rather hear a brazen canstick turned, / Or a dry wheel grate on the axle-tree, / And that would set my teeth nothing on edge, / Nothing so much as mincing poetry. / 'Tis like the forced gait of a shuffling nag" (3.1.127–31). For more on theatrical interpretations of Hotspur as a "provincial boor," especially in contrast to the "internationally educated" Hal, see Roberta Barker 294.
5 On this point, see Park and Kessler 455.
6 In addition, Wear notes that many of the same medical remedies prescribed for humans were also used on animals, a fact that "must have helped to produce a sense of interrelatedness" between humans and their environment (144).
7 On this point, see Siraisi 102.
8 For more on self-containment as the cultural standard for masculine gentility, and on "temperance" as a quality invoked to justify colonial endeavours, see Hutson, "Civility."
9 See also Craik for the idea of masculine self-mastery in travel contexts.
10 For examples, see Finch 70; Floyd-Wilson, *English Ethnicity*, passim; Paster 19; Poole 211; Schoenfeldt 9.

11 Jowitt, *Voyage* 84, 86, 90, 97; Lockey 208.
12 See Gowland on these conventional descriptions.
13 For further elaboration on Hamlet and Jaques as melancholic types, see Frye 217–18.
14 Qtd in Floyd-Wilson, *English Ethnicity*, 132.
15 On the alleged "coldness" of England, see Paster 14; Floyd-Wilson, *English Ethnicity* 28–30.
16 Simpson writes: "at the time when the controversy between the partisans of the soldier under the banner of Essex and the partisans of the civilian under that of the Cecils divided men's minds, and when at the same time the question of peace with Spain and that of the proper treatment for Ireland were occupying attention, Stucley was a useful and popular figure to be used by the political dramatist" (143).

2. "We Are of the Sea!": Masterless Identity and Transnational Context in *A Christian Turned Turk*

1 See Questier 3 for a fuller discussion of this pattern.
2 For an example, see the "Laudian Rite for Returned Renegades," reprinted in Vitkus, *Piracy, Slavery*, 361–6.
3 Examples include Bruster, Ingram, Leinwand, and Pye.
4 For an extended critique of Agnew, see Shershow; for remarks on economic criticism's specific neglect of labour, see Kendrick xi, 17.
5 Collections exploring early modern globalism include Sebek and Deng, and Singh. Studies that explore the relationship between romance and the global include Forman, "Comic-Tragedy" and *Tragicomic Redemptions*; Fuchs, "Faithless Empires" and *Mimesis*, chap. 5; Jowitt, *Culture of Piracy* and *Voyage Drama*; Lesser; Linton; Matar; Potter; and Robinson. Loomba uses the term "mercantile-colonial romance" to describe this particular development in the English theatre ("Break Her Will" 68). Of these sources, Fuchs, Jowitt, Matar, Potter, and Robinson address Daborne's play specifically.
6 This is not to dismiss the interventions of the cultural materialists who took on the character-centred work of A.C. Bradley to deconstruct and historicize the tragic subject; indeed, the work of such theorists as Francis Barker, Catherine Belsey, and Jonathan Dollimore did much to advance the scholarly conversation towards a consideration of social forces. Yet even studies that reflect this influence (see, for example, Sullivan and even Holbrook, who argues for tragedy as a meditation on "human freedom," including "social and economic freedom" [3]) alight mainly on the struggles of bourgeois and courtly figures.

7 For two discussions of genre and class conflict that inform this chapter, see Jean Howard, "Shakespeare"; Greenblatt.

8 During the reign of Elizabeth I, the Crown viewed pirates and privateers as a weapon against Spanish ships; a semantic slippage between "privateering" and "piracy" reflects this blurring of lines between legitimate and illegitimate activity, as other scholars have noted. The end of the Anglo-Spanish conflict under James I prompted a "war against the pirates," however, with the king taking an active interest in apprehending English subjects engaging in maritime plunder. For an account of how this political shift affected Ward and other English pirates, see Bak's chapter 10.

9 MacLean surveys these texts, including later ones that hailed Ward as a champion of free trade. See also Bak's chapter 11 and "AfterWard." Jowitt also reads the Jacobean pirate in an economic vein, as "a conflation of aspects of the 'heroic' gentleman adventurer and the 'shrewd' mercantile venturer" (*Culture of Piracy* 137).

10 Late Tudor fishermen did benefit from William Cecil's attempt to boost English ports, shipbuilding, and mariners by encouraging English Protestants to eat more fish. However, fishermen lived outside the protection of trade guilds, making fishing a relatively "masterless" occupation of men practising a "patchwork economy" (Bak 7–8). This status made them vulnerable to naval impressment. For more on the politics of impressment with respect to class and occupation, see Fury 27–32. For more on "masterlessness" as a Tudor and Jacobean phenomenon, see Beier, *Masterless*; Archer, *Pursuit of Stability*; Woodbridge; Carroll; and Fumerton, "Not Home" and *Unsettled*.

11 For the purposes of this chapter, I define "piracy" as attacking without legal authority, drawing on Haywood and Spivak's definition (7). Thomson, who also defines the difference between privateering and piracy as a matter of state authorization, supplies my working definition of "corsair" as a pirate who fought under the banners of Malta and along the Barbary coast instead of under the "Jolly Roger" (44–5).

12 All citations from the play come from Vitkus's edition.

13 See also "Comic-Tragedy."

14 For more on the politics of class subordination in tragicomedy and colonial romance, see Mason, Orkin, Kim Hall, and Kimbrell.

15 On seafaring and piracy in the classical Mediterranean world and medieval Europe, see Heller-Roazen's chapter 3. On the Tudor state's incursion into the traditional rights of seamen over their own labour, see Fury's chapter 1.

16 For expanded accounts of seamen's resistance to oppressive institutions, see Rediker; Linebaugh and Rediker; Hill, *Liberty* and "Radical Pirates."

17 See Scammell's discussion on 659.

18 For a detailed description of the seaman's labour inside and outside state service, see Fury's chapter 1.

19 For a theoretical articulation of the notion's alterity as a feature of the emerging "blue cultural studies," see Mentz, "Toward a Blue Cultural Studies." For readings of Shakespearean plays that treat the ocean as both menace and redemption, see Mentz's *At the Bottom*.

20 See Balasopoulos for the utopian implications of this oceanic "blank space" and its relationship to tragicomedy.

21 For captivity narratives of contemporaneous Englishmen faced with the temptations of conversion, see Vitkus's *Piracy*. For descriptions of pirate utopias, see Peter Lamborn Wilson and Scammell.

22 Netzloff elaborates on this history in *England's Internal Colonies*, chapters 1 and 2.

23 The phenomenon of "masterlessness," prevalent in the Tudor era's legal and literary texts, seems to represent the culmination of increasing associations of the poor – including the working poor – with vagrancy and restiveness throughout the Middle Ages; see Mollat on this history.

24 On the "low" perspectives embedded in ballad literature, see Fumerton, *Unsettled* 135–52. For a book-length treatment of cheap print and the "peasant reader," see Spufford.

25 On the cultural materialists, see note 6 above.

26 See Clark 70–1, 129–30, 136–7; Fumerton, "Not Home"; Fumerton, *Unsettled* 7.

27 On the authorship of *A General History*, see Jowitt, *Culture of Piracy* 6–7.

28 In addition to Woodbridge's examples, see also Thomas Dekker's *Lantern and Candle-light* (1608), which provides a clear example of such commentary: "Look what difference there is between a civil citizen of Dublin and a wild Irish Kern, so much difference there is between one of these counterfeit Egyptians and a true English beggar. An English rogue is just of the same livery" (qtd in Kinney 243).

29 According to the British Library catalog, versions of the ballad were printed in London around 1700 and 1820. Dates are not listed for other existing versions.

30 For more on Essex as representing a clash of values with the Elizabethan regime, see my discussion in chapter 1.

31 For more on the legal and geopolitical implications of the *Mare liberum* debates for the ocean as governable space, see Warren; Balasopoulos; Connery, "Ideologies" and "Oceanic Feeling"; and Schmitt 175–80.

32 For one outstanding example, see again *Lantern and Candle-light*, where Dekker applies his interest in pestilential disease to social diagnosis (Kinney 245 and passim).

33 A Venetian ambassador reported James's very public pronouncement at a dinner party at the end of 1609: "Throughout the dinner his Majesty indulged in pleasant talk. He told us how his ships had captured some pirates, and how he hoped to extirpate them. He dwelt at length on his hatred of such folk, many of whom he had put to death. He said he would never pardon them, and declared that one pirate had offered him 40,000 pounds sterling, equal to 160,000 crowns, to recover his favour, but he would not even consider the proposal" (Brown 430).

34 See Thomson's definition cited in note 11 above.

35 On this confusion, see Heller-Roazen 88; Thomson; Fuchs, "Faithless" 45–51. Fury notes that men often moved back and forth between both identities: "From the 1580s onward, it was not unusual to find former 'pirates' serving in the Queen's fleet; often these same men worked aboard merchant and privateering vessels as well" (250).

36 In a similar vein, Tarak Barkawi cautions against distinctions that privilege the juridical at the expense of the de facto and assuming too much about private/public distinctions and state/foreign boundaries.

37 See Scammell on this development.

38 See note 4 above.

3. "Lend Us Your Lament": Purser and Clinton on the Scaffold

1 See Forman, *Tragicomic Redemptions*; Lesser.

2 Ania Loomba uses the term "mercantile-colonial romance" to describe this type of early seventeenth-century English play ("Break Her Will" 68). Frequently discussed examples include Fletcher's *The Island Princess* (c. 1620), Massinger's *The Renegado* (pub. 1630), and Heywood's *The Fair Maid of the West, Parts I and II* (pub. 1631).

3 See also Forman's "Comic-Tragedy."

4 Here I draw partly on Bridget Escolme's critique of scholarly moves to discover "anxiety" in early modern drama: "There is a disjuncture between the notion of cultural anxiety and how it might somehow be immanent in cultural products and events, and the possible experiences of those who consumed or attended them. [… I]t is easier to uncover cultural anxiety in the discourses of artefacts and events, and either assume this anxiety was felt in their reception, or disregard whether or not it was" (xxvii). Escolme makes these remarks in the context of a book-length study of emotion in the early modern theatre. I apply them here with a broadly similar yet slightly different intent, which is to account for the possibility of audience responses that diverge politically from state policy and its didactic expressions.

5 See Thomson 22–3.

6 On the "Pax Hispanica" and its impact on English piracy, see Bak's chapter 10 and Senior 7–9. Jowitt's readings in *Culture of Piracy* and "Piracy and Politics" demonstrate a keen awareness of how piracy took on different cultural significations according to the politics of each reign.

7 See for example Dolan, "'Gentlemen'"; Lake and Questier; Laqueur; Shapiro.

8 Holinshed's inclusion in this list is not to suggest that Holinshed's *Chronicles* is the discrete, self-contained, creation of a single author; as scholars now acknowledge, the two editions of "Holinshed's" *Chronicles* contain many different hands – including Stow's. The 1587 edition, in fact, utilizes the same language about Clinton and Purser's giving away their clothing as we find in Stow's 1605 *Annales*. While acknowledging the common practice of sharing and repurposing passages between chronicle texts, here I will treat the *Annales* as a work of Stow's, compiled and arranged by him.

9 On this tendency, see Beer 25–9. For an influential account of the gradual bureaucratization of charity throughout the Middle Ages and into the early modern period, see Mollat.

10 See Beer 29–33.

11 Quoted in Netzloff, *England's Internal Colonies* 54. See also Senior 75 on the hardships of the navy and seamen's limited options outside of it.

12 See Lezra 273, which quotes extensively from Senior to support the point that pirates were embedded in their local communities and thus more difficult to distinguish than the authorities might hope. Whereas Lezra cites Senior to serve a reading of pirates as "interrupters" of the figurative boundary between "court and prison" (271), I apply it to Stow's chronicle to question a different figurative boundary, the one between the deviant renegade and the normative English subject.

13 See Netzloff, *England's Internal Colonies* 59–60.

14 See chapter 1 of Fury, where she argues this point despite signs of "otherness" she detects elsewhere in the culture of seamen. Her evidence indicates that even a self-conscious otherness – expressed as camaraderie among seamen – did not necessarily sever landed ties, economic or otherwise. On this point, see also Senior 36. For accounts of later periods, which describe pirates as conscious political actors and even principled rebels, see Linebaugh and Rediker; Rediker; Hill, "Radical Pirates."

15 For an Elizabethan chronicler of his times, Stow notably has little to say about the talented bureaucrats – the Cecils, Francis Walsingham, and Nicholas Bacon – who exerted such influence over state policy. See Beer 117.

16 On Stow's alleged nostalgia in general, see Archer, "Nostalgia" 20 and Manley, "Of Sites and Rites" 52.

17 On this tendency, see Beer 117.

18 All quotes from Holinshed come from the University of Oxford's *Holinshed Project*.

19 For a summary of Nussbaum, Berlant, and other theorists of compassion, see Woodward. The term "ameliorative actor" comes from Berlant, "Introduction," 1. For a summary of scholarship on the early modern passions and their somatic effects, see Craik and Pollard.

20 See Netzloff, *England's Internal Colonies* 59; Jowitt, *Culture of Piracy* 17.

21 For these views, see Jowitt, *Culture of Piracy* 36; Netzloff, *England's Internal Colonies* 66; Lezra 18.

22 Aristotle writes: "Pity is felt towards one whose affliction is undeserved; fear towards one who is like ourselves," a moment of identification apparently not troubled by the hero's social distinction: "He will belong to the class of those who enjoy great esteem and prosperity, such as Oedipus, Thyestes, and outstanding men from such families." See 44, 126.

23 On early modern English uses of Aristotle's theory of tragedy, see Cronk; Reiss 241–7; Orgel 117.

24 All passages from *Fortune* are cited from Doh's edition.

25 Lezra 279–80; Fuchs, "Faithless" 56; Jowitt, "Piracy and Politics" 226.

26 For more on debtors' prison, see Ahnert 36.

4. "Extravagant Thoughts": The Sherley Brothers and the Future of Renegade England

1 For an expanded account of Robert's English embassies, including reactions to his dress, see Arthur.

2 For a more thorough evaluation of scholarship that focuses on the Sherleys' more outrageous acts, see Subrahmanyam 116–17.

3 For more detail on the widespread suspicion aimed at travellers, see Hadfield and also Carey.

4 On the aristocracy, see Subrahmanyam 77–8; on commoners, see Fumerton, *Unsettled*. In discussing the word "sovereignty" and its variations, I take the term to signify not something immutable and essential, as some writers describe it, but something contested; for more sustained reflection on this debate, see Netzloff, "State." I also follow Christopher Warren's call for a more fluid view of the nation-state; Warren asks that we "dispense with the presumption of geographically stable, territorially bound citizens and start instead from the reality that early modern merchants, servants,

lovers, mariners, diplomats, warriors, scholars, students, and sovereigns regularly crossed national borders" (6). Carole Levin and John Watkins also usefully note the limitations of national unity and distinctiveness in their analysis of the "stranger," a term that increasingly applied to "native-born English men and women, such as religious dissidents, who resisted conformity to an increasingly narrow sense of English identity" (8).

5 On the usefulness of the Persian example for English imperialist thinking, see also Sahin and Schleck 88–9.

6 For elaborations of this process, see Fitzmaurice; Stern.

7 Cited from Parr's edition, which also contains the version of *Travels* I will cite here. For a reading of Brome's play within the context of early modern drama's engagement with vicarious travel, see McInnes's chapter 4.

8 Early English Books Online (EEBO) attributes one copy (STC 25022) of *Newes* to Anthony Nixon, the same author commissioned to write the 1607 defence of the Sherleys whom I discuss in the paragraph to follow. I do not know the rationale for this attribution. If it is accurate, however, it suggests that Nixon allotted space to defending the Sherleys even in a pamphlet dedicated to exploring Ward's misdeeds – that is to say, Nixon already had begun to concern himself with distinguishing Anthony from other renegade figures who invited comparison.

9 Although the Sherley family allegedly held Catholic sympathies, some Sherleys were recusants and others were Protestants, even Calvinists. Thus, D.W. Davies concludes that "what one can safely say about the religion of Sir Thomas [Senior] is very little" (6), and the behaviour of his sons suggests the same of them. On the Sherleys' religion, see also Penrose 3 and Subrahmanyam 91.

10 Following Nixon's apology for the resemblance to Stukeley, Parr speculates – not unreasonably – that *Travels of the Three English Brothers* was "probably designed to set them off against the eponymous hero in *Captain Thomas Stukeley*" (5), a play I examine in chapter 1.

11 For a wider exploration of Elizabethan nostalgia in Jacobean England, particularly in its literary culture, see Perry.

12 The scholarly literature on early modern concepts of honour is vast. It begins with the seminal work of Mervyn James, whose description of the transition from late medieval "warrior nobility" to early modern "service nobility" charts a process by which personal and state honour became one. Although later historians have critiqued James's narrative as overly schematic (see Kane 5–7 for a summary of these critiques), I find it valuable nonetheless for its distinction between personal and national honour and its acknowledgment of how early moderns sometimes

conflated the two for strategic ends. Ruff's remarks, and the scholarship on the early modern public sphere I cite here, advance James's narrative to more fully account for honour's indebtedness to rhetorical construction and public perception.

13 See Doty's "*Richard II*" and "*Measure.*"

14 A decade, ago Peter Lake and Steve Pincus initiated a look backwards from Habermas's Enlightenment historical framework into the multiple public spheres of pre-Enlightenment Europe. Since then, early modern literary scholars have found evidence of "publics" emerging across a variety of sixteenth- and seventeenth-century media; for a sampling of such scholarship, see the edited collections *Making Publics* (ed. Wilson and Yachnin) and *Forms of Association* (ed. Yachnin and Eberhart).

15 For some accounts of this development, see Barkawi, Gallant, Perotin-Dumon, and Thomson.

16 For an exploration of the "travail of travel" in other texts, see Vitkus, "Labor and Travel."

17 In this sense, the play exhibits what Yachnin calls the "populuxe," a kind of entertainment that presents the image of an exclusive world to common eyes and thus "reminds the playgoers of their exclusion from public life by inviting them to imagine their inclusion" ("*Hamlet*" 87).

18 For this history see Parr 6.

19 See Grogan 161 on this connection.

20 For more on the persistence of the "raging Turk" stereotype, which frequently existed alongside admiration for Muslim cultures, see Jonathan Burton's *Traffic and Turning* 37–8.

21 I borrow the terms "residual" and "emergent" from Williams' description of cultural process in *Marxism and Literature.*

22 See Parr 59, n. 0.1. Parr cites his description of Fame in a robe "thickly set" from Thomas Dekker's 1604 royal entry.

23 The play's cultivation of immediate approval demonstrates the special nature of the theatre as what Doty calls a "public-making space": "The theater is the ideal space for exploring the problem of popularity, since it was already a literal domain of popularity; the theater thrives on popular favor and applause" ("*Richard II*" 205, 191). As the following analysis will suggest, I believe that this dependence on audience feedback also makes the theatre ideal for considering the related topic of fame.

24 For more on the use of this device in *Travels*, *Henry V*, and *Pericles*, see H. Neville Davies 100.

25 The connection to Tamburlaine gains support from the fact that, as Publicover notes, Marlowe's play had just been revived at the Red Bull when *Travels* was first staged (701–2).

26 See chapter 1 for my earlier discussion of this term.
27 Sahin and Schleck similarly note the fundamental sameness that the play draws between the Persians and the English, although they argue in a somewhat different direction by observing that this sameness bolsters Anthony's claim to diplomatic skill: "Rather than a discoverer, navigator, or conqueror, Anthony is depicted as a consummate courtier and diplomat, skillfully negotiating a foreign court and accomplishing his goals through canny alliances and smooth persuasion. In order for this strategy to work, the court of Shah Abbas could not be cast as radically different from the European courts in which Anthony sought employment" (94).
28 For surveys of the "economy of ransom" in the late medieval and early modern Mediterranean, see Valerian; Backman.
29 See, for example, John Booker's *Uranoscopia* almanacs (1648–50). Notably, in keeping with the ambiguity surrounding the Sherleys' "fame," prospective glasses (and their variant, "perspective glasses") also were thought to held the potential for deceit; see Shickman.
30 For surveys of such humanist critique, see Fitzmaurice as well as Armitage, "Literature and Empire" 109–10.
31 On the interlopers, see Stern 515.
32 See Stern 521–2.
33 For iterations of this historical narrative, see Canny 1 and Armitage, "Literature and Empire" 102–11.

Coda

1 For an influential genealogy of these forms and their influence on the novel, see McKeon.
2 In *The Valley of Fear* (1915), Sherlock muses, "Everything comes in circles – even Professor Moriarty. Jonathan Wild was the hidden force of the London criminals, to whom he sold his brains and his organisation on a fifteen per cent commission. The old wheel turns, and the same spoke comes up. It's all been done before, and will be again" (Doyle 18).
3 Some scholars attribute this biography, as well as two biographies of Sheppard (*A Narrative of All the Robberies, Escapes, &c. of John Sheppard* and *The History of the Remarkable Life of John Sheppard, Containing a Particular Account of His Many Robberies and Escapes*) to Daniel Defoe. However, since no definitive evidence currently exists to support the attribution, I will treat these three texts as anonymous.
4 For a fuller discussion of the revolted apprentice in early modern print culture, see Rawlings 19–22. The story of Thomas Savage is told in the anonymous *Gods Justice against Murther, or The Bloody Apprentice Executed*

(1668 – the term "extravagancies" occurs on A3) and Richard Allaine's *A Murderer Punished and Pardoned, or, A True Relation of the Wicked Life and Shameful-happy Death of Thomas Savage Imprisoned, Justly Condemned, and Twice Executed at Ratliff for His Bloody Act in Killing His Fellow-servant* (1668).

5 The image in the database consulted, *Eighteenth Century Collections Online* (ECCO), is scanned in a way that cuts off the page number.

6 See Maxwell-Stewart 1226, Butler 17.

7 See Mackie 102.

8 The comparison is a common one. See, for example, Hobsbaum 44 and Paulson, *Sin and Evil* 142.

9 See also Moore 263.

10 Cannadine finds a similar trajectory in the later years of the British Empire, when non-aristocratic Britons abroad could attain "a status and a position to which they might never realistically have aspired at home." Cannadine further suggests that, ironically, such individuals may have felt especially invested in maintaining hierarchy within empire: "Small wonder, then, that many people who went out to the empire, as settlers or as administrators, or as proconsuls, sought to replicate Britain's social hierarchy overseas, on account of their *enhanced position within it,* rather than to overturn it" (130, emphasis in original).

Bibliography

Agnew, Jean-Chrisophe. *Worlds Apart: The Market and the Theater in Anglo-American Thought, 1550–1750*. New York: Cambridge UP, 1996.

Ahnert, Ruth. "The Prison in Early Modern Drama." *Literature Compass* 9, no. 1 (2012): 34–47.

Amussen, Susan Dwyer. *An Ordered Society: Class and Gender in Early Modern England*. New York: Columbia UP, 1994.

Andrea, Bernadette. "Lady Sherley: The First Persian in England?" *Muslim World* 95 (April 2005): 279–95.

"Apostasy Punish'd: or, A New Poem on the Deserved Death of Jonas Rowland, the Renegado, Lately Executed at Morocco." London, 1682.

Appleby, Andrew B. *Famine in Tudor and Stuart England*. Stanford, CA: Stanford UP, 1978.

Appleby, John C. "War, Politics and Colonization, 1558–1625." In Canny, pp. 56–78.

Arab, Ronda. *Manly Mechanicals on the Early Modern English Stage*. Selinsgrove, PA: Susquehanna UP, 2011.

Archer, Ian. "The Nostalgia of John Stow." In Smith et al., pp. 17–34.

– *The Pursuit of Stability: Social Relations in Elizabethan London*. Cambridge: Cambridge UP, 1991.

Aristotle. *The Poetics of Aristotle: Translation and Commentary*. Translated by Stephen Halliwell. Chapel Hill: U of North Carolina P, 1987.

Armitage, David. *The Ideological Origins of the British Empire*. Cambridge: Cambridge UP, 2000.

– "Literature and Empire." In Canny, pp. 99–123.

Arthur, Kate. "'You Will Say They Are Persian but Let Them Be Changed': Robert and Teresa Sherley's Embassy to the Court of James." *Britain and the*

Muslim World: Historical Perspectives, edited by Gerald MacLean. Newcastle, UK: Cambridge Scholars Press, 2011, pp. 37–51.

Aune, M.G. "Passengers, Spies, Emissaries, and Merchants: Travel and Early Modern English Identity." *Emissaries in Early Modern Literature and Culture: Mediation, Transmission, Traffic, 1550–1700*, edited by Brinda Charry and Gitanjali Shahani. New York: Routledge, 2016, pp. 129–44.

Authentic Memoirs of the Life and Surprising Adventures of John Sheppard. By G.E., Gentleman in Town. London, 1724.

Backman, Clifford R. "Piracy." In Horden and Kinoshita, pp. 170–83.

Bailey, Amanda. *Of Bondage: Debt, Property, and Personhood in Early Modern England.* Philadelphia: U of Pennsylvania P, 2013.

Bak, Greg. *Barbary Pirate: The Life and Crimes of John Ward, The Most Infamous Privateer of His Time.* Gloucestershire, UK: History Press, 2010.

Balasopoulos, Antonis. "'Suffer a Sea Change': Spatial Crisis, Maritime Modernity, and the Politics of Utopia." *Cultural Critique* 63 (Spring 2006): 122–56.

Barkawi, Tarak. "State and Armed Force in International Conflict." *Mercenaries, Pirates, Bandits and Empires: Private Violence in Historical Context*, edited by Alejandro Colas and Bryan Mabee. New York: Columbia UP, 2010, pp. 33–54.

Barker, Andrew. *True and Certain Report of the Beginning, Proceedings, Overthrows, and Now Present Estate of Captaine Ward and Danseker.* London, 1609.

Barker, Francis. *The Tremulous Private Body: Essays on Subjection.* 2nd ed. Ann Arbor: U of Michigan P, 1995.

Barker, Roberta. "Tragical-Comical-Historical Hotspur." *Shakespeare Quarterly* 54, no 3 (Fall 2003): 288–307.

Barret, J.K. *Untold Futures: Time and Literary Culture in Renaissance England.* Ithaca, NY: Cornell UP, 2016.

Bartolovich, Crystal. "'Travailing' Theory: Global Flows of Labor and the Enclosure of the Subject." In Singh, pp. 50–66.

Beer, Barrett L. *Tudor England Observed: The World of John Stow.* Gloucestershire, UK: Sutton Publishing, 1998.

Beier, A.L. *Masterless Men: The Vagrancy Problem in England.* London: Methuen, 1985.

– *The Problem of the Poor in Tudor and Early Stuart England.* London: Methuen, 1983.

Belsey, Catherine. *The Subject of Tragedy: Identity and Difference in Renaissance Drama.* London: Methuen, 1985.

Berckman, Evelyn. *Victims of Piracy: The Admiralty Court, 1575–1678*. London: Hamish Hamilton, 1979.

Berlant, Lauren. "The Epistemology of State Emotion." *Dissent in Dangerous Times*, edited by Austin Serat. Ann Arbor: U of Michigan P, 2010, pp. 46–78.

– "Introduction: Compassion (and Withholding)." In Berlant, pp. 1–13.

– ed. *Compassion: The Culture and Politics of an Emotion*. New York: Routledge, 2004.

Braddick, Michael J. *State Formation in Early Modern England, c. 1550–1700*. Cambridge: Cambridge UP, 2000.

Braddick, Michael J., and John Walter, eds. *Negotiating Power in Early Modern Society: Order, Hierarchy and Subordination in Britain and Ireland*. Cambridge: Cambridge UP, 2001.

Braudel, Fernand. *The Mediterranean and the Mediterranean World in the Age of Philip II*. 2 vols, translated by Sian Reynolds. New York: Harper Torchbooks, 1975.

Brome, Richard. *The Jovial Crew*, edited by Tiffany Stern. London: Bloomsbury Arden Shakespeare, 2014.

Brown, Horatio F., ed. *Calendar of State Papers and Manuscripts, Relating to English Affairs Existing in the Archives and Collection of Venice, and in Other Libraries of Northern Italy*. Vol. 11. *1607–1610*. London: Longman, Roberts, and Green, 1904.

Bruster, Douglas. *Drama and the Market in the Age of Shakespeare*. Cambridge: Cambridge UP, 2005.

Burckhardt, Jacob. *The Civilization of the Renaissance in Italy*. Oxford: Phaedon Press, 1981.

Burghley, William Cecil. *The Execution of Justice in England for Maintenaunce of Publique and Christian Peace, against Certeine Stirrers of Sedition, and Adherents to the Traytors and Enemies of the Realme*. London, 1583.

Burnett, Mark Thornton. *Masters and Servants in English Renaissance Drama and Culture: Authority and Obedience*. New York: St Martin's, 1997.

Burton, Jonathan. "The Shah's Two Ambassadors: *The Travels of the Three English Brothers* and the Global Early Modern." *Emissaries in Early Modern Literature and Culture: Mediation, Transmission, Traffic, 1550–1700*, edited by Brinda Charry and Gitanjali Shahani. Burlington, VT: Ashgate, 2009, pp. 23–40.

– *Traffic and Turning: Islam and English Drama, 1579–1624*. Newark: U of Delaware P, 2005.

Burton, Robert. *The Anatomy of Melancholy*. London, 1652.

Butler, James Davie. "British Convicts Shipped to American Colonies." *American Historical Review* 2, no. 1 (October 1896): 12–33.

Cannadine, David. *Ornamentalism: How the British Saw Their Empire.* Oxford: Oxford UP, 2001.

Canny, Nicholas. "The Origins of Empire: An Introduction." *The Oxford History of the British Empire.* Vol. 1. *The Origins of Empire.* Ed. Canny. Oxford: Oxford UP, 1998, pp. 1–33.

Capp, Bernard. "Popular Literature." *Popular Culture in Seventeenth-Century England,* edited by Barry Reay. London: Croom Helm, 1985, pp. 198–243.

Carey, Daniel. "Questioning Incommensurability in Early Modern Cultural Exchange." *Common Knowledge* 6 (1997): 32–50.

Carroll, William C. *Fat King, Lean Beggar: Representations of Poverty in the Age of Shakespeare.* Ithaca, NY: Cornell UP, 1996.

Chew, Samuel C. *The Crescent and the Rose: Islam and England during the Renaissance.* New York: Octagon Books, 1965.

Clark, Peter. *The English Alehouse: A Social History, 1200–1830.* New York: Longman, 1983.

"Clinton, Purser, & Arnold to Their Countreymen Wheresoever. Wherein Is Described by Their Own Hands Their Unfeigned Penitence for Their Offences Past: Their Patience in Welcoming Their Death, and Their Duetiful Minds towards Her Most Excellent Majestie." London: Imprinted by John Wolfe, 1583.

Cogan, Thomas. *The Haven of Health.* London, 1584.

Colley, Linda. *Captives.* New York: Pantheon Books, 2002.

Connery, Christopher L. "Ideologies of Land and Sea: Alfred Thayer Mahan, Carl Schmitt, and the Shaping of Global Myth Elements." *boundary 2* 28, no. 2 (2001): 173–201.

– "The Oceanic Feeling and the Regional Imaginary." *Global/Local: Cultural Production and the Transnational Imaginary,* edited by Rob Wilson, et al. Durham, NC: Duke UP, 1996, pp. 284–311.

Cooper, Helen. *The English Romance in Time: Transforming Motifs from Geoffrey of Monmouth to the Death of Shakespeare.* Oxford: Oxford UP, 2004.

Cormack, Bradin. *A Power to Do Justice: Jurisdiction, English Literature, and the Rise of Common Law, 1509–1625.* Chicago: U of Chicago P, 2007.

Craik, Katharine. "Reading *Coryat's Crudities* (1611)." *Studies in English Literature, 1500–1900* 44 (Winter 2004): 77–96.

Craik, Katherine A., and Tanya Pollard. "Introduction: Imagining Audiences." *Shakespearean Sensations: Experiencing Literature in Early Modern England,* edited by Craik and Pollard. Cambridge: Cambridge UP, 2013, pp. 1–25.

Cronk, Nicholas. "Aristotle, Horace, and Longinus: The Conception of Reader Response." In Norton, pp. 199–204.

Cunningham, Karen. *Imaginary Betrayals: Subjectivity and the Discourses of Treason in Early Modern England*. Philadelphia: U of Pennsylvania P, 2002.

Davies, D.W. *Elizabethans Errant: The Strange Fortunes of Sir Thomas Sherley and His Three Sons, As Well in the Dutch Wars as in Muscovy, Morocco, Persia, Spain, and the Indies*. Ithaca, NY: Cornell UP, 1967.

Davies, H. Neville. "*Pericles* and the Sherley Brothers." *Shakespeare and His Contemporaries: Essays in Comparison*, edited by E.A.J. Honingmann. Manchester: Manchester UP, 1986, pp. 94–113.

Davis, Robert C. *Christian Slaves, Muslim Masters: White Slavery in the Mediterranean, the Barbary Coast, and Italy, 1500–1800*. New York: Palgrave Macmillan, 2003.

Defoe, Daniel. *A General History of the Pyrates*. 2nd ed., edited by Manuel Schonhorn. Mineola, NY: Dover Publications, 1999.

Degenhardt, Jane Hwang. "Catholic Martyrdom in Dekker and Massinger's *The Virgin Martir* and the Early Modern Threat of 'Turning Turk'." *ELH* 73 (2006): 83–117.

Dimmock, Matthew. *New Turkes: Dramatizing Islam and the Ottomans in Early Modern England*. Aldershot, UK: Ashgate, 2005.

Doh, Herman, ed. *A Critical Edition of "Fortune by Land and Sea" by Thomas Heywood and William Rowley*. New York: Garland Publishing, 1980.

Dolan, Frances E. "'Gentlemen, I Have One Thing More to Say': Women on Scaffolds in England, 1563–1680." *Modern Philology* 92, no. 2 (November 1994): 157–78.

– "The Subordinate('s) Plot: Petty Treason and the Forms of Domestic Rebellion." *Shakespeare Quarterly* 43, no. 3 (Autumn 1992): 317–40.

Dollimore, Jonathan. *Radical Tragedy: Religion, Ideology, and Power in the Drama of Shakespeare and His Contemporaries*. Brighton, UK: Harvester Press, 1984.

Doty, Jeffrey S. "*Measure for Measure* and the Problem of Popularity." *English Literary Renaissance* 42, no. 1 (Winter 2012): 32–57.

– "Shakespeare's *Richard II*, 'Popularity,' and the Early Modern Public Sphere." *Shakespeare Quarterly* 61, no. 2 (Summer 2010): 183–205.

Doyle, Arthur Conan. *The Valley of Fear*. Oxford: Oxford UP, 1994.

Edelman, Charles, ed. *The Stukeley Plays: "The Battle of Alcazar" by George Peele; "The Famous History of the Life and Death of Captain Thomas Stukeley."* Manchester: Manchester UP, 2005.

The English Rogue Revived: Or, the Lives and Actions of Jonathan Wild, Thief-taker. Joseph Blake alias Blueskin Foot-pad and John Sheppard. London, 1725.

Escolme, Bridget. *Emotional Excess on the Shakespearean Stage: Passion's Slaves*. London: Bloomsbury Arden Shakespeare, 2013.

Ewen, C. L'Estrange. *Captain John Ward: "Arch-Pirate."* Printed for the author, 1939.

Faller, Lincoln B. *Turned to Account: The Forms and Functions of Criminal Biography in Late Seventeenth- and Early Eighteenth-Century England.* Cambridge: Cambridge UP, 1987.

A Famous Sea-fight between Captain Ward and the Rainbow. To the Tune of, Captain Ward, & c. London, c. 1700.

Finch, Martha L. *Dissenting Bodies: Corporealities in Early New England.* New York: Columbia UP, 2010.

Fitzmaurice, Andrew. "Introduction: Neither Neo-Roman nor Liberal Empire." *Renaissance Studies* 26, no. 4 *Special Issue: The Intellectual History of Early Modern Empire,* edited by Fitzmaurice (September 2012): 479–90.

Floyd-Wilson, Mary. *English Ethnicity and Race in Early Modern Drama.* Cambridge: Cambridge UP, 2003.

– "English Mettle." *Reading the Early Modern Passions: Essays in the Cultural History of Emotion,* edited by Gail Kern Paster, Katherine Rowe, and Mary Floyd-Wilson. Philadelphia: U of Pennsylvania P, 2004, pp. 130–46.

Forman, Valerie. "The Comic-Tragedy of Labor: A Global Story." *Working Subjects in Early Modern English Drama,* edited by Michelle M. Dowd and Natasha Korda. Burlington, VT: Ashgate, 2011, pp. 209–24.

– *Tragicomic Redemptions: Global Economics and the Early Modern English Stage.* Philadelphia: U of Pennsylvania P, 2008.

Frye, Roland Mushat. *Shakespeare: The Art of the Dramatist.* Boston: Houghton Mifflin, 1970.

Fuchs, Barbara. "Faithless Empires: Pirates, Renegadoes, and the English Nation." *ELH* 67, no 1 (Spring 2000): 45–69.

– *Mimesis and Empire: The New World, Islam, and European Identities.* Cambridge: Cambridge UP, 2001.

Fumerton, Patricia. "Not Home: Alehouses, Ballads, and the Vagrant Husband in Early Modern England." *Journal of Medieval and Early Modern Studies* 32, no. 3 (Fall 2002): 493–518.

– *Unsettled: The Culture of Mobility and the Working Poor in Early Modern England.* Chicago: U of Chicago P, 2006.

Fury, Cheryl A. *Tides in the Affairs of Men: The Social History of Elizabethan Seamen, 1580–1603.* Westport, CT: Greenwood Press, 2002.

Gallant, Thomas W. "Brigandage, Piracy, Capitalism, and State-Formation: Transnational Crime from a Historical World-Systems Perspective." *States and Illegal Practices,* edited by Josiah McC. Heyman. Oxford: Berg, 1999, pp. 25–61.

Garber, Marjorie. "Compassion." In Berlant, *Compassion,* pp. 15–27.

Garcia-Arenal, Mercedes, and Gerald Wiegers. *A Man of Three Worlds: Samuel Pallache, a Moroccan Jew in Catholic and Protestant Europe*, translated by Martin Beagles. Baltimore: Johns Hopkins UP, 1999.

Gladfelder, Hal. *Criminality and Narrative in Eighteenth-Century England: Beyond the Law.* Baltimore: Johns Hopkins UP, 2003.

Gowland, Angus. "The Problem of Early Modern Melancholy." *Past and Present* 191, no. 1 (2006): 77–120.

Graeber, David. *Debt: The First 5000 Years.* Brooklyn, NY: Melville House, 2011.

Greenblatt, Stephen. "Murdering Peasants: Status, Genre, and the Representation of Rebellion." *Representations* 1 (February 1983): 1–29.

Greenblatt, Stephen, et al., eds. *The Norton Shakespeare: Based on the Oxford Edition.* New York: W.W. Norton and Co., 1997.

Griffin, Eric. "Spain Is Portugal/and Portugal Is Spain: Transnational Attraction in the Stukeley Plays and *The Spanish Tragedy.*" *Journal for Early Modern Cultural Studies* 10, no. 1 (April 2010): 95–116.

Grogan, Jane. *The Persian Empire in English Renaissance Writing, 1549–1622.* New York: Palgrave Macmillan, 2015.

Hadfield, Andrew. "The Benefits of a Warm Study: The Resistance to Travel before Empire." In Singh, pp. 101–13.

Hall, Kim. "Sugar and Status in Shakespeare." *Shakespeare Jahrbuch* 145 (2009): 49–61.

Hall, Stuart, et al., eds. *Culture, Media, Language: Working Papers in Cultural Studies, 1972–79.* London: Routledge, 1992.

Harding, Christopher. "'*Hostis Humani Generis*': The Pirate as Outlaw in the Early Modern Law of the Sea." In Jowitt, *Pirates*, pp. 20–38.

Harris, Jonathan Gil. *Sick Economies: Drama, Mercantilism, and Disease in Shakespeare's England.* Philadelphia: U of Pennsylvania P, 2004.

Haynes, Jonathan. *The Humanist as Traveler: George Sandys' of a Journey Begun An. Dom. 1610.* Teaneck, NJ: Fairleigh Dickinson UP, 1986.

Haywood, Robert, and Roberta Spivak. *Maritime Piracy.* New York: Routledge, 2012.

Heller-Roazen, Daniel. *The Enemy of All: Piracy and the Law of Nations.* Cambridge, MA: Zone Books, 2009.

Hill, Christopher. *Liberty against the Law: Some Seventeenth-Century Controversies.* London: Penguin, 1996.

– "Radical Pirates." *The Collected Essays of Christopher Hill.* Vol. 3. Amherst: U of Massachusetts P, 1987, pp. 161–88.

Hillman, David. *Shakespeare's Entrails: Belief, Skepticism, and the Interior of the Body.* New York: Palgrave, 2007.

Hindle, Steve. *The State and Social Change in Early Modern England, c. 1550–1640*. New York: Palgrave, 2000.

The History of the Remarkable Life of John Sheppard, Containing a Particular Account of His Many Robberies and Escapes. London, 1724.

Hobsbaum, Philip. *A Reader's Guide to Charles Dickens*. Syracuse, NY: Syracuse UP, 1998.

Hogarth, William. *Industry and Idleness*. 1747. Reproduced in Paulson, *Hogarth's Graphic Works*.

Holbrook, Peter. *English Renaissance Tragedy: Ideas of Freedom*. London and New York: Bloomsbury Arden Shakespeare, 2015.

The Holinshed Project. The Holinshed Project, 2008–13, http://english.nsms.ox.ac.uk/holinshed/toc.php?edition=1587.

Holstun, James. *Ehud's Dagger: Class Struggle in the English Revolution*. London: Verso, 2000.

Horden, Peregrine, and Sharon Kinoshita, eds. *A Companion to Mediterranean History*. Oxford: Wiley Blackwell, 2014.

Howard, Clare. *English Travellers of the Renaissance*: London: John Lane, 1914.

Howard, Jean. "Gender on the Periphery." *Shakespeare and the Mediterranean: The Selected Proceedings of the International Shakespeare Association World Congress, Valencia, 2001*, edited by Thomas Clayton. Newark: U of Delaware P, 2004, pp. 344–62.

– "Shakespeare, Geography, and the Work of Genre on the Early Modern Stage." *MLQ: Modern Language Quarterly* 64, no. 3 (2003): 299–322.

– *The Stage and Social Struggle in Early Modern England*. London: Routledge, 1994.

Hudson, Nicholas. "Literature and Social Class in the Eighteenth Century." *Oxford Handbooks Online*. Oxford: Oxford UP, 2006.

Hutchings, Mark. "Acting Pirates: Converting *A Christian Turned Turk*." In Jowitt, *Pirates*, pp. 90–104.

Hutson, Lorna. "Chivalry for Merchants; or, Knights of Temperance in the Realms of Gold." *Journal of Medieval and Early Modern Studies* 26, no. 1 (Winter 1996): 29–59.

– "Civility and Virility in Ben Jonson." *Representations* 78, no. 1 (Spring 2002): 1–27.

Ingram, William. *The Business of Playing: The Beginnings of Adult Professional Theater in Early Modern London*. Ithaca, NY: Cornell UP, 1992.

James, Mervyn. "English Politics and the Concept of Honour, 1485–1642." *Society, Politics, and Culture: Studies in Early Modern England*, edited by James. Cambridge: Cambridge UP, 1986, pp. 308–415.

Jones, Ann Rosalind, and Peter Stallybrass. *Renaissance Clothing and the Materials of Memory*. Cambridge: Cambridge UP, 2000.

Jordan, Thomas. *Rules to Know a Royall King, from a Disloyall Subject.* London, 1642.

Jowitt, Claire. *The Culture of Piracy, 1580–1630: English Literature and Seaborne Crime*. Aldershot, UK: Ashgate, 2010.

– "Piracy and Politics in Heywood and Rowley's *Fortune by Land and Sea* (1607–1609)." *Renaissance Studies* 16, no. 2 (2002): 217–33.

– *Voyage Drama and Gender Politics, 1589–1642: Real and Imagined Worlds*. Manchester: Manchester UP, 2003.

– ed. *Pirates? The Politics of Plunder, 1550–1650*. New York: Palgrave Macmillan, 2003.

Judges, A.V. *The Elizabethan Underworld: A Collection of Tudor and Early Stuart Tracts and Ballads*. New York: Octagon Books, 1965.

Kane, Brendan. *The Politics and Culture of Honour in Britain and Ireland, 1541–1641*. Cambridge: Cambridge UP, 2010.

Kendrick, Matthew. *At Work in the Early Modern English Theater: Valuing Labor*. Teaneck, NJ: Fairleigh Dickinson UP, 2015.

Kimbrell, Garth. "Taste, Theatrical Venues, and the Rise of English Tragicomedy." *Studies in English Literature, 1500–1900* 55, no. 2 (Spring 2015): 285–307.

Kinney, Arthur F. *Rogues, Vagabonds, and Sturdy Beggars*. Barre, MA: Imprint Society, 1973.

Knapp, Jeffrey. *An Empire Nowhere: England, America, and Literature from "Utopia" to "The Tempest"*. Berkeley: U of California P, 1992.

Lake, Peter, and Steve Pincus. "Rethinking the Public Sphere in Early Modern England." *Journal of British Studies* 45 (April 2006): 270–92.

Lake, Peter, and Michael Questier. "Agency, Appropriation and Rhetoric under the Gallows: Puritans, Romanists and the State in Early Modern England." *Past and Present* 153 (November 1996): 64–107.

Laqueur, Thomas W. "Crowds, Carnival and the State in English Exeuctions, 1604–1868." *The First Modern Society: Essays in English History in Honour of Lawrence Stone*, edited by A.L. Beier, David Cannadine, and James M. Rosenheim. Cambridge: Cambridge UP, 1989, pp. 305–55.

Leinwand, Theodore. *Theatre, Finance and Society in Early Modern England*. Cambridge: Cambridge UP, 1999.

Lesser, Zachary. "Tragical-Comical-Pastoral-Colonial: Economic Sovereignty, Globalization, and the Form of Tragicomedy." *ELH* 74 (2007): 881–908.

Levin, Carole, and John Watkins. *Shakespeare's Foreign Worlds: National and Transnational Identities in the Elizabethan Age*. Ithaca, NY: Cornell UP, 2009.

Levine, Donald N., ed. *Georg Simmel on Individuality and Social Forms*. Chicago: U of Chicago P, 1971.

Lezra, Jacques. *Unspeakable Subjects: The Genealogy of the Event in Early Modern Europe*. Stanford, CA: Stanford UP, 1997.

Linebaugh, Peter. *The London Hanged: Crime and Civil Society in the Eighteenth Century*. Cambridge: Cambridge UP, 1992.

Linebaugh, Peter, and Marcus Rediker. *The Many-Headed Hydra: The Hidden History of the Revolutionary Atlantic*. Boston: Beacon Press, 2000.

Linton, Joan Pong. *The Romance of the New World: Gender and the Literary Formations of English Colonialism*. Cambridge: Cambridge UP, 2006.

Lockey, Brian C. *Early Modern Catholics, Royalists, and Cosmopolitans: English Transnationalism and the Christian Commonwealth*. Aldershot, UK: Ashgate, 2015.

Lodge, Thomas. *The Complete Works of Thomas Lodge*. 4 vols. New York: Russell & Russell, 1963.

– *Life and Death of William Longbeard, the Most Famous and Witty English Traitor, Borne in the Citty of London, Accompanied with Manye Other Most Pleasant and Prettie Histories*. London, 1593.

Loomba, Ania. "'Break Her Will, and Bruise No Bone, Sir': Colonial and Sexual Mastery in Fletcher's *The Island Princess*." *Journal for Early Modern Cultural Studies* 2, no. 1 (Spring/Summer 2002): 68–108.

– *Shakespeare, Race, and Colonialism*. Oxford: Oxford UP, 2002.

Lyons, Bridget Gellert. *Voices of Melancholy: Studies in Literary Treatments of Melancholy in Renaissance England*. London: Routledge and Kegan Paul, 1971.

Mackie, Erin Skye. *Rakes, Highwaymen, and Pirates: The Making of the Modern Gentleman in the Eighteenth Century*. Baltimore: Johns Hopkins UP, 2009.

MacLean, Gerald. "On Turning Turk, or Trying To: National Identity in Robert Daborne's *A Christian Turn'd Turke*." *Explorations in Renaissance Culture* 29, no. 2 (2003): 225–52.

Manley, Lawrence. *Literature and Culture in Early Modern London*. Cambridge: Cambridge UP, 1995.

– "Of Sites and Rites." In Smith, et al., pp. 35–54.

Marx, Karl. *Grundrisse*. London: Penguin, 1993.

Mason, Philip. *Prospero's Magic: Some Thoughts on Class and Race*. Oxford: Oxford UP, 1962.

Matar, Nabil. "The Renegade in the English Seventeenth-Century Imagination." *Studies in English Literature, 1500–1900* 33 (1993): 489–505.

Maxwell-Stewart, Hamish. "Convict Transportation from Britain and Ireland, 1615–1870." *History Compass* 8, no. 11 (November 2010): 1221–42.

McInnes, David. *Mind-Travelling and Voyage Drama in Early Modern England*. New York: Palgrave Macmillan, 2013.

McKeon, Michael. *The Origins of the English Novel, 1600–1740*. Baltimore: Johns Hopkins UP, 2002.

Mentz, Steve. *At the Bottom of Shakespeare's Ocean*. London: Continuum, 2009.

– "Toward a Blue Cultural Studies: The Sea, Maritime Culture, and Early Modern English Literature." *Literature Compass* 6, no. 5 (2009): 997–1013.

Mollat, Michel. *The Poor in the Middle Ages: An Essay in Social History*, translated by Arthur Goldhammer. New Haven: Yale UP, 1986.

Moore, Lucy. *The Thieves' Opera: The Remarkable Lives of Jonathan Wild, Thief-Taker, and Jack Sheppard, House-Breaker*. London: Viking, 1997.

Muldrew, Craig. *The Economy of Obligation: The Culture of Credit and Social Relations in Early Modern England*. New York: St Martin's Press, 1998.

Netzloff, Mark. *England's Internal Colonies: Class, Capital, and the Literature of Early Modern English Colonialism*. New York: Palgrave Macmillan, 2003.

– "The State and Early Modernity." *Journal for Early Modern Cultural Studies* 14, no. 1 (Winter 2014): 149–54.

A Narrative of All the Robberies, Escapes, &c. of John Sheppard: Giving an Exact Description of the Manner of His Wonderful Escape from the Castle. London, 1724.

Newes from Sea, of Two Notorious Pyrates Ward the Englishman and Danseker the Dutchman. With a True Relation of All or the Most Piraces by Them Committed unto the First of April. London, 1609.

Nocentelli, Carmen. "The Erotics of Mercantile Capitalism: Cross-Cultural Requitedness in the Early Modern Period." *Journal for Early Modern Cultural Studies* 8, no. 1 (Spring/Summer 2008): 134–52.

Norton, Claire. "Lust, Greed, Torture, and Identity: Narrations of Conversion and the Creation of the Early Modern Renegade." *Comparative Studies of South Asia, Africa and the Middle East* 29, no. 2 (2009): 259–68.

Norton, Glyn P., ed. *Cambridge History of Literary Criticism*. Vol. 3. *The Renaissance*. Cambridge: Cambridge UP, 1999.

Nixon, Anthony. *The Three English Brothers Sir Thomas Sherley His Travels, with His Three Yeares Imprisonment in Turkie: His Inlargement by His Majesties Letters to the Great Turke: and Lastly, His Ssafe Returne into England This Present Yeare, 1607. Sir Anthony Sherley His Embassage to the Christian Princes. Master Robert Sherley His Wars against the Turkes, with His Marriage to the Emperour of Persia His Neece*. London, 1607.

Orgel, Stephen. "Shakespeare and the Kinds of Drama." *Critical Inquiry* 6, no. 1 (Autumn 1979): 107–23.

Orkin, Martin. "Civility and the English Colonial Enterprise: Notes on Shakespeare's *Othello*." *Theoria: A Journal of Social and Political Theory* (December 1986): 1–14.

Ornstein, Robert. "Can We Define the Nature of Shakespearean Tragedy?" *Comparative Drama* 19, no. 3 (Fall 1985): 258–69.

Pagden, Anthony. *Lords of All the World: Ideologies of Empire in Spain, Britain, and France, 1500–1800*. New Haven, CT: Yale UP, 1995.

Park, Katharine, and Eckhard Kessler. "The Concept of Psychology." *The Cambridge History of Renaissance Philsophy*, edited by Charles B. Schmitt, et al. Cambridge: Cambridge UP, 1988, pp. 455–63.

Parker, Patricia. "Preposterous Conversions: *Turning Turk*, and Its 'Pauline' Rerighting." *Journal for Early Modern Cultural Studies* 2, no. 1 (Spring/Summer 2002): 1–34.

Parr, Anthony, ed. *Three Renaissance Travel Plays*. Manchester: Manchester UP, 2000.

Parry, William. *A New and Large Discourse of the Travels of Sir Anthony Sherley Knight, by Sea, and over Land, to the Persian Empire*. London, 1601.

Paster, Gail Kern. *Humoring the Body: Emotions and the Shakespearean Stage*. Chicago: U of Chicago P, 2004.

Paulson, Ronald. *Hogarth's Graphic Works*. New Haven, CT: Yale UP, 1965.

– *Sin and Evil: Moral Values in Literature*. New Haven, CT: Yale UP, 2007.

Pearson, M.N. "Merchants and States." In Tracy, pp. 41–116.

Penrose, Boies. *The Sherleian Odyssey, Being a Record of the Travels and Adventures of Three Famous Brothers during the Reigns of Elizabeth, James I, and Charles I*. Taunton, UK: Wessex Press, 1938.

Perotin-Dumon, Anne. "The Pirate and the Emperor: Power and the Law on the Seas, 1450–1850." In Tracy, pp. 196–227.

Perry, Curtis. *The Making of Jacobean Culture: James I and the Renegotiation of Elizabethan Literary Practice*. Cambridge: Cambridge UP, 1997.

Poole, Kristin. "The Devil's in the Archive: Doctor Faustus and Ovidian Physics." *Renaissance Drama*, n.s. 35 (2006): 191–219.

Porter, Roy. *London: A Social History*. Cambridge, MA: Harvard UP, 1995.

Potter, Lois. "Pirates and *Turning Turk* in Renaissance Drama." *Travel and Drama in Shakespeare's Time*, edited by Jean-Pierre Maquerlot and Michele Willems. Cambridge: Cambridge UP, 1996, pp. 124–40.

Publicover, Laurence. "Strangers at Home: The Sherley Brothers and Dramatic Romance." *Renaissance Studies* 24, no 5 (2010): 694–709.

Pye, Christopher. "The Theater, the Market, and the Subject of History." *ELH* 61, no. 3 (Fall 1994): 501–22.

Questier, Michael. *Conversion, Politics and Religion in England, 1580–1625*. Cambridge: Cambridge UP, 1996.

Rawlings, Philip. *Drunks, Whores and Idle Apprentices: Criminal Biographies of the Eighteenth Century*. London: Routledge, 1992.

Raymond, Joad. *Pamphlets and Pamphleteering in Early Modern Britain*. Cambridge: Cambridge UP, 2006.

Rediker, Marcus. *Between the Devil and the Deep Blue Sea: Merchant Seamen, Pirates, and the Anglo-American Maritime World, 1700–1750*. New York: Cambridge UP, 1987.

Reiss, Timothy J. "Renaissance Theatre and the Theory of Tragedy." In Norton, pp. 229–47.

Rice, Nicole R., and Margaret Aziza Pappano. *The Civic Cycles: Artisan Drama and Identity in Premodern England*. Notre Dame, IN: U of Notre Dame P, 2015.

Richetti, John J. *Popular Fiction before Richardson: Narrative Patterns, 1700–1739*. Oxford: Clarendon Press, 1969.

Robinson, Benedict S. *Islam and Early Modern English Literature: The Politics of Romance from Spenser to Milton*. New York: Palgrave Macmillan, 2007.

Rothman, E. Natalie. *Brokering Empire: Trans-Imperial Subjects between Venice and Istanbul*. Ithaca, NY: Cornell UP, 2012.

Ruff, Julius R. *Violence in Early Modern Europe, 1500–1800*. Cambridge: Cambridge UP, 2001.

Sahin, Kaya, and Julia Schleck. "Courtly Connections: Anthony Sherley's *Relation of His Travels* (1613) in a Global Context." *Renaissance Quarterly* 69, no. 1 (Spring 2016): 80–115.

Scammell, G.V. "European Exiles, Renegades and Outlaws and the Maritime Economy of Asia, c. 1500–1750." *Modern Asian Studies* 26, no. 4 (October 1992): 641–61.

Schleck, Julia. "'Plain Broad Narratives of Substantial Facts': Credibility, Narrative, and Hakluyt's *Principall Navigations*." *Renaissance Quarterly* 59, no. 3 (Fall 2006): 768–94.

Schmitt, Carl. *The Nomos of the Earth in the International Law of the Just Publicum Europaeum*, translated by G.L. Ulmen. New York: Telos, 2006.

Schoenfeldt, Michael. *Bodies and Selves in Early Modern England: Physiology and Inwardness in Spenser, Shakespeare, Herbert, and Milton*. Cambridge: Cambridge UP, 2000.

Schofield, R.S. "The Impact of Scarcity and Plenty on Population Change in England, 1541–1871." *Journal of Interdisciplinary History* 14 (1983): 265–91.

Sebek, Barbara. "'After My Humble Dutie Remembered': Factors and/versus Merchants." *Emissaries in Early Modern Literature and Culture: Mediation, Transmission, Traffic, 1550–1700*, edited by Brinda Charry and Gitanjali Shahani. New York: Routledge, 2016, pp. 113–28.

Sebek, Barbara, and Stephen Deng, eds. *Global Traffic: Discourses and Practices of Trade in English Literature and Culture from 1550 to 1700*. New York: Palgrave Macmillan, 2008.

Sell, Jonathan P.A. *Rhetoric and Wonder in English Travel Writing, 1560–1613*. Aldershot, UK: Ashgate, 2006.

Senior, C.M. *A Nation of Pirates: English Piracy in Its Heyday*. New York: Crame, Russak & Company, 1976.

Shakespeare, William. *The Complete Works of William Shakespeare*. 5th ed., edited by David Bevington. New York: Longman, 2003.

Shapiro, James. "'Tragedies Naturally Performed': Kyd's Representation of Violence." *Staging the Renaissance*, edited by David Scott Kastan and Peter Stallybrass. New York: Routledge, 1991, pp. 99–113.

Sharpe, J.A. "'Last Dying Speeches': Religion, Ideology, and Public Execution in Seventeenth-Century England." *Past and Present* 107 (May 1985): 144–67.

Shepard, Alexandra. *Accounting for Oneself: Worth, Status, and the Social Order in Early Modern England*. Oxford: Oxford UP, 2015.

Sheppard in Egypt, or News from the Dead. London, 1725.

Sherley, Anthony. *Sir Anthony Sherley: His Relation of His Travels into Persia. The Dangers, and Distresses, which Befell Him in His Passage, both by Sea and Land, and His Strange and Unexpected Deliverances. His Magnificent Entertainement in Persia, His Honourable Imployment There Hence, as Embassadour to the Princes of Christendome, the Cause of His Disapointment Therein, with His Advice to His Brother, Sir Robert Sherley, also, a True Relation of the Great Magnificence, Valour, Prudence, Justice, Temperance, and Other Manifold Virtues of ABAS, Now King of Persia, with His Great Conquests, Whereby He Hath Inlarged His Dominions. Penned by Sir Antony Sherley, and Recommended Brother, Sir Robert Sherley, Being Now in Precution of the Like Honourable Imployment*. London, 1613.

– *A True Report of Sir Anthony Shierlies Journey Overland to Venice*. London, 1600.

Shershow, Scott Cutler. "Idols of the Marketplace: Rethinking the Economic Determination of Renaissance Drama." *Renaissance Drama* (1995): 1–27.

Shickman, Allan. "The 'Perspective Glass' in Shakespeare's *Richard II*." *Studies in English Literature, 1500–1900* 18, no. 2 (Spring 1978): 217–28.

Sidney, Philip. *A Defence of Poesie and Poems*. Project Gutenberg, n.d. http://www.gutenberg.org/files/1962/1962-h/1962-h.htm. Accessed 16 November 2015.

Simpson, Richard. *School of Shakspeare*. London: Chatto and Windus, 1878.

Singh, Jyotsna G., ed. *A Companion to the Global Renaissance: English Literature and Culture in the Age of Expansion*. Hoboken, NJ: Wiley-Blackwell, 2009.

Siraisi, Nancy G. *Medieval and Early Renaissance Medicine: An Introduction to Knowledge and Practice*. Chicago: U of Chicago P, 1990.

Smith, Bruce R. *Shakespeare and Masculinity*. Oxford: Oxford UP, 2000.

Smith, David L., Richard Strier, and David Bevington, eds. *The Theatrical City: Culture, Theatre and Politics in London, 1576–1649*. Cambridge: Cambridge UP, 1995.

Spufford, Margaret. *Small Books and Pleasant Histories: Popular Fiction and Its Readership in Seventeenth-Century England*. London: Methuen, 1981.

Stern, Philip. "Corporate Virtue: The Languages of Empire in Early Modern British Asia." *Renaissance Studies* 26, no. 4 *Special Issue: The Intellectual History of Early Modern Empire*, edited by Andrew Fitzmaurice (September 2012): 510–30.

Stow, John. *The Annales of England, Faithfully Collected out of the Most Autenticall Authors, Records, and Other Monuments of Antiquitie, Lately Corrected, Increased, and Continued, from the First Inhabitation untill This Present Yeere 1600. By John Stow Citizen of London.* London, 1605.

Subrahmanyam, Sanjay. *Three Ways to Be Alien: Travails and Encounters in the Early Modern World.* Waltham, MA: Brandeis UP, 2011.

Sullivan, Jr, Garrett A. "Tragic Subjectivities." *The Cambridge Companion to English Renaissance Tragedy*, edited by Emma Smith and Garrett A. Sullivan Jr. Cambridge: Cambridge UP, 2010, pp. 73–85.

Tenenti, Alberto. *Piracy and the Decline of Venice, 1580–1615.* London: Longmans, Green, 1967.

Thomson, Janice E. *Mercenaries, Pirates, and Sovereigns: State-building and Extraterritorial Violence in Early Modern Europe.* Princeton, NJ: Princeton UP, 1994.

Tinniswood, Adrian. *Pirates of Barbary: Corsairs, Conquests, and Captivity in the Seventeenth Century Mediterranean.* New York: Riverhead Books, 2010.

Tracy, James D., ed. *The Political Economy of Merchant Empires.* Cambridge: Cambridge UP, 1987.

The True and Genuine Account of the Life and Actions of the Late Jonathan Wild; Not Made up of Fiction and Fable, but Taken from His Own Mouth, and Collected from Papers of His Own Writing. London, 1725.

A True Discourse, of the Late Voyage Made by the Right Worshipfull Sir Thomas Sherley the Yonger, Knight: on the Coast of Spaine. Written by a Gentleman That Was in the Voyage. London, 1602.

A True Relation, of the Lives and Deaths of the Two Most Famous English Pyrats, Purser, and Clinton Who Lived in the Reigne of Queene Elizabeth. Together with the Particular Actions of Their Takings and Undertakings. With Other Pleasant Passages Which Hapned before Their Surprizall Worth the Observing. London, 1639.

Tyerman, Christopher. *England and the Crusades, 1095–1588.* Chicago: U of Chicago P, 1988.

Valerian, Dominique. "The Medieval Mediterranean." In Horden and Kinoshita, pp. 77–90.

Vitkus, Daniel. "Adventuring Heroes in the Mediterranean: Mapping the Boundaries of Anglo Islamic Exchange on the Early Modern Stage." *Journal of Medieval and Early Modern Studies* 37, no. 1 (Winter 2007): 75–95.

– "Labor and Travel on the Early Modern Stage: Representing the Travail of Travel in Dekker's *Old Fortunatus* and Shakespeare's *Pericles*." *Working*

Subjects in Early Modern English Drama, edited by Michelle M. Dowd and Natasha Korda. Burlington, VT: Ashgate, 2011, pp. 225–42.

– *Piracy, Slavery, and Redemption: Barbary Captivity Narratives from Early Modern England.* New York: Columbia UP, 2001.

– *Turning Turk: English Theater and the Multicultural Mediterranean, 1570–1630.* New York: Palgrave Macmillan, 2003.

– ed. *Three Turk Plays from Early Modern England: "Selimus", "A Christian Turned Turk," and "The Renegado."* New York: Columbia UP, 2000.

Warren, Christopher. *Literature and the Law of Nations, 1580–1680.* Oxford: Oxford UP, 1986.

Watt, Ian. *The Rise of the Novel: Studies in Defoe, Richardson, and Fielding.* 2nd American ed. Berkeley: U of California P, 2001.

Wear, Andrew. "Making Sense of Health and the Environment in Early Modern England." *Medicine in Society: Historical Essays,* edited by Wear. Cambridge: Cambridge UP, 1992, pp. 119–47.

Williams, Raymond. *Keywords: A Vocabulary of Culture and Society.* Rev. ed. New York: Oxford UP, 1983.

– *Marxism and Literature.* Oxford: Oxford UP, 1977.

Wilson, Bronwen, and Paul Yachnin. "Introduction." In Wilson and Yachnin, pp. 1–21.

– eds. *Making Publics in Early Modern Europe: People, Things, Forms of Knowledge.* New York: Routledge, 2010.

Wilson, Peter Lamborn. *Pirate Utopias: Moorish Corsairs and European Renegades.* Brooklyn, NY: Autonomedia, 1995.

Woodbridge, Linda. *Vagrancy, Homelessness, and English Renaissance Literature.* Urbana: U of Illinois P, 2001.

Woodward, Kathleen. "Calculating Compassion." *Indiana Law Journal* 77, no. 223 (2002): 223–45.

Wright, Thomas. *The Passions of the Minde in Generall.* London, 1604.

Wrightson, Keith. "Estates, Degrees, and Sorts in Tudor and Stuart England." *History Today* 37, no. 1 (January 1987): 17–22.

– "The Social Order of Early Modern England: Three Approaches." *The World We Have Gained: Histories of Population and Social Structure,* edited by Lloyd Bonfield, Richard M. Smith, and Keith Wrightson. Oxford: Blackwell, 1986, pp. 177–202.

Yachnin, Paul. "*Hamlet* and the Social Thing in Early Modern England." In Wilson and Yachnin, pp. 81–95.

Yachnin, Paul, and Marlene Eberhart, eds. *Forms of Association: Making Publics in Early Modern Europe.* Amherst: U of Massachusetts P, 2015.

Index